Melville and His Circle

The University of Georgia Press   *Athens and London*

William B. Dillingham

Melville &

His Circle

THE LAST YEARS

Title page photo: Herman Melville, 1885. Gansevoort-Lansing Collection,
Rare Books and Manuscripts Division, The New York Public Library,
Astor, Lenox, and Tilden Foundations.

Designed by Louise OFarrell
Set in 10/14.5 Minion by Books International
Printed and bound by Thomson-Shore
The paper in this book meets the guidelines for
permanence and durability of the Committee on
Production Guidelines for Book Longevity of the
Council on Library Resources.

Printed in the United States of America

00   99   98   97   96   C   5   4   3   2   1

LIBRARY OF CONGRESS CATALOGING IN PUBLICATION DATA
Dillingham, William B.
Melville and his circle : the last years / William B. Dillingham.
p.   cm.
Includes bibliographical references and index.
ISBN 0-8203-1856-6 (alk. paper)
1. Melville, Herman, 1819–1891—Homes and haunts—New York (N.Y.)
2. Melville, Herman, 1819–1891—Friends and associates. 3. New York
(N.Y.)—Social life and customs—19th century. 4. New York (N.Y.)—
Intellectual life—19th century. 5. Novelists, American—19th
century—Biography. 6. New York (N.Y.)—Biography. I. Title.
PS2386.D55   1996
813' .3—dc20
[B]   96-767

BRITISH LIBRARY CATALOGING IN PUBLICATION DATA AVAILABLE

For

David Wayne Nunnery

Matthew Byron Briggs

Jennifer Dianne Briggs

Joshua Lance Harbin

Travis William Briggs

My youth is ever new like an eagle's.

Psalm 103

The walls of Gold entomb us.
The swords of scorn divide.
Take not thy Thunder from us,
But take away our pride.
From sleep and from damnation
Deliver us, good Lord!

G. K. Chesterton

Contents

Preface

Though "circle" books appear only seldom these days, they were once in great vogue: *Joseph Conrad and His Circle* (1935), *Michael Drayton and His Circle* (1941), *Dr. Johnson and His Circle* (1913), *Ruskin and His Circle* (1910), *Wordsworth and His Circle* (1907), *Hawthorne and His Circle* (1903), and so on. Such books constitute a biographical-critical genre: they usually deal with an important figure in the specific context of his or her close personal friends and colleagues. I hope that those who begin *Melville and His Circle: The Last Years* with the anticipation of such a treatment will not be disappointed, for this is not that kind of book. I have meant not to deceive but to suggest through the title contrast if not uniqueness. Unlike numerous other authors, Herman Melville had no circle in the usual sense. His difference, his rarity, is everywhere apparent. I have used the word *circle* in the sense of those persons with whom Melville associated only intellectually and imaginatively at a time when he had few if any actual friends, perhaps the most nearly solitary era of his life. This is a book about his reading of certain authors during the years indicated, about what he was like at that time, and about how the two are connected.

Not all the writers Melville became familiar with during this late period became members of his select circle. He read much that is not covered in this book, writings that did not much affect him one way or the other. He sometimes borrowed books from the New York Society Library that apparently made no lasting impression on him. He gave books as gifts that he thought family members would like, and he received books as gifts from others—works in which he showed no pronounced interest. For example, a fellow employee of the New York Customs Service, Robert Barry Coffin (who wrote under the pseudonym Barry Gray), presented him with at least four of his books, but neither Coffin nor any of the others who worked for the Customs Service and also wrote (Richard Grant White, Charles F. Briggs, and Richard Henry Stoddard) and with whose works Melville was familiar appealed deeply to his intellect and imagination. He could be gracious in his appreciation to another writer who seemed sincerely to admire him, as did the author of sea fiction, William Clark Russell, but it is clear that Russell did not really capture his imagination or truly command his highest degree of respect. Therefore, these and numerous other writers whose work Melville read in his late years are consciously omitted from the discussion that follows because they appear to have had minimum impact on the author of *Billy Budd.* Thus this book makes no attempt to be totally comprehensive in its treatment of what Melville read during the final years of his life. The focus is on those writers to whom Melville devoted the most attention, authors such as Matthew Arnold, Honoré de Balzac, James Thomson, Arthur Schopenhauer, and a few others.

Over the several years that this book has been in preparation, I have profited greatly from the work of numerous Melville scholars. There is not space enough to name them all—scores—but I wish to name just a few: Merton M. Sealts Jr., whose books and articles on almost every aspect of Melville's life and writings provide not only invaluable information but also a model of how to express it; William H. Shurr, whose pioneering book on Melville's poetry still startles with its insights and satisfies with its common sense; Harrison Hayford and his coeditors of the Northwestern-Newberry edition of Melville's works, whose devotion to background and text seem almost unequaled in American literature; Hennig Cohen, Donald Yannella, and John Bryant, whose leadership in the Melville Society and editorship of its journal, *Extracts,* through the years have furthered immensely the cause of Melville studies; Stanton Garner, whose persistent research into neglected areas of Melville's life has paid large dividends to us all. To these and many others whose names I have not listed, including students and colleagues who have listened, responded, stimulated, and corrected, I express my sincere gratitude. During the final stage of composition of this book, Emory University assisted enormously by generously providing me with a full-year research leave of absence. In that regard, I wish to thank especially Professor Walter Reed, then chair of the Department of English, for his faith in my endeavors and for his constant support.

Melville scholars who visit the collections housed in the Houghton Library of Harvard University and in the New York Public Library will encounter, as I have, eager and intelligent helpfulness from people who are professionals in the best sense of the word. I am also much in debt to the staff of the Woodruff Library of Emory University not only for their unfailing and friendly cooperativeness in untold ways but also for the quiet and thought-provoking atmosphere of a certain private place with which the library has furnished me so that I might muse and compose in solitude.

Melville and His Circle

One

THE SOUL SELECTS

ITS OWN SOCIETY

*T*he period covered in this book, 1877–91, is perhaps the most neglected in the life of Herman Melville. Biographers have seen little in these years—the "silent years," as one critic called them—to write about. It is astonishing how few pages are devoted to the period after the publication of *Clarel* in the biographies by Raymond Weaver, John Freeman, Lewis Mumford, Leon Howard, and Edwin Haviland Miller.

Admittedly, Melville's life as a senior citizen does not appear very exciting. Occupying a rowhouse with his family at 104 East Twenty-Sixth Street in New York City, he worked in a humdrum position as customs inspector until his retirement in December 1885. Before and after that date, he severely restricted his circle of acquaintances. He answered most letters as briefly as possible, and he politely declined invitations to social functions. When he died in September 1891, the *Press* published a notice that reads in part:

> There died yesterday at his quiet home in this city a man who, although he had done almost no literary work during the past sixteen years, was once one of the most popular writers in the United States. . . . Of late years, Mr. Melville—probably because he had ceased his literary activity—has fallen into a literary decline, as the result of which his books are now little

A Luncheon at Delmonico's, Corner of Fifth Avenue and 26th Street. From a sketch by Smedley, 1890. *Harper's Weekly.*

known. Probably, if the truth were known, even his own generation has long thought him dead, so quiet have been the later years of his life.[1]

We like to scoff at such obituaries of now famous writers, but the truth is that something of the same attitude as indicated in the above notice remains current among critics and biographers. A feeling persists that with the exception of *Billy Budd*, Melville's work after *Clarel* reflects a precipitous "literary decline," as the *Press* put it, that during these years he essentially "ceased his [serious] literary activity." Such an assumption proves the validity of Stanton Garner's view that the Melville of these later years is "the Melville who awaits discovery."[2] In his brief but imaginative and sometimes even poetic account of how Melville lived during this period, Lewis Mumford writes: "The days pass and one day is like another: there is comfort in monotony."[3] The quietness of Melville's outer life naturally invites such a view. When a person pretty much hides himself away, he most likely is also retiring from all kinds of activity, internal as well as external. Melville's own statements in his correspondence about his approaching old age and his "lassitude" add brush strokes to the portrait of a tired old titan of an artist now tinkering with small matters but incapable of the great conceptions and experimentations of former times and no longer interested in them.

But is that portrait an accurate representation of the man? Does disengagement from many of the busy activities of life, even to the extent of becoming known as a recluse, necessarily entail disengagement from a busy internal life, the life of the imagination? The career of Emily Dickinson provides the answer. One of the most profound mistakes that a critic or biographer can make is to assume that in Melville's last fourteen or so years he had for all practical purposes "ceased his literary activity." *Billy Budd* is not the result of ceased literary activity, and in addition to that great short novel, Melville composed (or in some instances reworked) an impressive number of poems during this period, most of them gathered into three volumes but a substantial number of them together with an assortment of prose sketches left uncollected and unpublished. Since he worked at full-time employment for more than half of these final fourteen years, this body of work is no small achievement, especially for an aging artist.

What he actually produced after *Clarel,* however, is not so much the point here as what was his state of mind. As he narrowed his circle of sociality, he committed himself consciously and unswervingly to the life of the artist. The truth is that Melville did not cease his literary activity after *Clarel,* if by activity one means thinking as well as the actual act of writing, but concentrated and intensified it. Thoughts about the essence of art and the process of creativity probably occupied his mind more during these years than during any other period of his life. In fact, these subjects became his preoccupation. A highly productive, forceful, and sometimes intuitive artist earlier in his career, he became if anything a more conscious artist late in life as he increasingly pondered the nature of art and the workings of the imagination. What kept him going during these difficult years of diminished physical powers was not family or friends or religious faith but his imagination and his meditations on artistry.

One of the best illustrations of these concerns is a two-part poem that he probably began earlier in his life but worked on together with several related prose sketches during this period and left unpublished at his death. "At the Hostelry" and "Naples in the Time of Bomba" constitute the main part of what Robert A. Sandberg argues is an unfinished book, which he chooses to call *The Burgundy Club*.[4] Using such evidence as is available, Sandberg attempts to date the composition of these various pieces, but he confesses that "even after careful consideration of the physical evidence provided by the manuscripts themselves, it may never be possible finally to determine exactly what years Melville was working on any given piece."[5] The soundness of Sandberg's conclusion is evident from the variety of scholarly conjectures about composition dates.[6] What is clear, however, is that no matter how soon he began this poetic work after his trip abroad in 1856–57, which furnished him with materials, he continued to rethink the concepts behind the project, to add, subtract, and revamp. In its extant form, the work is the product of and reflects the thought and artistry of Melville's post-*Clarel* years.

Most particularly, it embodies his late-life thoughts about art and the creative imagination, and it manifests his continued vigor with regard to artistic experimentation. What Melville was attempting in "At the Hostelry" and "Naples in the Time of Bomba" is similar to his experimentation in the 1850s with such two-part (or bipartite) stories as "The Paradise of Bachelors and the Tartarus of Maids," "The Two Temples," and "Poor Man's Pudding and Rich Man's Crumbs," all of which reveal two ways of dealing with the same basic subject, theme, or idea. But it is even bolder and more original. At one stage of the composition, Melville had in mind combining "At the Hostelry" and "Naples in the Time of Bomba" with several sketches, thus making up a new kind of work, a bipartite poem with related prose. He experimented a good deal during his later years with the combination of prose and poetry, but I believe this is the only instance in which the poem involved is bipartite.

The degree of experimentation with the mode of narration is startling. Melville the author creates an "editor" as the supposed author, who in turn creates the work from materials he heard from two men, the Marquis de Grandvin and Major Jack Gentian, the supposed narrators of "At the Hostelry" and "Naples in the Time of Bomba" respectively. The complexity increases as the "editor" explains in his preface that the "true" author of both parts of the poem is the Marquis de Grandvin since he so inspired and motivated Jack Gentian, his devoted disciple, that when we hear Jack speaking, it is essentially the Marquis. Thus the narrative voice of "Naples in the Time of Bomba" seems to be Jack Gentian's, but it is in a way that of the Marquis, who is the force and spirit behind the entire work. However, nearly all the cantos are introduced by remarks in prose that obviously do not come from either Jack Gentian or the Marquis de Grandvin but emanate from another source, the "editor" or, as it seems sometimes, Melville himself. So Jack Gentian ostensibly narrates one part of the work, but he is the mouthpiece for the Marquis. The Marquis seems to narrate the other part, but, again, an authorial or editorial voice introduces most of the cantos, and to complicate matters further, in the forefront of the scene enacted in this section are many individual speakers revealing directly their separate and distinct personalities and thus displacing the voice of the Marquis. Furthermore, the Marquis has in reality written nothing; his table talk has been molded into poetry and art by the real narrator, the "editor," who refuses to take credit for being anything but an observer and compiler and who is a character in the work distinct and different from the real author, Herman Melville, who remains hidden, as it were, in the center of these concentric circles of narration. An illusion of group effort emerges in which the work is the product not of a single creator but the result of a collective endeavor.

The illusion of art by committee, which Melville creates through multiple levels of narration, naturally sustains another illusion, that of randomness or fragmentation. Although "At the Hostelry" and "Naples in the Time of Bomba" may appear to be two distinct poems with little in common and although a great variety of subjects and diversity of views may seem to characterize the two parts of the work, it is in actuality a cohesive bipartite poem growing out of a central concern, namely, Melville's desire to articulate his thoughts on the essence of art.

Centering on the concept of the picturesque, the first part of the work, "At the Hostelry," is a deliberation on artistic perception and on the nature of art. The second part, "Naples in the Time of Bomba," is an *example* of the picturesque, an actual manifestation in poetic form of the aesthetic theory developed in the first part. "At the Hostelry" and "Naples in the Time of Bomba" were intended as a unit. It is for this reason that Melville did not include in his Burgundy Club materials two other poems that have much in common with both "At the Hostelry" and "Naples in the Time of Bomba." Combining a prose introduction with a poem, "Rip Van Winkle's Lilac" deals with the precise subject of "At the Hostelry," the picturesque. Aaron Kramer comments that "Rip Van Winkle's Lilac" "actually belongs with 'At the Hostelry,'" and so it would seem.[7] The fact that Melville did not include it nor another poem, "Pausilippo (in the Time of Bomba)," which is related to "Naples in the Time of Bomba," with the Burgundy Club materials suggests that he intended that work to consist not of a collection of poems but of one long bipartite poem with perhaps appropriate accompanying prose. (He apparently never settled on whether or not he would include the various prose sketches.)[8]

Melville relies heavily upon the willing suspension of disbelief as he depicts in "At the Hostelry" an imaginary symposium (in the older sense of the term: a convivial drinking party with conversation) made up of about two dozen dead artists, not only dead, in fact, but long dead and some not contemporaneous in life with others. Together, they represent some three centuries of painting: from Fra Angelico (1387–1455) to Antoine Watteau (1684–1721), brought together in a modern setting—a private room in Delmonico's restaurant in the New York City of Melville's later life. The greatest number of the painters, however, are seventeenth-century artists who were either Italian or had strong Italian connections or attachments. In his choice of painters, Melville obviously kept in mind the opening section of the poem and the Italian setting of the second part.

The opening section, printed as the first canto of "At the Hostelry," seems actually more suited as a prologue to the entire bipartite poem. If content dictates structure, these opening stanzas should be set aside as introductory to both parts of the poem, and "At the Hostelry" should begin with what is now designated as the second canto. The introductory section merges the subjects of both parts of the poem. Ostensibly "touching Italian affairs," as does "Naples in the Time of Bomba," the prologue deals with the Italian heroes Garibaldi and Cavour and with Italy as a metaphor for the picturesque. Italy is "Art's Holy Land." The picturesque and Italy come together in these opening stanzas through the idea of unification, that is, the process by which Italy became unified suggests metaphorically the process through which certain alien materials are unified into art. Whitmanlike, Melville uses events in Italy's history as manifestations of the poetic mission—to combine, to unite the oppositions of life into art. The separate and disparate city states of Italy represent the material with which the picturesque artist works.

The history of the term *picturesque,* beginning in the eighteenth century and continuing on well into the nineteenth, is long and tangled.[9] Originally, the term meant "that a landscape looked as though it came straight out of a picture," such as in a painting by Claude or by Gaspar Poussin.[10] Through the writings of its most prominent advocates, Uvedale Price and Richard Payne Knight (who could not agree on its meaning), the picturesque emerged in the late eighteenth century as one of the most important concepts in painting. Significantly, Melville selects artists who generally put into practice (in varying degrees) certain aspects of the picturesque aesthetic but who ironically would not have been familiar with the term previous to the symposium since it came into widespread use only after their deaths. Equally significant is the fact that by the time Melville wrote "At the Hostelry" and "Naples in the Time of Bomba," the keen interest in and the controversy over it had subsided, and *picturesque* had fallen in importance from being a serious and complex aesthetic term to one applied with vague approval by people who do not know art but who know what they like, to scenes that they consider pleasing charming, and quaint.

Melville knew precisely what he was doing here; he was aware of all the angles involving this term. He knew the long history of the concept, but he did not want his characters to know it; so he chose painters who lived and died too early to be aware of either the controversy over the term in the late eighteenth century or the disrepute into which over time it had fallen by the late nineteenth century. Consequently, they would have to respond to the question of what the picturesque consists of in a fresh and original manner, thus revealing in their comments their personal perceptions of the nature of art. Those painters in the symposium who do not speak reveal much by their silences; they allow their artistic productions to talk for them. The term under discussion performs essentially the same function as an "original character." Melville explains in *The Confidence-Man* that such a character reveals little about himself but is the means of showing much about those who respond to him. An original term, like *picturesque,* reveals much about those who discuss it but is not itself completely defined in the discussion.

Melville did not choose the picturesque as the principal subject for his imaginary symposium, however, merely because a discussion of it would afford a splendid opportunity to show the relativity of perception in those who create art, though that was unquestionably one reason. He chose it also because of his own attraction to it. He was so strongly drawn to painting and sculpture that he appropriated a concept from the visual arts to represent his own aesthetic as a writer.[11] Advocates of the picturesque in the late eighteenth century disagreed among themselves about several aspects of that aesthetic concept, but they concurred on certain basic matters—for example, that the picturesque is made up of contrasting elements, that it embraces roughness as well as smoothness, the bleak as well as the cheerful, irregularity as well as the seamless, and so forth. The mixture or fusion of these disparate elements constitutes the very essence of the picturesque. The challenge of the artist is to select materials that manifest these oppositions and then to mate them in a work of art that leaves the impression of being less finished than it could have been.[12] Melville's adherence to such a theory is clearly stated in a late poem, one that he could well have entitled "The Picturesque" but that he called instead "Art." "What unlike things," he writes, "must meet and Mate":

> A flame to melt—a wind to freeze;
> Sad patience—joyous energies;
> Humility—yet pride and scorn;
> Instinct and study; love and hate;
> Audicity—reverence. These must mate.

The symposium in "At the Hostelry" results in "an inconclusive debate," as the prose headnote to the second canto says, but along the way various speakers in defining the picturesque echo Melville's aesthetic. For example, Herman van Swanevelt (1600–1655), who was born in Holland but like several others in the group spent much of his career in Italy, remarks that in art beauty is often allied with horror, as in the instance of Leonardo's painting of the Medusa. The picturesque, he implies, is a mixture in which both grace and terror can be ingredients. Another Dutch painter, Jan Steen (1625–79), makes the point that the stuff of art is life itself, which is made up—as is the picturesque—of "wine and brine"; the picturesque is "the mingled brew."

In Melville's thought, the perception of the picturesque results when the creative imagination acts upon the sense of sight. The artist of the picturesque must possess above all a picturesque eye. Art results when, as a further step, the creative imagination then acts upon the intellect, intuition, and will to transform the perception into a work of the picturesque. If "At the Hostelry" deals primarily with perceptions of the picturesque, "Naples in the Time of Bomba" is the picturesque, as Melville conceived it, exemplified.

Melville's fascination with Naples was more than the shallow affection tourists often hold for favorite faraway places that they have visited. A large framed print depicting the Bay of Naples occupied a prominent place in Melville's home at 104 East Twenty-Sixth Street because Naples occupied a prominent place in his imagination. Of all the locations he knew, Naples at the time he knew it represented most poignantly the combination of elements associated with the picturesque. Joy and tragedy walked hand-in-hand in a setting objectifying nature's proclivities toward the disparate. Freedom and despotism vied with each other and with religiosity, and the past continually cast its haunting shadow upon the present. Naples was the very "type" of the picturesque: "Funeral urns of time antique / Inwrought with flowers in gala play." The importance of Naples as the "type" of the picturesque is suggested by the fact that at one point Melville gave the title "Parthenope," another name for Naples, to the projected book consisting of the bipartite poem and several sketches.[13] Naples was made up of "the brine and wine" that Jan Steen spoke of as the essence of the picturesque, and throughout "Naples in the Time of Bomba," Melville keeps in the foreground these coeval oppositions. Indeed, the main character of "Naples in the Time of Bomba" is not Major Jack Gentian, despite his ostensible role as protagonist and narrator, but Naples itself. This remarkable second part of Melville's bipartite poem is actually a series of sharp, unforgettable images—or pictures— of the setting and the humanity of Naples, thus picturesque in still another meaning of the word, "evoking mental images." "Naples in the Time of Bomba" is a written picture, and to echo the words of the Dutch painter Gerard Dou (1613–75) in "At the Hostelry": "Agree, the picture's *picturesque*."

If "At the Hostelry" and "Naples in the Time of Bomba" reveal an older Melville deeply occupied with thoughts about art and still actively engaged in creative experimentation, the two prefaces and seven prose sketches that he composed in conjunction with the bipartite poem suggest much about how this intensified concern with the life of the imagination relates to his impulses toward sociality.

In the two sections of the bipartite poem, the Marquis de Grand-vin and Major Jack Gentian are somewhat shadowy figures, little more than narrative devices. Therefore, Melville probably set out sometime after seeing *Clarel* through the press to introduce these putative narrators, as Merton Sealts Jr. has argued, to fill out the portrait of them so that their roles in the poem would be more understandable.[14] Then after composing at various times over a considerable span of years the seven sketches, Melville began to have second thoughts about using them with the poem. He explains in one of the two prefaces he composed that including character sketches of the two narrators "would overmuch enlarge the volume."[15] Although the other preface, "House of the Tragic Poet," indicates that he would incorporate certain prose sketches into the projected volume, it is clear that he was not entirely comfortable with them.[16]

Perhaps his reason was simply the one that he gave in the preface— he did not want to lengthen the volume—but more than likely he had something else in mind, such as the thought offered by Sealts: "As the book took form, however, the prose sketches threatened to eclipse the poetry."[17] It is also likely that Melville recognized that the sketches as he had written them did not fit well with the poetry. His delineations of the Marquis de Grandvin and Major Jack Gentian in the prose pieces are so ambivalent that authorial direction and intention become intriguingly foggy. He may well have worried that his characterization of Jack Gentian in the sketches was that of a somewhat different person from the Major who ostensibly narrates "Naples in the Time of Bomba."

At any rate, these sketches are an invaluable resource for what they reveal about Melville's state of mind in this last period of his life, particular in reference to two long conflicting tendencies within him: geniality and privacy. Because Melville created the Burgundy Club, of which Major Jack Gentian is the highly respected "Dean," critics and biographers have often assumed that in the loneliness of these dreary final years, he was expressing in the Burgundy Club sketches a longing for those early times when he, Evert Duyckinck, and a few others called themselves "the Knights of the Round Table" and, as Leon Howard writes, "gathered in the basement of No. 20 Clinton Place and talked of old books and faraway lands over their punch and cigars."[18] An aging and nostalgic Herman Melville thus indulges himself by creating imaginary playmates, as it were, to recapture some of the pleasure of the past. Hershel Parker believes that the sketches served Melville as "self-consolation" in these years, "content to hold genial converse with his invented characters" so like himself.[19]

Love of geniality unquestionably played a role in Melville's life, as Merton M. Sealts Jr. has convincingly documented.[20] In answer to a critic who disagreed with his position, Sealts wrote: "You think I overstate HM's inclination toward the genial; I hope I've also pointed to his equally strong feelings that geniality can be whaleishly alluring, deceptive, even destructive."[21] Sealts's insistence upon Melville's duality in this regard is precisely correct. Even in his younger days as one of the "Knights of the Round Table," his impulse toward good fellowship was tempered with a desire for privacy and a strong self-caution about the ill effects of gregariousness. As he grew older, he did not lose the appetite for companionship, especially intellectual companionship, but he came to satisfy it in a different way, largely by selecting writers (and in a few instances painters) with whom he discovered some soul-depth common denominators and by getting to know their works, sometimes exhaustively. These creative geniuses, none of whom Melville knew or associated with personally, became his circle, and it was upon them that he lavished his attention. He came to select his own society more from the kind of people from which he formed his imaginary symposium in "At the Hostelry" than from those who belonged to the clubs of New York City.

The Burgundy Club sketches should be considered in the context of Melville's New York in the last fourteen years of his life. Clubs surrounded him in every sense during this period. In 1873, Francis Gerry Fairfield wrote: "At no time, probably, in the history of the metropolis, has there been a movement so marked in the direction of club-life: New York being the second city in the world in the number of membership of its clubs, London standing first."[22] The period in New York between the end of the Civil War and shortly after Melville's death has been called "the flowering of clubdom": "Club membership became a matter of prestige, of social and of business importance. It became the badge of social rank."[23] Melville's home on East Twenty-Sixth Street was only short blocks away from many of these clubs, the oldest of which was the Union, formed in 1836. A few years later came the New York Club (1845), which at one time looked "out on Madison Square at the Worth monument," which Melville mentions in his sketch "To Major John Gentian, Dean of the Burgundy Club."[24] As time passed, Fifth Avenue (two blocks over from the Melville residence) became lined with prestigious clubs. "Clubs and clubmen," wrote Moses King near the time of Melville's death, "are legion throughout New-York City. Every conceivable social, political, religious, professional and business interest is concentrated in this manner." He points out that "there are fully 300 clubs of good standing in New York, with a membership of upward of 100,000. Few men of New York do not belong to at least one club, and most of them have membership in several."[25]

Many of the clubs held dinner meetings at Delmonico's famous restaurant, where a private room and impeccable service awaited them.[26] In his walks, Melville often passed this symbol of New York's elite society, for Delmonico's had moved from Fourteenth Street and Fifth Avenue in 1876 to East Twenty-Sixth Street and Fifth Avenue, just two blocks from Melville's home and opposite Madison Square Park, which he liked to frequent in his last years. According to Henry Collins

Brown, "nightly the great dining salon was filled with beautiful women and men of national celebrity, while the men's cafe . . . [was] the best club in the city, owing to the infinite variety of its members." It was the "trysting place of men from the Union, Knickerbocker, Calumet, and Manhattan Clubs, the great meeting ground of business men, actors and other professional men, leaders of the financial world, sportsmen and men who have nothing to do save enjoy themselves."[27] Melville's selection of the men's cafe of Delmonico's for the setting of "At the Hostelry" thus appears a supreme stroke of irony, for Rembrandt, Tintoretto, Rubens, Rosa, Michelangelo, and company do not appear to be the kinds of patrons usually found at Delmonico's.

Melville was one of those "few men of New York" who did not belong to a club, but he was surrounded by those who did. Almost everyone who was anyone in New York was a member of at least one club. From 1859 to his death in 1872, Melville's brother Allan, a prominent attorney, was a member of the prestigous Century Club.[28] Other members of the same club included Melville's ministers at the All Souls Unitarian Church, Dr. Henry W. Bellows and later Dr. Theodore Chickering Williams; the Reverend Orville Dewey, who baptized the Melville children in Pittsfield in 1863; Richard Henry Stoddard, whom Melville knew when they both served with the Customs Service; Edmund C. Stedman, one of few literary men who manifested continuing interest in the aging Melville; and Titus Munson Coan, who—according to his own account—visited Melville during the 1880s "repeatedly in New York, and had the most interesting talks with him. What stores of reading, what reaches of philosophy, were his! He took the attitude of absolute independence toward the world."[29]

Melville's staunch sense of independence, which so forcefully impressed Coan, accounts in part for his remaining aloof from club life even though he was surrounded by this phenomenon of the times. Another factor may have been the expense of joining and maintaining membership. James Herbert Morse pointed out to Edmund C. Stedman, who supported an increase in membership fees for the Century Club, "that the Century would have been impossible for Hawthorne, even after he had arrived at the 'Scarlet Letter' period; for Emerson, at almost any period during his best productive days, for Thoreau at any time; for Whittier, Poe, and for Lowell while he was writing his forceful poems in those years when he was eagerly looking for $15 a week."[30] However, when in 1882 certain members of the Century decided to found the Authors Club, and asked Melville to join, they purposely kept the expenses of membership to a minimum, an entrance fee of fifteen dollars and annual dues of only ten dollars.[31] Even Melville could probably have afforded this, though he did not have the financial resources needed for some of the ancillary social activities.[32] Nevertheless, given the fact that he knew a number of the members of the new club, such as George W. Curtis, Richard H. Stoddard, Julian Hawthorne, and Edmund C. Stedman, he was tempted to accept the invitation.

In fact, he did accept it. In one of the most telling and curious episodes of his last years, he responded favorably to the invitation of the founding committee to become a member of the Authors Club. Then, almost immediately, he thought better of it and wrote to decline. According to the secretary of the new club, Charles De Kay: "Rather to my surprise Herman Melville the elusive accepted the original invitation, but as he soon wrote, he had become too much of a hermit, saying his nerves could no longer stand large gatherings and begged to rescind his acceptance."[33]

What Melville, the nervous hermit, would have encountered had he become a club member was a great deal of good fellowship, good storytelling, good wine, and good food. James Herbert Morse describes an evening of geniality and stories sometime after 1875 at the Century Club:

> As I now see the picture, [Bayard] Taylor was the central
> figure, in a full grown arm-chair—and he quite filled it too
> with his two-hundred-odd pounds of bigness—more than
> did the honors of it with his rich voice, his ripe experience of
> men and of the world; with a laugh that was contagious, an
> eye that was gloriously sympathetic, a head that was more
> than "leonine,"—for no lion would have unbent so naturally
> to become a splendid boy again as Taylor did that night.
> Richard Henry Stoddard sat by him, mostly silent, abiding the
> moment when the conversation might perchance need one of

his keen, bright flashes of wit to give it a fresh twist. Taylor was telling some tale of the Old World—I know not what it was—and Stedman sat on the arm of the big chair, with one arm round the shoulders of the narrator.[34]

Suggestions about the extent to which Melville may or may not have been genuinely drawn to such activity could well be hidden in the pages of his Burgundy Club sketches, for he created there figures very much like those Morse describes in his reminiscence. An understanding of the tone of the sketches, which projects his attitude toward such types, helps to clarify whether his decision to reject membership in a club—to which he was attracted perhaps because of a lingering inclination toward geniality—was more the result of frayed nerves, as he claimed in his polite note, or of a deep and fundamental inclination to form his circle of companionship elsewhere and by other means. One side of him, just for a moment, wanted to join the Authors Club, but he found, as did Emily Dickinson, that his soul selected its own society, and it was not to be from the club life of New York.

The two sketches that Melville devoted to the Marquis de Grandvin are both dedicatory in nature, one less than a single printed page and the other some seven pages in length and offering more detail about the Marquis as a type. Just what he is meant to be the type of seems to have been largely settled since Merton M. Sealts Jr. pointed out in 1958 that Melville "considered referring to [him] not as the Marquis but as the 'Magnum.'"[35] Since then and Sealts's later characterization of him in his *Melville's Reading* (1966) as "a personification of wine," critics have largely agreed that this is the intended function of the Marquis de Grandvin.[36] With his usual perspicacity, Sealts was unquestionably right on two counts, his reading of the Marquis as an abstraction and his recognition that Melville associated him with wine. Building on Sealts's observations, I suggest a further and somewhat broader interpretation: the Marquis is not merely the personification of wine but the very spirit of club life (which includes wine). He is geniality personified.[37]

The issue of whether Melville meant the Marquis de Grandvin to function as a personification of wine or in a more comprehensive role as the spirit of geniality is fundamental to a consideration of the Burgundy Club sketches. If the Marquis represents wine and its effects, the sketches devoted to him and the scattered references to him in the other pieces appear to add up to a kind of affected joke about drinking, and the strange tone of playful exaggeration that runs through the sketches seems to be simply a part of the good-humored, if somewhat precious, fun. If the materials are to be considered in a more serious vein, then either the Marquis must be the representative of more than wine or wine must be a symbol of something beyond, as in the reading of William Bysshe Stein, who argues that wine symbolizes Dionysian power, the power "to deliver man from the suffering and anxiety of temporal existence."[38] Stein may be off target in his claims that Melville in his later years was "an apostle of Bacchus or Dionysus," but he is sound in his conviction that the the Burgundy Club materials are worthy of the most serious consideration, and he is correct that they are highly revealing (even if one disagrees with him about what it is that they reveal).[39]

They reveal, among other things, not only Melville's inclination toward geniality, as many critics have suggested, but his pronounced distrust of it as well. In "The Marquis de Grandvin," the narrator (or "editor") writes that his subject is "a person of genial temper," a "genial foreigner." He is a "genial paragon," a man who causes a "genial flood" in others (346, 347, 348).[40] Though he is "an honorary member of most of the Fifth Avenue Clubs," as the spirit of geniality would naturally be, he is not strictly an American or French phenomenon, for "in the high circles of every European capital he is received with even more than good-will" (346, 347).

Praise of geniality, however, almost imperceptively turns into condemnation. For what but condemnation is it to point out that geniality is highly transitory, that it is incapable of embodiment in literature, and that its influence is similar to that of a mere magnet: "withdraw the magnet and all is over"? (351). The Marquis possesses what appears a "talismanic something" that "can operate upon another nature though of a temper not favourably disposed to receive its benign influence" (349–50). But Melville did not place much reliance in a "Talismanic Secret"—as he makes clear in *Pierre*.[41] The Marquis possesses a "fine, open, cheery aspect . . . that conveys a thrill to these frames so exquisitely strung to happiness" (346–47), but such a bearing (resembling the friendly, open expression of Captain Delano in "Benito Cereno") is not characteristic of those whom Melville most admires. Searching his mind for someone else who manifests the sterling qualities of geniality found in the Marquis, the narrator claims that he can come up only with "that oratorical pyrotechnist" (350–51), Rufus Choate (1799–1859), a criminal defense lawyer (and sometime politician) noted for his ability to spellbind juries with his purple oratory and thus win cases.[42] Overtly praising the Marquis by comparing him with Choate, the narrator creates through irony the opposite effect.

Such irony crackles through this sketch as it does elsewhere in the Burgundy Club materials. The extent to which the narrator should be seen as the conscious creator of such irony is difficult to determine. This character appears to be a fawning sycophant whose prose reeks of the obsequiousness that marks every aspect of his relationship with the Marquis de Grandvin and Major Jack Gentian. His praise of the Marquis so lacks meditative restraint that it counters itself. He declares in purple hyperbole that he will force the gods to make room for the Marquis on "their golden benches" and proclaims that he will "monumentalise him to the remotest posterity in a book fragrant as violets, yet lasting as the Pyramids!" (352). So artificial is his language at times that he seems to be either a disingenuous cynic or a total fool. The complexity of his role in the Burgundy Club materials deepens with the realization that he is the poetic creator of "At the Hostelry" and "Naples in the Time of Bomba," certainly not the product of a superficial and pedestrian mind.

Whether the undercurrent of irony flows directly from Melville or through a narrator who pretends to be more naive and direct than he really is, it flows nevertheless, and it makes for writing that in its doubleness challenges and finally delights. Its presence forces an illuminating reexamination of such issues as Melville's late-life attitude toward geniality. Above all, recognizing the presence of irony preserves one from the misperception inherent in the remark of one critic that these sketches are "sentimental" and "little more than nostalgia."[43]

Melville's delineation of Major Jack Gentian is much more detailed than that of the Marquis de Grandvin and even more complexly double-edged. Of the seven Burgundy Club sketches, five deal directly or indirectly with this character. Leon Howard calls him one of the author's "favorite characters" and argues that "Melville could not let him alone. He sketched him and revised and elaborated his sketches more often than he did those of Captain Vere, John Claggart, and Daniel Orme." Howard speculates that Melville never finished the project because he "could not forget Jack long enough to characterize the other members of the club."[44]

From the several sketches, a composite portrait of Major Jack Gentian emerges. He was born about the same time as Melville of, as the narrator of "Portrait of a Gentleman" explains, "a transplanted shoot of Southern stock for two generations taking root and branching out in the North" (1). Both his maternal and paternal ancestors fought in the Revolutionary War. He attended Harvard University and graduated. He is childless, a lifelong bachelor. In the American Civil War, he served as a major under Grant in the Wilderness Campaign and lost an arm in combat. He lives in (or, in another sketch, near) the Burgundy Club building on Fifth Avenue, and he devotes himself to club life. He is not employed—probably because he has a substantial amount of money, and at one time was the director of at least one bank. In the past he has run for public office but was defeated. He was nominated by Grant to fill a consulship in Naples, but the appointment was not confirmed. He is socially notable, recognized almost everywhere he goes in the city. He is unpretentious and straightforward, incapable of double-dealing. He is patriotic especially with regard to the Revolutionary War, and he wears with pride the Badge of the Society of Cincinnati on all appropriate occasions. He speaks no ill of the South and refers seldom to his part in the late war. He is charitable and compassionate and manifests a high degree of lovingkindness. He keenly recognizes that he is growing old and that his powers are in decline. He is an avowed and unashamed disciple of the Marquis de Grandvin.

Unquestionably, one reason Howard and others feel that Gentian is a highly favored character is that Melville made him in some respects like himself. Certain details in the character's background match those in the life of the author: the approximate date of birth, "double Revolutionary descent," and an unsuccessful attempt to secure a consulate appointment. These similarities notwithstanding, Jack Gentian is not Herman Melville. The composite offered above reveals far more differences than likenesses. Melville was not of southern background;[45] he did not graduate from Harvard University; he was not a bachelor; he did not fight in the Civil War, much less lose a limb in battle; he was not wealthy; he was never a director of a bank; he never ran for office; and so forth. Nor is Jack Gentian a projection of what Melville would like to be. In his life and works, Melville clearly rejects much of what this character stands for.

Indeed, a great deal of the praise that the narrator of the sketches heaps upon Jack Gentian smacks of the eqivocalness of irony. The narrator's overt purpose in repeating the criticisms of the Major by his detractors is to show their cruelty and unfairness and thus by contrast the nobility of Jack Gentian. Colonel Josiah Bunkum, who once ran against Gentian for public office, is a self-serving politician. His very name suggests insincere and foolish talk, hot air. Consequently, when the narrator relates Bunkum's condemnation of Jack's aristocratic tendencies in "Major Gentian and Colonel J. Bunkum," he blisters the Colonel by indirection and thus praises Jack by implication. The same technique is employed in "Jack Gentian," which depicts the Major in decline, an aged and pitiable figure attacked by unfeeling and narrow-minded hypocrites (none of whom belong to the Burgundy Club), who claim that he is no longer as dignified as he should be and needs an "attendant" (371). To these despicable people, Colonel Bunkum and the crooked-mouthed hypocrites, Jack is the enemy. But Melville makes Jack's enemies our enemies through his negative depiction of them. If Jack Gentian is their foe, then he merits our approval, for the enemy of our enemy is our friend.

Nevertheless, upon closer examination it becomes apparent that some of the charges against Jack Gentian are true, howsoever unsavory be the accusers. Toward the end of "Jack Gentian," the narrator writes: "I will not gainsay these young roosters and old hens, since on some points upon which they click-clock the basis of their talk is true enough" (372). And tucked away in "Major Gentian and Colonel J. Bunkum" is a criticism that Jack makes of the Colonel, which is as invidious as Bunkum's attack on the Major. He claims that the Colonel's so-called valor in the Civil War was "contorted," that it was "quite at odds with the magnanimities and martial amenities." He charges Bunkum with rashness and ignorance: "Not a man of broad judicial temper, sir" (376). Mockingly, he concludes that Bunkum is a crude and wisdomless boor, incapable of understanding a man like Jack Gentian. Irony runs through the final paragraph of this sketch as the Major's friends interpret as "charity" his biting estimate of Colonel Bunkum: "That is charity, Major, Christian charity with a vengeance. But some of us ere now have thought that by such charitable construings (or, are they indolently stoical ones?) of words and actions not charitable, thy failing to take the trouble to resent them, however absurd they may be, and vindicate thyself, thou hast—and more than once or twice—been something of a loser" (377). The Major's remarks about Bunkum are not charitable; he certainly does resent the Colonel's charges; and he has made an attempt to vindicate himself through his counterattack, which is "vengeance" but not in the sense his friends mean. He has been "something of a loser" in that he was not elected to office and that his friends have not had the opportunity to see him publicly put his critics in their place. But these final words, ironically intended as praise, speak the deeper truth of Jack Gentian's life and mind. As Melville depicts him, he is, indeed, something of a loser.

Though most of the sketches are seemingly dedicatory, they frequently border on the subtly condemnatory. All the narrator's praises notwithstanding, the one overwhelming characteristic of Jack Gentian is shallowness. In "The Portrait of a Gentleman," the Dean of the Burgundians is labeled the "captain of the good fellows" (353). Since the Civil War, his mission in life had been merely "the dispensing of those less abbreviated greetings on the Avenue and considerate old-school hospitalities" (353). In short, his entire existence is devoted to socializing. He is a sort of Jimmy Rose who has never had to face bankruptcy. In "To Major John Gentian, Dean of the Burgundy Club," his simplicity of mind, his lack of complexity, is suggested through the narrator's ostensible praise of his "single-mindedness, so resented by the ambidextrous double-dealers" (358). Melville himself, however, was an accomplished literary double-dealer, and this proclivity is evident in his portrait of Jack Gentian. The narrator's admiring description of "the genial humour of thy club-chat," as he calls Gentian's monologues in the same sketch, is cloaked in terms that suggest not profundity but superficiality. The Dean's talk is "garnished . . . even like to a holiday barn, with sprigs of classic parsley set about it or inserted cloves of old English proverbs, or yet older Latin ones equally commonplace, yet never losing the verity in them, their preservative spice" (358). In stark contrast to such conversation, decorated with parsley and flavored with cloves and other spices, are the comments of the artists in "At the Hostelry" or, indeed, the silence of those great talents present who merely muse and ponder.

With his profound admiration for the attitudes and ways of the Marquis de Grandvin, the Major is, like one of his detractors in "Jack Gentian," "a sort of man the natural product of the clubs and club-life," writes the narrator, who quickly adds, "so at least the moralising enemies of clubs would doubtless maintain" (371). Himself drawn to the spirit of geniality, Melville perceived clearly its dangers. Thus through irony, he allies himself with the "enemies of clubs" whom the editor mentions with scorn. He realized that a lifelong devotion to good fellowship and genial companionship in social clubs leads ultimately to emptiness. He depicted those perils years before in the first section of his bipartite story "The Paradise of Bachelors and the Tartarus of Maids" (1855), where English club life is brought under close scrutiny and where Melville's technique is similar to that in the Gentian sketches. The narrator lavishly praises the Templars of London and the elaborate dinner he attended at their invitation, but a strong undercurrent of irony tellingly washes away the paradisaical hedonism, exposing below the grinning specter of human suffering and death. The bachelors are finally revealed as superficial disciples of routine and order who are trying desperately to escape the realities of life and death.

Melville's delineation of Jack Gentian is permeated with melancholy. Grown old in his pursuit of good company and conversation, Jack now finds himself alone, the most terrible fate possible for the consummate clubman. In an extended scene in "To Major John

Gentian, Dean of the Burgundy Club," Melville depicts him in his "customary place at the club's bay-window" overlooking Fifth Avenue on a Fourth of July morning, "discoursing at whiles with whomsoever may, fortunately for himself, happen to be at hand" (360). There is something profoundly sad in the spectacle of this good and respected man sitting all morning in his long-used chair of the club looking for someone to talk to and starting a conversation with anyone he encounters. Practically abandoned now and having no life outside his club, he gazes around the almost empty room, waiting for lunch. He engages in conversation the only other member present, a "somewhat reserved gentleman of mature years," who is presumably the "editor" of the Burgundy Club materials (361). Major Gentian's comments reflect his despair over loneliness. "Not good for a man to be alone," he says, "especially on the immortal Fourth" (364). But he is alone, "gazing out of the open window for a time, noting the strange Sabbatarian quiet of the Avenue" and turning his eyes with disappointment to the "vacant lounges and sofas" of the room (360). Reduced to fussing over trivial details, he calls to the server: "Go, see if the steward has ordered it [the wine] as I directed, kept that *chambertin* three leagues from his refrigerator and the bottles in readiness to be gently immersed up to the neck—mind, up to the neck in a water-cooler, the water of its natural temperature at this season. Go, lad, it is important" (364).

Although he goes on to say that in insisting on such meticulous detail in regard to the luncheon wine he is merely humoring the tastes of the two friends who will dine with him, it is clear that such unimportant particulars have indeed become important to him, and what is important to Jack Gentian is the crux of these sketches about him. He holds "good fellowship" to be the highest goal of life, and even in death, he will, predicts the narrator in "Jack Gentian," respond to his circle of fellows with a "genial spirit" reflected in his "waning eyes" (372).

Next in importance to him is his badge of the Society of the Cincinnati and what he associates with it. Melville devotes an entire sketch to this emblem so highly valued by Jack Gentian and mentions it in all but one of the other prose pieces about him. It is this badge that Colonel Bunkum objects to as an indication of Jack's aristocratic tendencies.

Refusing to wear the badge of the Grand Army of the Republic, though he was a field officer and maimed hero of the Civil War, Major Gentian never misses an opportunity to exhibit, writes the narrator of "To Major John Gentian, Dean of the Burgundy Club," the "cherished eagle of the Society of the Cincinnati," a "golden eagle suspended by the white-bordered blue ribbon," and representing "an order which Washington and Lafayette" and Jack's "grandfather and father wore before" him (358, 360). He is sure to polish up and sport the emblem of the Cincinnati not only on every Fourth of July, but also "at certain grand banquets," the narrator writes in "Portrait of a Gentleman," "where as an honorary guest he sits at the high table" (356). The badge "descended to the Major from his great-grandfather, a South Carolinian, a white-haired captain of infantry at the battle of Saratoga Springs, who therefore, being eligible as a Revolutionary officer, was enrolled in the order upon its formation just after the Peace" (356–57). Jack Gentian's inordinate pride in this insignia is unusual if not strangely peculiar. The Cincinnati badge is so weighted with importance for him that he considers other such symbols—even those of religious orders—to be insignificant. He "once demanded, and with some animation—'Compared with this bit of old gold,' tapping it with his hand, 'what is the insignia of the Knights of the Golden Fleece or the Knights of the Spanish Order of the Holy Ghost? Gimcracks, sir!'" (357).

The true reason for Jack's devotion to the Cincinnati is not the explanation that the Colonel offers in "Major Gentian and Colonel J. Bunkum": "I remember long ago in my youth the eldest son of a revolutionary officer, and as such an inheritor of the Cincinnati badge, saying, over the Madeira, to his own son, then a stripling, 'My boy, if ever there is a recognised order of nobility in this land, it will be formed of the sons of the officers of the Revolution'" (373). Since, as Merton M. Sealts Jr. has pointed out, a Cincinnati badge was passed down in the Gansevoort branch of Melville's own family—from his maternal grandfather, General Peter Gansevoort—the above remark could well be a part of the family history.[46]

One has to look elsewhere, however, to find the meaning of the badge to Jack Gentian. His interest in the insignia does not grow out of a desire to be an aristocrat, a part of the nobility of a monarchy, but out of his romantic nature. He romanticizes the Revolutionary War and patriotism. The most important day of the year for him is the Fourth of July, which he calls "the immortal Fourth." He romanticizes boyhood and his days of travel in Europe. He cannot romanticize the Civil War, however, because its carnage is vivid in his mind (his own stump of an arm a harsh reminder) and its outcome less than glorious; consequently, he tries to blot it from his thinking and wears no emblems to memorialize his part in the terrible struggle. It is not that he is modest or that he is ashamed of his having been a combat soldier, far from it; memories of the war simply conflict with his strong romantic tendencies, which he prefers to follow. That is why he exhibits the Cincinnati badge but refuses to wear that of the Grand Army of the Republic. The emblem of the Cincinnati is really all that he has left. It is the manifestation of what passes as his identity—his family roots and his nature as a romantic.

Like Melville's paternal grandfather, the sociable but ever more isolated Major Thomas Melvill, Jack Gentian outlives his "usefulness" and in his advanced years becomes something of an anachronism, the "Last Leaf," as Oliver Wendell Holmes termed Major Melvill.[47] He is similar to the organization whose insignia he wears as it is described by the "philosopher" of the Burgundy Club in "The Cincinnati": "If the Society of the Cincinnati, a heritage from the Fathers, be really worthy of a respect bordering upon reverence, it is of the sort that the Catholics pay to the bones of the saints; for, indeed, this venerable institution survives but as a relic. . . . [It] attests a temper and an era that shall never be restored. It is a remarkable monument of the times. . . . In short, the Society is archaic" (380).

This is not to say that Melville's portrait of Jack Gentian is totally negative, for despite his shallowness, his unswerving (and misguided) devotion to club life, and his overly romantic nature, the Dean of the Burgundians is admirable for his charity and loving-kindness, his honesty and his forthrightness. Melville's basic disapproval of such a man bleeds through the narrator's almost mock heroic praise, but occasionally bleeding through the disapproval is a hint of respect and understanding. The reason for this ambivalence may be that Melville based his characterization of Jack Gentian on a family member—like

Major Thomas Melvill—about whom he held feelings of both sad disapproval and affection. Or in the exploration of Gentian's character, Melville could have been exploring the territory Henry James covered in his story "The Jolly Corner," where the aging Spencer Brydon encounters a specter figure who is very much unlike himself but who presumably manifests what he could have been had he followed another course in life, had he remained in New York, pursued a career in business and finance, and fought in the Civil War. Brydon finds himself drawn to this ghostly presence, though he does not approve of him. His confronting the ghost of what he might have been is difficult and even traumatic but ultimately cathartic. The similarities of James's story with Melville's portrait of Jack Gentian are striking. As William Bysshe Stein observes, Gentian "suggests what Melville might have been if he had not become immersed in the insoluble metaphysical and theological problem of good and evil."[48]

Detailed speculation about what one might have become under different circumstances is, of course, always futile if not silly, but it is not unusual among thoughtful and sensitive people whose lives are more than ordinarily self-centered. It is unhealthy only if the imagined other self turns out to be more attractive, in which case deep regret and self-pity ensue. If in his creation of Major Jack Gentian, Melville was, indeed, imagining what he might have been, the exercise resulted not in guilt and disappointment but in a rush of self-esteem and justification. For he clearly is glad that he did not turn out like the Dean of the Burgundians, though he naturally feels some affection for and kinship with him. He is glad that he never wished to pursue membership in the Society of the Cincinnati, though he might have been successful had he tried.[49] He neither longed to wear the badge that another member of his family inherited nor wished to join with those who totally disapproved of such emblems. As Hershel Parker astutely observes, Melville mocked "both those who affect aristocratic 'gew-gaws' and those levelers who would destroy anything hinting of inherited privileges, such as the badge of the Order of the Cincinnati."[50] He did not himself cherish the badge, but he did not like those who railed against it.

Melville's attitude toward Jack Gentian is important because it is one key to his values and to his self-conceived identity in these late years of his life. If the Major is not a projection of what Melville most admired in others and wished to be, neither is the old sailor of "Daniel Orme," who is Gentian's very antithesis. This sketch was found in a folder with the manuscript of *Billy Budd* after Melville's death and published in the Constable Edition in 1924. The editor, Raymond Weaver, has been the target of much abuse as has been a later editor, F. Barron Freeman, because they assumed that the sketch was once meant to be a part of *Billy Budd.* Not so, argue other critics, some of whom believe that "Daniel Orme" is Melville's self-portrait in his old age.[51] Philip Young writes of the sketch in a manner reminiscent of critics years ago who argued that *Billy Budd* is Melville's personal testament of acceptance, that it manifests his final peace with himself and his reconciliation with God. To Young, "Daniel Orme" appears to be Melville's new testament of acceptance: "The force of 'Daniel Orme' rests substantially in the realization that it is Melville's portrait of himself as an old man approaching death willingly, hoping to depart without remorse, penitence, or confession, and completely resigned to obscurity after a life of extraordinary vicissitude and long disappointment."[52]

Some of the details of "Daniel Orme" appear to support Young's biographical reading of the sketch, and old sailors such as Orme obviously did command Melville's respect if not admiration. One might also argue that if Major Jack Gentian is not Melville's self-portrait, then Daniel Orme could be because the aged tar is in essential ways the opposite of the clubman. Gentian is sociable in the extreme, is of a prominent family, is a Harvard graduate, is an ex-officer of the Union Army, and is independently wealthy. Orme is unsociable in the extreme, is of the lower class, is uneducated, is an ex-common sailor, and is poor. Gentian's emblem is that of the Cincinnati; Orme's is a tattooed red and blue cross on his chest over the heart crossed with a scar. Neither person is Herman Melville, who was not much given to painting self-portraits as such but who chose to manifest his characteristics and struggles in more subtle ways. He was somewhat sympathetic with both Gentian and Orme, but he did not pour his own identity into either. It may be pleasant to contemplate a resigned and reconciled Herman Melville realizing his guilt for wrongs he perpetrated on his family, as Young suggests, remembering his seagoing days of yore, and finding a place across the river and into the trees where he could die in serenity. That attractive but sentimental scenario, however, does not match up with the real Melville.

During his last years, Melville was a far different person from Daniel Orme, whose allegiance even in death is not to art and the creative impulse but to the memory of military life and engagement. Unlike Melville, the old sailor cannot be said to have a vital life after his retirement. Forced from sea duty by age, he simply spends his last years remembering what he once was. In brief, he was "a man-of-war's man."[53] That is his total identity. Nothing is known about his early history, and now that he is old, he is still at heart a man-of-war's man. His life has been one devoted conscientiously and constantly to "discharging his duties" to the God of War (118). His face is "peppered all below the eyes with dense dottings of black-blue," the result of "a cartridge explosion" during battle (118). He does not regret his life of devotion to Mars but misses it intensely. This is the reason that he sometimes looks under his shirt at his chest. As his shore acquaintances discover surreptitiously, he has "a crucifix in indigo and vermilion tattooed on the chest and on the side of the heart. Slanting across the crucifix and paling the pigment there ran a whitish scar, long and thin, such as might ensue from the slash of a cutlass imperfectly parried or dodged" (120). As for the cross, Melville explains that it was not unusual for a sailor of those days to have this symbol tattooed on his body (though having it on the "trunk" was somewhat rare). It does not suggest religiosity so much as fad or cultural identification. The scar happens to run through the cross because "the old mastman had in legitimate naval service known what it was to repel boarders and not without receiving a sabre mark from them" (120).

The cross and the scar in conjunction serve to project Melville's conclusions about Daniel Orme. His reason for gazing in later life upon the scarred cross has nothing to do with "something dark" in his past. Among the various rumors that circulate about him is one that claims he feels remorse and is doing penitence, but this gossip is no more reliable than the other superstitious nonsense circulated by his fellow lodgers: that he had been a notorious and murderous pirate, that he was "branded by the Evil Spirit," and so forth (119, 120). The idea that Orme has some dark secret that leaves him guilt-ridden goes back to his days on the sea when he was given to moodiness. When from "muttered soliloquy he would sometimes start" and appear uncheerful if not quarrelsome, the "Calvinistic imagination of a certain frigate chaplain" declared that the sailor's actions indicated "remorseful condemnation of some dark deed in the past" (118). But what, in Melville's mind, is such an opinion from such a one worth? From the time he served aboard the frigate *United States*, Melville was convinced that naval chaplains were hypocrites because of their sworn allegiance to the military. In *White-Jacket*, he wrote:

> How can it be expected that the religion of peace should florish in an oaken castle of war? How can it be expected that the clergyman, whose pulpit is a forty-two-pounder, should convert sinners to a faith that enjoins them to turn the right cheek when the left is smitten? How is it to be expected . . . when . . . the chaplain shall receive "two twentieths" of . . . [the] price paid for sinking and destroying ships full of human beings? How is it to be expected that a clergyman, thus provided for, should prove efficacious in enlarging upon the criminality of Judas, who, for thirty pieces of silver, betrayed his Master?[54]

Melville expressed a similar opinion in *Billy Budd*, composed about the same time as "Daniel Orme." In his sensitivity and genuineness, the chaplain in that work seems somewhat exceptional, but Melville leaves no doubts about his opinion in general of military clergy: "Bluntly put, a chaplain is the minister of the Prince of Peace serving in the host of the God of War—Mars. As such, he is as incongruous as that musket of Blucher, etc., at Christmas. Why then is he there? Because he indirectly subserves the purpose attested by the cannon; because too he lends the sanction of the religion of the meek to that which practically is the abrogation of everything but brute Force."[55] At the end of "Daniel Orme," Melville rejects the view of the naval chaplain with the "Calvinistic imagination" that Orme in his final years suffered from remorse: "No, let us believe that . . . he fell asleep recalling through the haze of memory many a far-off scene" (122).

Thus in retirement, this "old man-of-war's man," peppered and scarred by battle, has no regrets about his life but misses so keenly all that he has identified himself with, namely war, that he spends his time remembering those beautiful days of military engagement, and when it comes time for him to die, he selects an abandoned fort for that purpose. It was a place "destined for use in war" (121).[56] Significantly, Orme props himself against one of "an obsolete battery of rusty guns" and breathes his last (121).

The Christian references in "Daniel Orme" create an effective undercurrent of irony and establish poignantly and eloquently Melville's point that this man of Mars has but one religion, one god—War. The Christian cross over his heart ultimately means nothing to him though it implies much about him. When he puts aside his garment and stares at his chest, he is not contemplating the cross but the real insignia of his identity, the battle scar that runs through it; he is not hungering for Christ or recognizing his past sinfulness but longing for the old days when he was a warrior. The scar is his most forceful reminder of those times. Any spiritual impulse in Orme (the cross) has been negated by his devotion to Mars (the scar). That he dies on Easter, the holiest and perhaps most meaningful of Christian holidays, shows but the plainer how far his life has been removed from the teachings of the Prince of Peace.

Yet Melville does not delineate Daniel Orme with hostility or even condescension. The tone that permeates this sketch is not one of contempt but one of pathos. Melville is not chiding the old sailor but portraying him from a motive of curiosity mixed with a feeling of respectful melancholy. He appeals to Melville's imagination. Here is an admirable person but a shallow and misguided one, a person who has devoted himself to and totally identified himself with the world of the man-of-war. Conscientious as has been his devotion to duty, his devotion has been to the wrong cause. Melville finds such allegiance praiseworthy in some ways but curious, curious because it is so shallow and shortsighted. A character who embodies this trait is scarcely his "literary double," as one critic claims.[57] In fact, such a person could never be a member of Melville's circle. Major Jack Gentian and Daniel Orme represent what Melville was not in his old age far more than what he was.

The Melville of the Burgundy Club materials and "Daniel Orme" was a man who, unlike the genial clubman and the old sailor, carefully and consciously devoted his late years to the life of the imagination and who clearly realized that such a commitment, combined with his particular temperament, left little room for a wide circle of friends in the usual sense. The bipartite poem, "At the Hostelry" and "Naples in the Time of Bomba," manifests Melville's continuing vitality as a creative experimenter and his growing interest in the nature of art. The accompanying prose sketches reflect his intensified conviction that a life dedicated to the spirit of geniality is but vaporous. On the other hand, "Daniel Orme" suggests that "unsociability," as Melville describes the sailor's disposition, is not meaningful and productive in and of itself. Disengagement with sociality must be accompanied by engagement with the creative imagination. These complimentary stances represent Melville's own strongest proclivities during the final fourteen years of his life.

He did enjoy a kind of circle, one formed largely from his reading, not a circle in the usual sense of the word, but a group of artistic and philosophical compatriots with whom he communicated only through the intellect and imagination. His basic nature determined who would make up this circle. It consisted largely of the creative minds whose ideas—Buddhism and Pessimism, for example—he explored. The writers who are discussed in connection with Melville in the chapters that follow form the core of his circle: Sir Edwin Arnold and the Buddhist commentators, James Thomson, Arthur Schopenhauer, Matthew Arnold, Honoré de Balzac, Sir Walter Scott, William Dean Howells, S. Reynolds Hole, Omar Khayyám, and the artist Elihu Vedder. They were his company, his provokers, and his support, though he neither agreed with them always nor allowed them to form or change his own views. He gave them his attention and his respect but never his allegiance. The soul selects its own society, but that society does not fundamentally change it. This book is not an influence study in the usual sense but an attempt to understand what was going on in Melville's mind and imagination during these years to draw him to these particular authors or artists, seeking not new ideas but justification and encouragement.

Two

DISENCHANTMENT

Sometime in the 1870s—Merton M. Sealts Jr. places the time between 1871 and 1875—Melville purchased a copy of William Rounseville Alger's *The Solitudes of Nature and of Man* (1869), which contains a section of some eighteen pages on Buddha.[1] From 1874 to 1878, Alger, a Unitarian minister, was pastor of the fashionable Church of the Messiah in New York City, where Dr. Orville Dewey, who in 1863 baptized all of the Melville children (except Malcolm) in Pittsfield, had preceded him and where at one time "could occasionally have been heard the eloquence of Dr. Channing."[2] Whether the Melvilles actually knew Alger is difficult to ascertain, but they definitely knew of him, for he was not only minister of a sister church to their own All Souls Unitarian Church in New York City but also one of the most famous local men of letters and a brilliant speaker in the lyceums. Liberal in theological as well as political matters, he had made himself something of an authority on Eastern religion and thought. In 1856 he published *The Poetry of the East,* and a few years later he came out with a massive work of scholarship, *A Critical History of the Doctrine of a Future Life* (1864), which went through at least ten editions and which treats in detail, among numerous other things, Buddhist beliefs.[3]

What Melville encountered in Alger's *The Solitudes of Nature and of Man* in regard to Buddhism was a genuine admiration of Gautama and a profound respect for his beliefs. Buddha, Alger wrote, "was endowed with surprising personal beauty and with the noblest traits of character."[4] He was "a genius and hero of the most exalted order," a "cosmopolitan hero of the mysteries of human life and destiny," and he "stands out as one man from amidst thousands of millions."[5] In Alger's hands, Sakya-Muni, the Buddha, becomes personally as appealing as Jesus Christ, and his doctrine perhaps even more magnetic, for Buddhism, he points out, is "the most numerously followed of all religions that have ever prevailed on the earth."[6] So compelling does Alger, himself a Christian, find "the power" of Gautama's appeal that he calls it "the most wonderful psychological phenomenon in the history of the human race."[7]

In order to convey the attractiveness of Buddhism, Alger delineates and by implication agrees with its view of "all finite existence as made up of unreality, pain, and impermanence."[8] Once the reality of that insight is grasped, it becomes logical to find the means of escaping "the intolerable evil of existence." Buddha clearly outlines those means: "self-renunciation, disinterested sympathy, the common virtues of life, and meditative aspiration, carried to their last terms."[9] Throughout his analysis of Buddhism, in which he treats all the major tenets, Alger stresses the attractiveness of escape, rest, and renunciation. Through enlightenment and self-discipline, he says, the Buddhist sets out to "break the chains of desire, and achieve an absolute detachment, and absolute indifference to everything."[10] By his system Gautama "sought . . . to guide all beings to the shoreless ocean of exemption, to the wall-less city of rest."[11] Those in this city of rest enjoy "a perfect detachment and equipoise."[12]

Such are the rewards for the faithful Buddhist in this life—an end to striving, a defeat of human desires and ambitions, a deliverance from the world's illusions. The reward hereafter—nirvana—Alger describes in highly positive terms: "By Nirwana the Buddhist thinkers mean a boundless affirmation, the resumption of that relationless, changeless state of which every form of existence is the deprivation; and they regard it as an infinite entrancement."[13] Though difficult for Western minds to grasp, nirvana is the very foundation of Buddhism: "It is the inspirer of their toils and aspirations, the receptable of their exhaling worships."[14]

Melville seemed to grasp the centrality of nirvana in Buddhist belief, for in his poem "Buddha," published in *Timoleon*, he has created the prayer of a devotee whose aspiration is to achieve the state of nirvana, "the receptacle," as Alger put it, of his "exhaling worships." "Nirvana!" Melville writes, "absorb us in your skies. / Annul us into thee." Years before he published "Buddha," Melville referred to Gautama in *Clarel,* where he comments on both his personal attractiveness and on the extent to which his teachings spread over the East. Tender and unselfish, Gautama suffered for humankind:

> How Buddha pined!
> Pierced with the sense of all we bear,
> Not only ills by fate assigned,
> But misrule of our selfish mind,
> Fain would the tender sage repair.[15]
> (4.18.252–56)

Earlier in the poem, Melville depicts Clarel's envisioning swarms of Mongolians making a pilgrimage to India in order to visit in reverence a Buddhist shrine, driven by some compelling hunger not easily explained:

> Far afloat,
> From eras gone he caught the sound
> Of hordes from China's furthest moat,
> Crossing the Himalayan mound,
> To kneel at shrine or relic so
> Of Buddha, the Mongolian Fo
> Or Indian Savior. What profound
> Impulsion makes these tribes to range?
> (1.5.199–206)

By the mid-1870s, Melville thus appears to have acquired some knowledge of Buddhism (indeed, enough to know that in parts of China and Mongolia, Gautama was known as Fo).

This knowledge was greatly enriched by his reading of Sir Edwin Arnold's highly popular account of Buddha's life and thought, *The Light of Asia.* This long poem in blank verse was included in *The Poems of Edwin Arnold,* which Melville read and annotated.[16] An Englishman who spent a portion of his early life in India, Arnold was for some forty years an important writer on the staff of the London *Daily Telegraph*. Through his second wife he became related to the American Channings: his father-in-law was William Henry Channing, Unitarian minister and nephew of the more famous William Ellery Channing. From this connection and another with Thomas Wentworth Higginson, Arnold became acquainted with some of the most prominent Americans of the day (one of his sons was named after Emerson, who had been a guest in the Arnold home and had blessed the infant in prayer). A friend and cowriter for the *Daily Telegraph* was W. Clarke Russell, an avid admirer of Melville to whom *John Marr and Other Sailors* was dedicated after Russell had for some years expressed profusely in print his enthusiasm for the man he considered America's greatest author, not only as a novelist but also as a poet—"leagues ahead of Longfellow and Bryant."[17] A popular writer of sea fiction, Russell later dedicated one of his novels to Melville.

Edwin Arnold's American connections insured him of immediate attention in this country upon the publication of *The Light of Asia* in 1879. Bronson Alcott and George Ripley praised it lavishly, and Melville's onetime physician Oliver Wendell Holmes reviewed it with enthusiasm. "Partly because of this distinguished sponsorship," according to Arnold's biographer Brooks Wright, "*The Light of Asia* was probably more widely known in America than in England."[18] That is not to say that this tender and sympathetic account of Buddha was not popular in Arnold's own country, for by 1885 its original publisher had issued more than thirty editions. Wright estimates that it may have had a sale of a million copies and was "once to be found side by side with *The Idylls of the King* and *Evangeline* in middle-class parlors throughout Great Britain and America."[19] It is almost impossible to say how many editions appeared by American publishers, for though it was issued in an authorized form by Roberts Brothers, pirated versions abounded.[20]

The reasons for the immense popularity of *The Light of Asia* are numerous, but certainly one of them was the fascination of the times with comparative religions. The opening lines of one of Arnold's early poems, *The Feast of Belshazzar*, expresses the inclination of this period to explore and understand the worship systems of other lands: "Not by one portal, or one path alone / God's holy messages to man are known." By the time *The Light of Asia* appeared, Britain and America had been broadening their theological horizons. Brooks Wright comments that "*The Light of Asia* could hardly have been better timed. For several decades the controversy over the relative merits of Buddhism and Christianity had been developing, and just as that quarrel came to a head, Arnold's poem appeared. Coming when it did, it seemed to many people the climactic utterance of the whole debate. Its literary charm and human appeal gave it a circulation far wider than any other book on Buddhism."[21]

Melville's natural curiosity about comparative theology and his objections to narrow sectarianism drew him toward a mind like Edwin Arnold's. He also appreciated the effort that Arnold put into a long, sustained poetic endeavor on a religious subject, for he had himself gone through such a trial in his composition of *Clarel.* He found in *The Light of Asia,* as he had found in Alger, a glorification of the life of Gautama and a detailed (if sometimes oversimplified) account of his philosophy. Not much of the basics of what is called Theravada, the older and original form of Buddhism, is omitted from *The Light of Asia.* In his preface, Arnold states that "my purpose has been obtained if any just conception be here conveyed of the lofty character of this noble prince, and of the general purport of his doctrine."[22] Several times Arnold stresses that Buddhism is no exotic and rare cult but the "great faith of Asia": "Four hundred and seventy millions of our race live and die in the tenets of Gautama. . . . More than a third of mankind, therefore, owe their moral and religious ideas to his illustrious prince, whose personality . . . cannot but appear the highest, gentlest, holiest, and most beneficent, with one exception, in the history of Thought."[23]

The eight blank-verse books that make up *The Light of Asia* follow Prince Siddhartha from his birth to his death, frequently stopping to explore such concepts as karma, metempsychosis, meditation (to a lesser degree), the doctrine of mind only (no soul), the four sublime truths, the noble eightfold path, and nirvana. Not of lesser interest to Melville was the Buddhist observation on the "delusion" of life, which breeds "Sankhara," defined as "Tendency Perverse: Tendency Energy."[24]

The right path is to reject ambition and all other forms of perverse energy and seek rest:

> . . . Man hath no fate except past deeds,
> No Hell but what he makes, no Heaven too high
> For those to reach whose passions sleep subdued.[25]

Melville had long believed at least part of this doctrine—that a person constitutes his or her own fate—and now that he was in a time of his life when, as Leon Howard has put it, "his greatest desire seems to have been to live quietly," he felt the strong pull of the other aspect of it—rest from striving.[26] Whether he attempted any of the meditative practices he read about is doubtful, but in *The Light of Asia* he discovered in more than one place the most prevalent of Buddhist mantras used in meditation: "Om, mani padme, hum." The poem ends on this note of reverence and meditative worship:

> OM! The Dew is on the lotus!—rise, Great Sun!
> And lift my leaf and mix me with the wave.
> Om mani padme hum, the Sunrise comes!
> The Dewdrop slips into the shining Sea![27]

Three of the volumes of Honoré de Balzac that Melville read late in his life contain lengthy introductions by George Frederic Parsons that deal principally with Balzac's interest in Eastern religions, especially Buddhism.[28] Running through all three of these introductions is Parsons's conviction that Balzac's thought was grounded in Buddhism. He frequently quotes Edwin Arnold admiringly and explores the basic concepts of Buddhism, stressing "the illusiveness of material existence."[29] He claims that nirvana is not annihilation but a positive and desirable state of unsurpassed peace and cites contemporary scholars who have commented on the subject; he explains the Four Noble Truths; and in a long and involved section on number, he explores the Buddhist chant and the mantra. If Melville had not already learned the characteristics and the glories of Buddhism, he found them delineated in abundance in Parsons's introductions.

Among the most widely read writings on Buddhism at this time in America were those of the Reverend James Freeman Clarke, a prominent Boston Unitarian minister whose study of comparative religions, he claimed in the preface to his popular *Ten Great Religions* (1871), spanned twenty-five years. That volume, the outgrowth of a series of articles that he published in the *Atlantic Monthly* in 1868, went through several editions, and his interest in Buddhism continued to be reflected into the 1880s with such articles as "Affinities of Buddhism and Christianity," published in the *North American Review* in 1883. Clarke found himself at times so enthusiastic about Buddhist principles and so moved by the figure of Gautama that he felt the need to correct his perspective and to remember that he was a Christian (and a minister at that). Still, he always remained receptive to such glowing accounts of Buddha as he found in Edwin Arnold. His article in the *North American Review* concludes: "Let us still be grateful for the influence which has done so much to tame the savage Mongols, and to introduce hospitality and humanity into the homes of Lassa and Siam. If Edwin Arnold, a poet, idealizes him [Buddha] too highly, it is the better fault, and should be easily forgiven. Hero-worshipers are becoming scarce in our time; let us make the most of those we have."[30]

Melville may or may not have read Clarke's *Ten Great Religions* or the articles on Buddhism that he published in prominent American journals, but he certainly knew Clarke personally and knew of his work in comparative theology. On her wedding day, Elizabeth Melville received Communion from Clarke, and he officiated at the funeral in August 1879 of Melville's mother-in-law (Elizabeth's stepmother), Hope Savage Shaw. Clarke's enthusiasm for Buddhist teachings is evident in *Ten Great Religions,* where in one place he warns against considering these convictions as debasing superstition and concludes that they "must have come from the sight of truth, not the belief in error."[31] Part of Clarke's admiration for this great Eastern faith was based upon its similarity to biblical teachings. He points out a parallel that must also have occurred to Melville, given his lifelong attraction to the "strong hammered steel of woe," the book of Ecclesiastes. Toward the beginning of his discussion of "Leading Doctrines of Buddhism," Clarke writes:

> [Sakyamuni] might have used the language of the Book of
> Ecclesiastes, and cried, "vanity of vanities! all is vanity!" The

profound gloom of that wonderful book is based on the same course of thought as that of the Buddha, namely, that everything goes round and round in a circle; that nothing moves forward; that there is no new thing under the sun; that the sun rises and sets, and rises again; that the wind blows north and south, and east and west, and then returns according to its circuits. Where can rest be found? where peace? where any certainty? Siddârtha was young; but he saw age approaching. He was in health; but he knew that sickness and death were lying in wait for him. He could not escape from the sight of this perpetual round of growth and decay, life and death, joy and woe. He cried out, from the depths of his soul, for something stable, permanent, real.[32]

The spirit of antidogmatism in Buddhist belief (as Clarke presents it) greatly appealed to Melville. "In this respect," Clarke remarks, "it can teach Christians a lesson. Buddhism has no prejudices against those who confess another faith. The Buddhists have founded no Inquisition. [They exhibit] . . . a toleration almost inexplicable to our Western experience."[33] Like many commentators on Buddhist practices, Clarke describes their incantationlike chant: "All kneel and begin to chant their prayers in a low and musical tone" from which arises "an immense and solemn harmony, which deeply impresses the mind."[34] On the question of nirvana, Clarke in one place refers his readers to Alger's able treatment of that thorny concept. He does comment, however, that there is a "profound sadness" in Buddhism: "To its eye all existence is evil, and the only hope is to escape from time into eternity,—or into nothing,—as you may choose to interpret Nirvana."[35]

Indications from the poems, as William H. Shurr points out, "clearly show that Melville was reading Buddhist literature during these years."[36] If we consider what he is known to have had in his personal library on Buddhism, what he is likely to have known about or read, and what was readily available to him on the subject, a substantial body of writing emerges. Melville's final fourteen years saw an explosion of Western interest in this light of Asia. In 1881 a reviewer of Arthur Lillie's *Buddha and Early Buddhism* commented in the *Atlantic Monthly* that there were "many who say that they approve of

Buddhism, or admit, as the cautious gentleman did of Niagara, that they have heard it very highly spoken of."[37] So rapidly did the American curiosity about Buddhism spread and so pronounced did it become that at the Chicago World's Fair in 1893 (only two years after Melville's death), some Americans worried that it and other religions might supplant the nation's traditional faith. Writing the year after, Paul Carus stated that at the fair, the "interest taken in other religions, especially Buddhism, grew to such an extraordinary degree that some Christians began to fear for Christianity and tried to counteract the favorable impression which the foreign delegates had made on the Chicago public."[38] Leaflets were hastily composed and distributed in an attempt to point out the evils of Buddhism and thus kill the growing acceptance of it as a legitimate faith and an alternative way of arriving at the same end that Western believers seek. In his article on "Buddhist Charity" in the *North American Review,* the great Buddhist scholar Max Müller commented in 1885: "My dear friend, the late Dean of Westminster, once said: 'I remember the time when the name of Gautama, the Buddha, was scarcely known, except to a few scholars, and not always well spoken of by those who knew it; and now—he is second to One only.'"[39] Müller finds that "so much has been written of late on Buddhism" that he must explain early in the essay what form of that faith he is discussing.

The point here is that in addition to what Melville is known to have read on Buddhism, he had the easy opportunity to read much more and probably did. Indeed, during the years 1877–91, current periodicals abounded in articles on Buddhism. Their proliferation was insured not only because of the current interest in comparative religions, in what Melville called in *Clarel* "the intersympathy of creeds," but also because of the debate on several issues that drew in that large segment of readers who thrive on controversy and argument. Especially heated was the debate raging on two aspects of Buddhism: its historical relationship with Christianity and the nature of its concept of nirvana. Since Gautama lived five centuries before Jesus and since, as numerous writers pointed out, startling similarities exist between Buddhism and Christianity, a controversy arose on whether the latter could have been based on the former. Arthur Lillie hotly pursued his conviction that "Buddha is the only true reformer who has ever existed and that the influence of his teachings was the inspiration" of others, including Jesus.[40] Some who espoused this view went so far as to claim that Buddhist missionaries discovered America in the fifth century. Half in humor, half in pique, a reviewer of Lillie's *Buddha and Early Buddhism* wrote in the *Nation*: "Surely Mr. Lillie would not contend that Buddhist missionaries ever found their way to Mexico *via* Behring's Straits and Alaska. If so, we give it up."[41]

Discussions of works in foreign tongues, such as that by the prolific Rudolf Seydel, also appeared in American journals. In several books, Seydel argued that the Christian Gospels were based on Buddhist scriptures, that in all likelihood the first four books of the New Testament were composed at Antioch or Ephesus by a Christian who had been influenced by a traveling Buddhist monk.[42] Others, who noticed the intriguing parallels in the two faiths, tried to find a way to prove that Christianity shaped later Buddhism. The Jesuits, for example, insisted that missionaries of the Roman Catholic Church visited Asia in the fourteenth century and provided Buddhists models for their ritual practices.[43] Such theories were vehemently disputed by Buddhist authorities like Max Müller and T. W. Rhys Davids.

An aspect of this same debate involved the question of legitimacy and rank—whether the teachings of Buddha should be considered as truth. Some Christians seemed determined to study Buddhism if for no other reason than to reveal its inferiority to Christianity. Best known in this group was the Reverend R. Spence Hardy, whose *A Manual of Buddhism* (1853) was widely read. Other writers on Buddhism, like the eloquent W. L. Courtney, argued that the same truths lie at the heart of both faiths.[44] Still other Western apologists appeared convinced of the basic superiority of Buddhism.

The most fascinating single facet of Buddhism for Western minds and certainly the most controversial is that of nirvana. Since the teachings of Gautama were introduced into this country in the nineteenth century, nirvana has been its most debated concept. James Freeman Clarke took an optimistic view of nirvana, as did many American writers on the subject; he explained in his *Ten Great Religions* that it means not *nothing* but *no thing*, that is, "it is the opposite to all we know, the contradiction of what we call life now, a state so sublime, so wholly different from anything we know or can know now, that it is the same thing as nothing to us."[45] Others agreed that we cannot in our present finite state understand nirvana but that it is certainly the opposite of nothing. Yet even some who were sympathetic with Buddhism argued with this view. A writer for the *North American Review* objected strongly to Clarke's representation of nirvana and insisted that to Buddhists nirvana is, indeed, nothingness, total annihilation, which to the peculiar Eastern mind is desirable, though damnable to us.[46] The combatants in this lively and sustained debate, the degrees of disagreement, and the variety of individual interpretations are too numerous even to sketch. But whether nirvana meant a peace that could actually be appreciated by the recipient or merely a total disappearance as if one had never lived, the controversy was interesting enough to enough people to help keep Buddhism before large numbers of readers, especially those who, like Melville, had a philosophical mind.

Buddhism is a wonderfully attractive philosophy for a tired man, a welcome alternative to the philosophy represented by the word *excelsior*. It seeks not a continuance of but an end to grasping and striving, which it perceives as but futile. It offers rest and peace. Melville's interest in Buddhism derived partly from his longtime fascination with "the intersympathy of creeds" and partly from the fact that it is a congenial philosophy for a seeker who has learned that he is not going to find the answers to life's maddening riddles. A. J. Bahm points out that Buddhism "argues the futility of seeking answers to metaphysical questions."[47] This had become Melville's position, so when he found the same conclusion expressed in Gautama's thought, he felt that he had discovered a worldview that in many ways—though not all—paralleled his own. Buddhism is essentially concerned with facing squarely the ugliness, the deceptiveness of existence, especially self-deception. For someone like Melville who had become deeply involved in self-exploration and the attempt of self-mastery, Buddhism could not fail to attract interest. Gautama taught that nothing should stand in the way "of your own self-conquest."[48]

Hints occur throughout Melville's later poems that he is turning his eye toward the East. With references like that in "To Ned" to "the Indian Psyche's languor won," he manifests an appreciation for the goal of certain Eastern religions. After a "dull day's work" in the customs service, he dreams, he writes in "My Jacket Old" of Asia, "Old Asia of the sun," where "other garbs prevail." Though Melville recognized clearly that some aspects of Buddhism were alien to his creative impulse (partly the subject of my next chapter), certain elements of Buddhist thought remained congenial to him.

In writers like James Thomson and Arthur Schopenhauer, he found much of what appealed to him in Buddhism combined with a rebellious spirit that he enjoyed. Thomson, Schopenhauer, Giacomo Leopardi, and others in the school of Pessimists were Buddhist-like in basic vision but men full of fire and fight, men who shouted angrily from a peak the glories of the downward way. Their very complexity was enough to attract the complicated mind of an aging Herman Melville, though as ever he retained his open independence of sea.

"Systematic" or "scientific" Pessimism, as it came to be known, emerged from the seed of Eastern Buddhism planted in the last half of the nineteenth century in a new and different soil, that of the Western world. The basic doctrines of Pessimism (especially those shared with Buddhism) can be summed up in a few sentences. The world as we see and experience it is an illusion. It appears to be reality, but it is not. In fact, it bars our way to reality, which is within rather than without. Freeing oneself of this illusion that the world around us is ultimate reality is the highest and noblest purpose, but it is extremely difficult. Detachment and indifference to things of the world must be cultivated and, most important, our cravings, our wills, must be overcome in order to obtain peace. Since the world is illusory and corrupt, the desires of humankind lead only to suffering. Life by its very nature is affliction. To be liberated from this City of Dreadful Night, as James Thomson called it, one must not rely upon a Creator.

In his book on nineteenth-century Pessimism, *The Philosophy of Disenchantment* (1885), Edgar Saltus observed:

> Within the last few years Buddhism has spread into Russia,
> and from there into Germany, England, and the United States,
> and wherever it spreads it paves in its passing the way for

pessimism. The number of pessimists it is of course impossible to compute: instinctive pessimists abound everywhere, but however limited the numbers of theoretic pessimists may be, their literature at least is daily increasing. For the last twenty years, it may safely be said that not a month has gone by unmarked by some fresh contribution; and the most recent developments of French and German literature show that the countless arguments, pleas, and replies which the subject has called forth have brought, instead of exhaustion, a new and expanded vigor.[49]

Saltus and other late nineteenth-century students of philosophical thought recognized that the new Pessimism, "theoretic" Pessimism he called it, was at its most fundamental level Buddhism stripped of its Eastern mythology and ritualistic practices. The worldviews of both were essentially the same. It was important, however, to distinguish between a traditional dark view of existence to be traced all the way back to ancient times, to thinkers such as the Cyrenaic philosopher Hegesias (whose pupils, it is said, made practical application of his teachings by killing themselves) and the more systematized beliefs of certain nineteenth-century Europeans led by Arthur Schopenhauer. The one, a generic mode of thought that has existed since the beginning of time, was called *pessimism;* the other, a recent phenomenon and recognizable chiefly from its basic similarity to Buddhism, was called *Pessimism* (with a capital *P* and often linked with one of the labels *scientific, philosophic, systematic,* or *theoretical*). The latter, said Saltus in 1885, "came into general notice not more than twenty-five years ago; at that time it aroused in certain quarters a horrified dislike; in others it was welcomed with passionate approval; books and articles were written for and against it in much the same manner that books and articles leaped into print in defense and abuse of the theory generally connected with Darwin's name."[50]

Melville's last fourteen years thus coincided with the rapid spread of a philosophical movement in America and Europe that evoked such interest and controversy that it has been compared in its effects with Darwin's theory of evolution. Biographers and critics have commented on Melville's reading of Schopenhauer and Thomson, but what has not been made clear is the extent to which these two writers, as different as they were from each other in some ways, shared a similar worldview and were members of a larger movement. They were part of what was a late nineteenth-century phenomenon, a trend that was influencing the intellectual world not just in philosophy but in belletristic literature as well. Systematic Pessimism was a magnet drawing to itself many who had independently arrived at various similar positions but did not heretofore have a name for their vision or a system into which to order it. All indications are that Melville was well aware of Pessimism as a movement, that he sensitively witnessed its impact on the contemporary scene, and that he felt its compelling power.

Even in the early 1870s, articles and books on the subject began to appear that set the stage for a lengthy controversy. In a two-part series in *The Contemporary Review,* for example, J. Frohschammer sought to define the issues and to make clear that philosophic Pessimism was challenging the established premises of the Western world. He states that "through the decided and very prevalent Pessimism of the philosopher Arthur Schopenhauer," this set of beliefs has "recently come into great prominence."[51] The seriousness with which Pessimism was taken in philosophic circles is suggested by the numerous studies devoted to the subject, books like James Sully's *Pessimism: A History and a Criticism* (1877) and R. M. Wenley's *Aspects of Pessimism* (1894). Sully begins his lengthy volume by pointing out that systematic Pessimism "stands for a recent development of speculations which provides a complete theory of the universe, and which appears to be adopted . . . by a large and growing school."[52] Wenley sees "the importance of recent Pessimism . . . to be gauged by the assurance with which its professors advance it as a working theory of the world," and he describes it as having "swelled into an inharmoniously harmonious symphony of despair."[53]

Much of what was published in this period about Pessimism was unfavorable, but instead of making the movement fade, such writings added to its notoriety. Agnes Repplier bemoaned the prevalence of this mode of thinking in an article in the *Atlantic Monthly* in 1887 and tried to show that Saltus, Schopenhauer, Sully, and others notwithstanding, there was nothing new about the new Pessimism: "From the misty flower-gardens of Buddha have been gathered for centuries the hemlock and nightshade that adorn the funeral-wreaths of literature."[54] There *was* something new about it, however, as Repplier herself (perhaps unwittingly) makes clear even in her condemnation of its followers: "They are full of the hopefulness of despair, and confident in the strength of the world's weakness. They assume that they not only represent great fundamental truths, but that these truths are for the first time being put forth in a concrete shape for the edification and adherence of mankind."[55]

Repplier pointedly set out the features of Pessimism that distinguished it from the more general darkness of numerous writers and thinkers over the centuries and from Buddhism, its undisputed parent: it was different because of the evident pleasure that its advocates took in pronouncing this the worst of all possible worlds, in proclaiming with gusto, "I am; therefore, I suffer." There was zeal in such pronouncements because the Pessimists considered themselves not disillusioners but truth speakers, who with ardor were freeing people of their illusions. Theirs was the philosophy of disenchantment, not enslaving enchantments. Their evident delight came not just from telling the truth as they saw it but also from destroying old and cherished notions. They were much louder than the modest Buddhists, more boisterous; they were in personalities as well as in message iconoclasts. Saltus commented that wherever Pessimism "rears its head, it does so amid a swirl of vanishing illusions and a totter and crash of superstitions."[56]

To read today the Pessimists that Melville read, the German philosopher Arthur Schopenhauer (1788–1860) and the British essayist and poet James Thomson (1834–82), sometimes called the "Laureate of Pessimism," is to be impressed with the vigor of their voices, the quickness of their minds, the profound sincerity of their convictions, and the rebelliousness of their combative spirits. Their essays are not heavy and melancholy but infinitely readable with flashes of great insight and frequent flourishes of genuine wit. The wonder is not that Melville read them but that he did not openly acknowledge more admiration for them, that he did not state what is obvious—his emotional and intellectual kinship with them. Such affinity is evident throughout his writings. He was unquestionably what Saltus called an "instinctive pessimist." In his late poems, in works like "The Berg" and those epigrams that make up the section in *John Marr* called "Pebbles," he reveals a philosophical stance much in line with that of the Pessimists. In other poems of the period he sounds like the inconoclastic Pessimists taking their shots at illusions that make life unalteringly optimistic. Satirically he assumes the voice of one of these optimists in "Merry Ditty of the Sad Man," positing the theory that a tragic vision should never be faced but covered up with a song. Similarly, in "Fruit and Flower Painter," he depicts the essential ingredient of optimism, self-deception:

> December is howling,
>> But feign it a flute:
> Help on the deceiving—
>> Paint flowers and fruit!

He was writing even closer to his heart in "The Medallion," where he attacked readers and critics who insist upon undiluted optimism in poetry. Why do you complain of poets, he asks, who present life as it is, "where no glossings reign?" Such poems illustrate sympathy for the Pessimist vision, but Melville's involvement in this movement and his debt to the Pessimists were far more specific.

The precursor of systematic Pessimism was the Italian poet and philosopher Giacomo Leopardi (1798–1837), often quoted admiringly by James Thomson and Arthur Schopenhauer. Leopardi's work did not become widely known to the English-speaking world until the middle of the nineteenth century, when William E. Gladstone wrote with what has been called "admiring disapproval" of him in an article in the *Quarterly Review*.[57] Saltus devoted about twenty pages to Leopardi in *The Philosophy of Disenchantment*, and James Sully refers to his thought as representative of the "pessimistic movement in modern poetry." Sully is struck not only with Leopardi's sense of despair but also with the "positive gratification" that he appeared to derive from it. "I rejoice," Sully quotes Leopardi as writing, "to discover more and more the misery of men and things, to touch them with the hand, and to be seized with a cold shudder as I search through the unblessed and terrible secret of life."[58]

Melville's interest in Leopardi goes as far back as his reading of Valery's *Historical, Literary, and Artistical Travels in Italy* (1852), a book that he acquired in Florence in 1857. In that volume he marked Leopardi's name and underlined a passage detailing the poet's death. In *Clarel*, he referred to Leopardi as having been "stoned by Grief" (1.14.3).[59] Later while reading James Thomson's essay "Proposals for the Speedy Extinction of Evil and Misery," he made a vertical line by a quotation from Leopardi: "But the lofty spirits of my century discovered a new, and as it were divine counsel: for not being able to make happy on earth any one person, they ignored the individual, and gave themselves to seek universal felicity; and having easily found this, of a multitude singly sad and wretched they make a joyous and happy people."[60] Still later Melville checked a passage in Schopenhauer's *The Will as World and Idea* regarding Leopardi: "[Leopardi] is entirely filled and penetrated by it [the idea that life is a tragic farce]: his theme is everywhere the mockery and wretchedness of this existence; he presents it upon every page of his works, yet in such a multiplicity of forms and applications, with such wealth of imagery, that he never wearies us, but on the contrary, is throughout entertaining and exciting."[61]

Melville's acquaintance with this great Italian Pessimist was possibly secondhand, but it was of long standing, and it stimulated obvious interest, which never waned. In Alger's *The Solitudes of Nature and of Man*, Melville found sections on both Leopardi and Schopenhauer. Already fascinated with Leopardi, he discovered in Alger's book an account of the man and his ideas that amounts to a tribute. According to Alger, Leopardi's intellect and "heart" were "remarkable for their scope and fervor. He dared to think without checks, and to accept as truth whatever he saw as such."[62] A thinker of this sort could not but command the respect of Herman Melville.

Alger also refers to Schopenhauer in various places and devotes an entire section to him, stressing his major personality traits and ideas, especially his indebtedness to Buddhism. Though not in agreement with Schopenhauer's philosophy, Alger finds him "our chief of modern Pessimists."[63] Melville probably did not read extensively if at all in Schopenhauer's writings until early 1891, but the point should not be missed that he was familiar with the German philosopher and his position in the new Pessimist movement before that, at least as early as 1871–75; sometime within that period he acquired and read Alger's book.

Years later, probably in 1889 or 1890, he found in George Frederic Parsons's introductions to Balzac's *Seraphita, Louis Lambert,* and *The Magic Skin* lengthy commentary on Schopenhauer's philosophy, particularly Schopenhauer's indebtedness to Buddhism. Parsons felt that Schopenhauer's "theory of the functions of the Will" was "at bottom a Germanization of the law of Karma."[64] Furthermore, Parsons insisted that Schopenhauer's belief in the nobility of denying the will reflected the principal motivating force of Buddhism. Thus Parsons not only explored the chief themes of Schopenhauer's belief but claimed him together with Buddha as Balzac's intellectual and spiritual kin. In one place, Parsons breaks into an impassioned defense of the so-called Apostle of Pessimism as one of the most misunderstood philosophers of all time: "Those only can regard him as a true pessimist and as a believer in annihilation, who expose their own narrow limitations."[65] The characterization of Schopenhauer as a pessimist, charges Parsons, "is emphatically Philistine, Materialist, shallow, and misleading."[66] Through his exposure to such an onslaught against the Philistines and materialists in defense of Schopenhauer, Melville was primed to read for himself the German philosopher many people were talking and writing about.

By the time Melville began his reading of James Thomson, probably in 1884, he was thus already aware of systematic Pessimism as a movement and no doubt recognized Thomson not as a voice crying alone in the wilderness but as one in an influential group of writers espousing a vision with which he had sympathies. This is an important factor because it is much more tempting to identify oneself with a significant trend in thought than with an individual who is alone and isolated in his views. During the next several years after 1884, when he was reading Thomson on and off, Melville might have found himself under the sway of this Scottish spellbinder because in a good many ways Thomson mirrored his concerns, echoed his feelings, matched his courage, and approached his depth of genius. In addition, Thomson was part of a fairly new philosophical revolution that included great minds like Leopardi and Schopenhauer.

In fact, Melville did derive much from Thomson and had to resist the temptation to accept more. From the several references Melville made to Thomson in letters to James Billson, an English correspondent who sent him copies of Thomson's works, and to Henry Stephens Salt, Thomson's biographer, it is clear that Melville was impressed with Thomson and admired his writings. Biographers and critics have quoted these comments as proof of Melville's approval.[67] What is surprising about these several letters, however, is not the praise they express for Thomson but the brevity and restraint that characterizes this praise. Melville is saying what is sincerely on his heart, but he is holding his heart in rein and is being careful not to give the impression of enthusiasm. A stranger from abroad, sensing that Melville would be struck with Thomson's work, sent him a volume of poems by that author. In a brief letter, Melville replied with politeness, thanked Billson, called the verse "supremely beautiful," and compared it to the work of Keats. He concluded his remarks by saying that it must have been rewarding to have known Thomson personally, sensing that Billson is proud of that distinction.[68]

Early the next year, 1885, Billson followed up with another gift, Thomson's best known volume, *The City of Dreadful Night and Other Poems*. Again Melville thanked him with obvious restraint, and in just a few lines made further comments about Thomson as "a sterling poet." Now it was time for him to make a disclaimer, however, and an odd one, indeed, it was. Though Melville's statement has often been quoted, no one to my knowledge has pointed out its strangeness or tried to explain why he felt compelled to make it. What he said was that he liked Thomson but that he was not himself a Pessimist, though he liked some things about Pessimism, too: "As to his [Thomson's] pessimism, altho' neither pessimist nor optomist [sic] myself, nevertheless I relish it in the verse if for nothing else than as a counterpoise to the exorbitant hopefulness, juvenile and shallow, that makes such a bluster in these days—at least, in some quarters."[69] By 1885, Melville had become a man of great dignity, private though his life was. He was not going to be swept off his feet by any writer—as he had once been by Nathaniel Hawthorne—no matter how much of himself he saw in that other genius. He was too seasoned and too proud to go any further than to be polite and moderate in his response to someone who was recommending another's writings. He wanted it clearly understood before this correspondence went any further that Billson could not expect from him enthusiastic admissions of intellectual discovery for which the Englishman could take credit. What Billson could expect was brief and restrained expressions of thanks for his thoughtfulness and carefully crafted appreciative remarks by a great writer on another author whose most basic vision, that of consistent despair, he could not share. Melville's disclaimer was, therefore, a declaration of dignity and independence to someone who completely unknowingly was threatening both.

Melville was also making the statement for his own benefit. In the face of Thomson's appeal and the call of Pessimism in general, he found it necessary to stop and remind himself that he could not give his emotional and intellectual allegiance to any system of thought. That being done, he could loosen up somewhat more in later remarks to Billson about Thomson, and he did so, always restraining his enthusiasm and avoiding extensive personal involvement. The closest he came to showing his affinity for Thomson and to revealing just how deeply Thomson was touching him was in a letter of December 20, 1885. It was the two books of Thomson's essays that Billson sent him, *Essays and Phantasies* (1881) and *Satires and Profanities* (1884), to which Melville was most responsive. To Billson he wrote: "It is long since I have been so interested in a volume as in that of the 'Essays & Phantasies.'—'Bumble'—'indolence'—'The Poet' etc., each is so admirably honest and original and informed throughout with the spirit of the noblest natures, that it would have been wonderful indeed had they hit the popular taste."[70] As Melville proceeded in this his most extended evaluation of Thomson's work, he appeared to warm to his subject and for the first time to link Thomson's thinking with his own. "It is good for me to think of such a mind," he continues, "to know that such a brave intelligence has been—and may yet be, for aught anyone can *demonstrate* to the contrary."[71] Melville made comments about Thomson in several letters after this but never again as lengthy or as self-revelatory. He guardedly uses expressions such as "extremely pleasing" and "highly interesting." He continues to praise "The City of Dreadful Night" as "massive and mighty" (the "modern Book of Job"), and he calls Thomson's "criticisms in general . . . very refreshing." In a letter to H. S. Salt, he seems on the verge of opening up, but he says simply: "Much more might be said; but enough." His final pronouncement on the subject came in another letter to Salt, where he comments that Thomson was "a very remarkable poet and man."[72]

There is so much in Thomson's works, especially his essays, for Melville to agree with and admire that his responses to Billson and Salt appear to be calculated understatements designed to protect his own privacy, dignity, and independence. Even in matters not particularly related to the doctrines of Pessimism, Melville found close kinship with Thomson. They shared an admiration for Spenser and Blake. They both held dogmas and creeds in great distrust. Often Thomson sounds much like Melville in describing the inadequacy of dogma. In the essay "An Evening with Spenser," Thomson's voice could easily be mistaken for Melville's: "A creed or system is a strait-waistcoat for Nature; and if you will persist in trying to force it upon Her, you will soon experience that the great Titaness not only flings it off with wrathful disdain, but makes yourself fit for a strait-waistcoat in recompense for your trouble."[73] In another essay, he writes that "dogmas are but empty bottles and barrels into which each believer pours as much spirit as he has, and of such kind and quality as he has."[74]

In his dogma, his reliance upon established forms and his resistance to any new ideas, Melville's character Captain Vere of *Billy Budd* is closely related to Thomson's "Bumble." The passage in which Melville describes these characteristics of Captain Vere strikingly parallels sections in Thomson's "Bumble, Bumbledom, Bumbleism," sections that Melville read and marked.[75] Vere's "settled convictions were as a dike against those invading waters of novel opinion, social, political, and otherwise, which carried away as in a torrent no few minds in those days, minds by nature not inferior to his own."[76] Thomson wrote of Bumble:

One thing he does hate. . . . This thing is a new idea, or even the semblance of a new idea such as a novel opinion. . . . Every new idea is a reproach and insult cast upon our old doctrines and institutions. . . . If things as they immemorially have been and as they now are—our holy Church and noble State, as by law and the wisdom of our ancestors established—be worthy of the most reverent conservation; what pretence can there be for changing them by the application of new ideas? . . . For ideas are most perilous things to handle; suddenly explosive as gunpowder and gun-cotton, no one is safe to be blown up by them: Guy Fawkes may go in fragments through the air, the Parliament Houses with king, bishops and nobles are sure to, if once the confounded train catches.[77]

In his objection to "novel opinion," Captain Vere is no hypocrite; he is sincere and unselfish in rejecting the "invading waters" of new ideas. He "disinterestedly opposed them not alone because they seemed to him incapable of embodiment in lasting institutions, but at war with the peace of the world and the true welfare of mankind."[78] "With mankind," he claims, "forms, measured forms, are everything."[79] This rigidity comes not from ulterior motives but from genuine conviction. Such is also precisely true for Thomson's Bumble, for whom "good habits are the ideal" in moral behavior. Nevertheless, Thomson continues, "let no one accuse Bumble of conscious insincerity; dissimulation he detests. . . . He is doing what he is doing with the very best intentions, and the saintliest anxiety for the continuation of the stability and prosperity . . . which he honestly loves and venerates."[80] This passage Melville marked with both a vertical line in the margin and a check. The qualities he was struck with in Bumble, traits that Thomson delineated with obvious disapproval, became essential characteristics of Vere. This fact may thus help us to understand more clearly Melville's own attitude toward his often puzzling captain.

Vere's character can also be examined profitably in the light of what Melville read in Thomson and Schopenhauer about self-fidelity. During his last years, this subject appeared to be especially on his mind. In fact, on his portable writing desk, he pasted a slip of paper on which these words were printed: "Keep true to the dreams of thy youth."[81] Melville discovered that Thomson repeatedly shows his disgust with those "who violate their own nature," who "force themselves" to take courses of action "for which they have no liking," who "sacrifice themselves" to codes and mores that happen "to be fashionable." He finds it saddening to witness people acting "against their own inclinations."[82] Melville marked with both line and check Thomson's statement of his mission to encourage others to "keep true to themselves" rather than "succumb to the amiable cowardice of seeking to pretend to believe otherwise than they really do believe."[83] Thomson thus insists upon the necessity of fulfilling one's "own nature, as it is right for him."[84]

Melville found precisely the same theme developed and buttressed in Schopenhauer. During the time when he was developing Captain Vere's character, the third stage of his composition of *Billy Budd* according to Hayford and Sealts, he read in *Counsels and Maxims* a passage that establishes the difference between self-fidelity and self-betrayal. Like Thomson, Schopenhauer stresses the importance of being true to oneself. He appears almost to be describing Captain Vere's dilemma when his heart tells him that Billy is innocent but the code that he follows tells him that Billy must hang. "In the great moments of life," Schopenhauer writes, "when a man decides upon an important step, his action is directed not so much by any clear knowledge of the right thing to do, as by an inner impulse—you may almost call it an instinct—proceeding from the deepest foundations of his being."[85] Such is the impulse Vere experiences—to let Billy off—but he does not consider it "the right thing to do," so he proceeds "to criticize," in Schopenhauer's words, this impulse "by the light of hard and fast ideas of what is right in the abstract—those unprofitable ideas which are learnt by rote, or, it may be, borrowed from other people; if he begins to apply general rules, the principles which have guided others, to his own case, without sufficiently weighting the maxim that one man's meat is another's poison, then he will run great risk of doing himself an injustice," that is, running the risk of not being true to himself.[86] Judged in the terms of Thomson and Schopenhauer, then, Vere is not heroic in his determination to do his duty but deeply flawed and misguided.

On another issue, Thomson's essay "Per Contra: The Poet, High Art, Genius" does not reflect Melville's belief in the importance of an artist's commitment to art, but it does echo his conviction that books constitute an imperfect reflection of what is in the artist and in life. In *Pierre,* Melville wrote that "all great books in the world are but the mutilated shadowings-forth of invisible and eternally unembodied images in the soul; so that they are but the mirrors, distortedly reflecting to us our own things; and never mind what the mirror may be, if we would see the object, we must look at the object itself, and not at its reflection."[87] In Thomson's essay, Melville read: "Yet life remains and ever is as superior to art as a man to the picture of a man. Man abounding and pictures rare, a picture will often be valued by us for more than would the original; similarly, life being abundant and art rare, we often value a fraction of art more than the fraction of life of which it is the shadow or symbol: but our valuations do not affect the absolute and relative worth of the things in themselves."[88]

Thomson echoed, too, Melville's conviction that ultimate truth is inexpressible, that language is incapable of relating essences, and that even universal nature, symbolic though it is, fails ultimately to convey full spiritual meaning. "Although the world consummates itself to our senses and intellect by expression," Thomson wrote, "the innermost and purest and loftiest soul or essence of all things is supremely inexpressive; and . . . its expression in the sensible universe, in suns and planets, in trees and animals, is a degeneration."[89] In addition, Thomson shared Melville's distrust of journalism and lack of confidence in the unenlightened and materialistic masses (whom Thomson called "Bumble" and Melville the "dead level of the masses"). In Thomson's essay "Bumble, Bumbledom, Bumbleism," Melville marked passages such as the following that acidly attack the newspapers: "Of course, the Press, while thus continually boasting of its freedom, knows quite well, and has a comfortable understanding with Bumbledom, that it is, in fact, only free to glorify Bumble."[90] Thomson charges that the journalist is a tool of the mediocre, and Melville seemed to agree, for he continued to place vertical lines by (or enclose in penciled brackets) all comments that bear on the subject. "A journalist," Thomson wrote, "could no more live by producing opinions too large for Bumble, than a tailor by making coats to the size of Daniel Lambert, or a boot-maker by proportioning boots from the ground plan of Adam's foot in Celon."[91] Melville's implied attack on newspapers as manifested in his account of how the weekly *News from the Mediterranean* distorted facts in the death of Claggart in *Billy Budd* reveals if not Thomson's influence on this chapter at least the kinship of mind shared by the two authors.

Melville could not fail to be struck with the brilliance of Thomson's essays and the surprising degree to which repeatedly they reflected his own interests and convictions. He found in Thomson a person with his own views of missionaries and the attempts at proselytizing. In "Sayings of Sigvat," Thomson wrote: "Can you convert another man to your own height, figure, complexion, constitution, temperament?—if you can, you may also convert him really and truly to your own faith."[92] Later in that essay, Thomson issues a blistering attack on those who would "get us civilised off the face of the earth," echoing a sentiment that Melville had exhibited frequently in his writings.[93] When Thomson speaks of "this high confraternity" of true thinkers and poets in "Open Secret Societies," of those "men in great cities who will never get on in the world," of certain "sailors with the rhythm of the ocean-tide in their blood," those who are the real deep divers of life, he could be mistaken for Herman Melville praising the "choice hidden handful of the Divine Inert."[94]

A measure of Melville's continuing interest in Thomson is the fact that after reading the several volumes of the Pessimist's poems and essays, he read through and annotated Salt's *The Life of James Thomson* (1889). The copy of this biography now in the Houghton collection at Harvard University is the one Salt himself presented to Melville in 1890. It includes several newspaper clippings about Thomson mounted on the inside front cover and reveals Melville's penciled markings. It is significant that Melville was so eager to read a life of Thomson that he sought out and purchased a copy of the Salt volume before the author sent one to him. Elizabeth Melville apparently gave this copy, its present location unknown, to Arthur Stedman after Melville died. Merton M. Sealts Jr. quotes Stedman as saying in a letter to Salt: "Mrs. Melville has given me the copy of the life of James Thomson which her husband purchased before you sent him one. He paid $3.75 for it at a time when he was a very poor man."[95]

From Salt, Melville received glimpses of Thomson that were not furnished in the poetry and essays, for generously sprinkled throughout are quotations from Thomson's letters, many of which Melville marked. It is clear that Melville's interest in Thomson had gone beyond his art and ideas to his personality and struggles in life. He found portrayed in Salt a complicated genius of profound honesty who made pronouncements without regard to personal consequences, a person of great melancholy who also relished life, a lover of the tobacco pipe and a drinker too fond of Bacchus. The son of a sailor and thrown upon his own at a fairly early age to come up the hard way, Thomson could command the respect of an American who had been forced into similar circumstances. Melville marked passages that deal with Thomson's troubles with his publishers, and he seemed impressed, if his vertical lines and checks offer such an indication, by Thomson's expressions of independence and self-respect. It does not take a strong act of the imagination to perceive that in marking some of these passages, Melville was thinking of himself. He checked, for example, the following words that Salt quotes from Thomson on a subject unquestionably close to his heart in this late time of his life: "No wealthy life, fearless and free, will suffer itself to be pitied. . . . Let not the ordinary cabman despise Phaeton because he could not control the sun-steeds."[96]

Salt quotes Thomson so extensively, not just from the letters but also from the essays, that Melville was reading some of the material at least twice. In doing so, he marked numerous passages quoted in Salt that he had previously marked in the essays themselves. Evidently he was not tiring of these ideas and Thomson's poignant and often witty expression of them. In the final long chapter on "General Characteristics," however, Melville found in Salt's biography something new—a treatment of Thomson in the context of Pessimism. There Thomson's indebtedness to Leopardi is explored as is his connection with Buddhism and with Arthur Schopenhauer. By the time Melville finished his reading of Salt, he had extensive knowledge of a writer of brilliance who could command his respect and offer by example and by association a way of thinking that would represent for Melville a turning of the corner. If he had followed anyone as far as the City of Dreadful Night, it would have been James Thomson, but Melville was not a follower.

Early in this century, Thomas Whittaker, author of numerous volumes on philosophy, opened his book on Schopenhauer with the following statement: "Arthur Schopenhauer may be distinctively described as the greatest philosophic writer of his century."[97] The century he was referring to was the nineteenth, but Schopenhauer did not come into the prominence Whittaker credits him with until after 1851, when his collection of essays *Parerga and Paralipomena* appeared. It was even later before his works were translated into English. When recognition came, late in his life, it was with the force of a great rain, washing away some established houses of tradition but preparing the ground for a vigorous new growth. Such growth was not to prove to be of the enduring banyan variety, but nevertheless at the turn of the century his reputation was such that an eminent scholar of philosophy could call him the "greatest philosophic writer" of his time, and he did shape later minds like Eduard von Hartman and Philip Mainlander. The period of his most profound influence in the world, the time when he stirred the greatest excitement, was the last decade or so of Melville's life. When Melville "discovered" him, Schopenhauer was not a writer and thinker long known in America; his name, in fact, created the interest and conveyed the excitement associated with newness.

Melville was familiar with Schopenhauer's thought at least as early as the 1870s, when he read about him in Alger's book. By the time he actually began to purchase copies of Schopenhauer's works, he certainly knew, and had known for a good while, what the German philosopher stood for. No one sent him copies of Schopenhauer's works; apparently no one urged him to read this powerful writer whose name was newly on the lips of many. The motivation seems to have been entirely his own. In February 1891, he checked out from the New York Society Library a copy of Schopenhauer's *Counsels and Maxims* translated into English by T. Bailey Saunders and published just the previous year. Whether he had actually read anything by Schopenhauer previously is with current evidence impossible to say, but what is clear is that he was so impressed with the essays in *Counsels and Maxims* that after returning the volume to the library, he bought a copy of it together with four of Schopenhauer's other works, all of which he read and in varying degrees marked. Since his own copy of *Counsels and Maxims* is marked, he presumably read the work at least twice—the library copy and then his own.

Considering the fact that he was in the final year of his life, when his health was failing, the attraction of Schopenhauer must have been extremely powerful for him to engage in such an extensive and systematic program of reading. Schopenhauer's most acclaimed work, *The World as Will and Idea,* is a three-volume giant that would in itself constitute a substantial challenge even to a much younger and healthier person than was Melville at the time. The very fact that he read so much of this material in his last year speaks eloquently of his positive responses to it. In fact, some of Melville's very late writings occasionally reflect a Schopenhauerean tinge. William H. Shurr has argued convincingly that chapter 44 of *The World as Will and Idea* plays an important role in "After the Pleasure Party," which was probably begun before Melville's reading of Schopenhauer but not completed before he read the great German Pessimist.[98] In this particular chapter, "The Metaphysics of the Love of the Sexes," Schopenhauer develops his theory that sexual love is so strong that it overcomes dignity and reason in its blind desire for fulfillment. His ultimate point, however, is that the sexual urge is merely another manifestation of the will-to-live—in this instance, to reproduce. Melville's portrait of the woman Urania in the poem reflects Schopenhauer's insistence that sexual love is "the strongest and most powerful of motives," but it does not embody the principal theme of chapter 44 of *The World as Will and Idea,* that the will-to-live is the source of it.[99]

An additional and perhaps even more important influence in the creation of Urania (if, indeed, the shadow of Schopenhauer does hang over "After the Pleasure Party") is another section in *The World as Will and Idea,* chapter 19, "On the Primacy of the Will in Self-Consciousness." The thoughts of this chapter bear a close resemblance to those in Melville's poem concerning the way true motivations are frequently hidden from oneself. The complex force that Schopenhauer calls the "will" attempts to control all else including consciousness, which is "like the *valet de place* who conducts the stranger [the will]. In truth, however, the happiest figure of the relation of the two is the strong blind man [the will] who carries on his shoulders the lame man [the intellect] who can see."[100] In characterizing Urania, Melville follows Schopenhauer's belief in the need to understand the deep urges of the will. Melville read in chapter 19 of *The World as Will and Idea:* "Often we don't know what we wish or what we fear. We may entertain a wish for years without even confessing it to ourselves, or even allowing it to come to clear consciousness; for the intellect must know nothing about it, because the good opinion which we have of ourselves might thereby suffer."[101] It is difficult to imagine a clearer or more accurate description of the internal life of Melville's Urania, who for years would not admit her sexual desire, would not allow "it to come to clear consciousness," because the "good opinion" she has of herself would "suffer thereby." Schopenhauer continues: "Indeed we are often in error as to the real motive from which we have done something or left it undone, till at last perhaps an accident discovers to us the secret, and we know that what we have held to be the motive was not the true one, but another which we had not wished to confess to ourselves, because it by no means accorded with the good opinion we entertained of ourselves."[102] In Schopenhauer's extensive discussion, the subject of repressed desire that erupts when the will is ready plays a major part—as it does in "After the Pleasure Party."

As was true with his reading of Thomson's works, Melville found in Schopenhauer a fascinating array of sentiments that paralleled his own. Though his masterpiece, *The World as Will and Idea,* is often intricately complex and sometimes tedious, his essays, like Thomson's, are full of the keen insight of a sensitive observer of life who has the gifts of penetrating honesty and winning wit. In these shorter works, he does not write like an academic philosopher coolly pursuing a narrow problem in the approved and exclusive jargon of his circle. He is sophisticated, brilliantly incisive, full of common sense, ever ready and adept with metaphors, clear as spring water, fiercely independent, and sometimes disgustingly (but colorfully) prejudiced. Even his prejudices, however, create acute interest.

The essay "Human Nature," which Melville may or may not have read, contains Schopenhauer's most extended and clearest delineation of a type of person he mentions elsewhere, a type that greatly interested Melville: the man of envy. Melville read about envy as a compelling force in *The Wisdom of Life*, where Schopenhauer quotes Cicero on its power to control.[103] The person Schopenhauer describes in "Human Nature" is so similar to Melville's Claggart of *Billy Budd* as to suggest if not direct influence, then a remarkable affinity between the two authors.

> In the envy that is directed to natural gifts and personal advantages, like beauty . . . there is no consolation or hope of one kind or the other; so that nothing remains but to indulge a bitter and irreconcilable hatred of the person who possesses these privileges; and hence the only remaining desire is to take vengeance on him.
>
> But here the envious man finds himself in an unfortunate position; for all his blows fall powerless as soon as it is known that they come from him. Accordingly, he hides his feelings as carefully as if they were secret sins, and so becomes an inexhaustible inventor of tricks and artifices and devices for concealing and masking his procedure, in order that, unperceived, he may wound the object of his envy. For instance, with an air of the utmost unconcern he will ignore the advantages which are eating his heart out; he will neither see them, nor know them, nor have observed or even heard of them, and thus make himself a master in the art of dissimulation. With great cunning he will completely overlook the man whose brilliant qualities are gnawing at his heart, and act as though he were quite an unimportant person. . . . But at the same time he will before all things endeavour by secret machination carefully to deprive those advantages of any opportunity of showing themselves and becoming known. Then out of his dark corner he will attack these qualities with censure, mockery, ridicule and calumny, like the toad which

spurts its poison from a hole. No less will he enthusiastically praise unimportant people. . . . In short, he will become a Proteas in stratagem, in order to wound others without showing himself. . . . He betrays himself . . . by the causeless hatred which he shows—a hatred which finds vent in a violent explosion at any circumstance however trivial, though it is often only the product of his imagination.[104]

Schopenhauer goes on to point out that envy is "to be found and always goes about *incognito;* or, as I have said, like a venomous toad it lurks in dark corners."[105] At the end of this depiction of the man of envy, he concludes: "We have been taking a look at the *depravity* of man, and it is a sight which may well fill us with horror."[106] So many obvious parallels does this characterization have in common with that of Claggart that it would be unnecessary and perhaps tedious to list them. The first few paragraphs of chapter 13 of *Billy Budd,* which contains Melville's discussion of envy and its horrors, are in themselves enough to establish the astonishing links between John Claggart and Schopenhauer's "envious man."

Schopenhauer was, like Melville, a lifelong student of human nature. His astute observations on the subject abound in his works and embue them with an authenticity far greater than that of his more esoteric and abstract philosophical theories. Melville's markings of passages in *Counsels and Maxims* and *The World as Will and Idea* reveal his interest in Schopenhauer's remarks about the relationship between a person's knowledge of the world and the ability to read human nature. In the latter work, Melville penciled a vertical line by Schopenhauer's remark that "human nature has depths, obscurities, and perplexities, the analysis and elucidation of which is a matter of the very greatest difficulty."[107] In *Counsels and Maxims,* Melville marked a passage that explains both the importance and the limitations of what Schopenhauer terms "experience of the world." While it is useful, "a great deal of experience with little reflection and scanty knowledge, give us books like those of the *editio Bipontina,* where there are no notes and much that is unintelligible."[108] Such observations are interestingly similar to those Melville makes in chapter 11 of

Billy Budd, where the narrator speaks of an "honest scholar," one who "is now no more" (perhaps a member of Melville's circle of imaginary friends—possibly Schopenhauer?), an "adherent of no organized religion," who spoke to him of the complexities of human nature and the limited function of knowledge of the world in interpreting it.[109]

Melville seemed especially interested in what Schopenhauer had to say about fate or necessity. He marked in the index to *The World as Will and Idea* the entries on *Necessity,* and in an essay in *Counsels and Maxims* he placed a heavy vertical line by a passage discussing the importance of understanding the role of fate in life.[110] Generally, Melville found echoed in Schopenhauer's writings his own conviction that people create their own destinies because of what they are.

In the period 1877–91, then, Melville's reading about and in the Pessimists was substantial. He read James Thomson and Arthrur Schopenhauer in depth because he found in them kindred spirits. To be even more specific, however, he discovered that they addressed themselves repeatedly not just to matters that he had long been interested in, such as those discussed above as constituting general parallels and affinities of mind, but also to several concerns that preoccupied him in his final years.

Melville's first and perhaps primary concern of these years was that of self. His mental state during this period was sometimes close to self-absorption. Evidence abounds that in the final fourteen years, he had become decidedly less interested in matters external to himself. As early as June 1876, Elizabeth Melville wrote to cousin Kate Gansevoort Lansing that she was glad for the opportunity to get away with her two daughters for a while because she thought that their absence from Herman would not only benefit them but also help to "take him out of himself."[111] Some years later, in July 1885, she commented in another letter to Kate that she would be sorry for Herman to lose his job in the Customs Service partly because it helped him to think about something besides himself; it kept him *occupied.*[112]

To read Melville's correspondence during this period is to be impressed with a sort of sameness of tone. He did not write much or often. He seems to have written only when necessary to prevent hurt feelings or rudeness. His letters in general suggest a person taking care of chores rather than one genuinely anxious to keep open channels with the world. Seldom does he appear truly interested in the person to whom he is writing. Loss of energy as old age closed in, problems with his eyes, and other factors may account for the brevity of some of his letters, but still one cannot escape the impression that he is just not much interested in the lives and happenings of others. When he does appear stirred, it is because of something that concerns himself. With a few exceptions, Melville's extant letters of his last fourteen years are among the dullest of those of any major author, but on the other hand, they are revealing for what they suggest of his general state of mind in his late life, and when he does write something out of the ordinary, it stands out with rare power. Though he was known to be on occasion entertaining and talkative during this time, he impressed others as being extremely moody, nervous, or even shy. Most of his agitation and reserve, however, can be attributed to impatience and disinterest. When one is simply not interested in the people and everyday events surrounding him, this state of mind can be interpreted as shyness, and his impatience can look like irritability or even unpredictable mood changes.

An event suggestive of Melville's self-absorption is recorded by his granddaughter, Frances Thomas Osborne. In the spring of 1887, Melville took Frances for a walk to nearby Madison Square. Once there Frances began to cavort while her grandfather occupied a bench. When she tired of running about, she glanced at the bench and found her grandfather gone. He had returned home to Twenty-Sixth Street without her. Francis made her way back, meeting Melville and his daughter Bessie coming to get her.[113] This incident became a family joke, not so funny, though, in its implications. Melville appeared to be forgetful almost to the point of senility; tragedy could have been the outcome of such an episode involving a child. This event is not symptomatic of Melville's sad loss of memory or of general mental deterioration, however. No senile grandfather composed *Billy Budd* and the rich poetry of these later years. What it does suggest is the extent to which he was at that moment self-absorbed, a condition that has nothing to do with loss of powers. It does have to do with a changing perception of what is real—only that which directly bears on the self.

Such self-centeredness, developing as it could into a perception of reality, was an arch sin in the dominant culture of Melville's world. An amorphous but large group of "optimists"—inspirational speakers and writers, ministers (no doubt including Melville's own), popular novelists and poets, politicians—all carried the message of service to others. In Schopenhauer's *The Wisdom of Life*, Melville marked a passage written by the translator, T. Bailey Saunders, which quotes one of the leading optimists of the day, Sir John Lubbock, by way of contrasting him with Schopenhauer.[114] It was Lubbock's view in *The Pleasures of Life* (1887) that our existence can be "a glorious inheritance" if we live correctly, which means making "ourselves useful" to others. "We need certainly have no . . . fear," he states, "if we have done our best to make others happy."[115] Pressures came from all sides, then, to get outside oneself, as Elizabeth Melville wanted her husband to do, but though he tried as best he could to hide an increasing degree of self-absorption, he could not drastically change.

To be sure, there were times when this condition offered psychological protection from what could have been devastating blows. The many deaths in his family circle during this period no doubt hurt him and added to the crisis atmosphere, but it is somewhat shocking that Melville did not respond to them with more heightened displays of feeling. News of the death of Stanwix, his son, in 1886, left Elizabeth incapacitated for a long time as she noticeably grieved over this wayward son who had died of tuberculosis in San Francisco. Melville, on the other hand, seemed not deeply shaken. Saddened by the news, he nevertheless responded somewhat like a person in whom the reality of the event had not taken hold. He reacted to Stanwix's death with less emotion than he displayed at the death in 1867 of his other son, Malcolm. Of course, the circumstances were different: Malcolm died by his own hand in the Melville household whereas Stanwix had become a wanderer and had not been part of the family circle for some time. Still, a pattern of behavior can be seen developing in which Melville reacted to death with less of what is ordinarily considered bereavement. Leon Howard has explained this behavior by positing that Melville by this time "had become used to death."[116] It seems more likely, however, that the deaths of others, even that of his son Stanwix and his affectionate and admiring brother-in-law John C. Hoadley, who died the same year, touched him less as he progressed toward an unarticulated feeling of unreality in regard to matters outside himself.

Given the pressures on him to conform to the virtue of living for others rather than for himself and the guilt that he could not escape for too much self-involvement, it is not surprising that he found comfort in the Pessimists. In "Sympathy," an essay in *Essays and Phantasies,* James Thomson argues that most of the activity performed in the name of living for others is motivated by selfish reasons. Melville placed a vertical line and three overlapping check marks by the following statement: "So far is sympathy from abounding in the works called 'charitable,' that the people who are most energetic in such works are usually very unsympathetic."[117] Rather than endeavoring to sympathize with and serve others, Thomson asserts, we should direct our sympathy toward ourselves, especially toward what we have been in the past. Cultivate self-directed compassion, he suggests, and not the sentimental charity so valued by ordinary society. Schopenhauer goes even further in the direction of commending self-centeredness. The man of genius, he says in *The Wisdom of Life,* the person with "the highest intellectual power," is by his very nature self-absorbed:

> Hence, undisturbed occupation with himself, his own thoughts and works, is a matter of urgent necessity to such a man. . . . This is the only type of man of whom it can be said that his centre of gravity is entirely in himself; which explains why it is that people of this sort—and they are very rare—no matter how excellent their character may be, do not show that warm and unlimited interest in friends, family, and the community in general, of which others are so often capable; for if they have only themselves they are not inconsolable for the loss of everything else.[118]

Schopenhauer further states that such people "get accustomed to move about amongst mankind as alien beings, and in thinking of humanity in general, to say *they* instead of *we*."[119] Such bold realigning of values, such self-confident attacks upon the key concept of civilization's idealism, shocked and repulsed many who read Schopenhauer, but not Melville.

In the Pessimists, Melville found repeatedly the notion that life is an illusion or a dream, an idea probably derived from Buddhism. Melville placed a line in the margin beside Schopenhauer's statement in *The World as Will and Idea* that "fools take the world as perfectly real, and place the end of it in the poor earthly happiness, which, however much it may be fostered by men and favoured by fate, is a hollow, deceptive, decaying, and sad thing, out of which neither constitutions and legal systems nor steam-engines and telegraphs can ever make anything that is essentially better."[120] One of Schopenhauer's recurrent themes is that what we take for reality is "permanently shifting and, this being so, evanescent and insubstantial, a world of appearance only." It is an "illusion that the world of experience is the world of permanent reality."[121] In *Religion: A Dialogue*, Schopenhauer insisted upon the truth of the Buddhist position that all that goes on around one is "in the nature of a dream."[122]

Of course, dreams can be nightmarish; the illusory nature of experience does not abolish suffering, as the Buddhists and the Pessimists constantly reiterate. Melville takes up the paradox of this position in one of his miscellaneous poems "To ———":

> Ah, wherefore, lonely, to and fro
> Flittest like the shades that go
> Pale wandering by the weedy stream?
> We, like they, are but a dream:
> Then dreams, and less, our miseries be;
> Yea, fear and sorrow, pain, despair
> Are but phantoms. But what plea
> Avails here? phantoms having powers
> To make the heart quake and the spirit cower.

In another poem, "Profundity and Levity," left unpublished at his death in the collection *Weeds and Wildings,* he depicts in the prose introduction "an owl in his wonted day-long retirement ruffled by the meadow-lark curvetting and caroling in the morning-sun high over the pastures and woods." While the lark, Melville's metaphor for an optimist, flits about happily in its ignorance and shallowness, the owl—perhaps Melville himself—dwells on "this latest theme," that "life wanders in night like a dream." The owl concludes: "Is then life worth living?" Essentially the same idea is developed in "Old Counsel," a poem in *John Marr*, and several other poems of this period. To a man questioning the reality of what goes on around him and feeling inclined toward self-absorption, the philosophy of disenchantment may not have offered a total system that he could accept and follow, but it certainly made him feel less isolated in his attitudes.

An aspect of Melville's preoccupation with himself during this period was his recurring consideration of his career as a writer. Pondering—as he did frequently—the nature of his career and the responses he had received from the reading public and from critics, he discovered little to encourage him. In considering what he should do with the years that remained, he found himself engaged in a major psychological stuggle. The warring factions within him consisted of, on the one hand, an ambitious nature, a thirst for fame, and on the other hand, a fear of rejection and shame and a contempt for fame, which he knew to be empty. This war he had fought for a long time, but in these final years, it intensified with the keen awareness that his reputation was so diminished as to make him almost a forgotten writer. If he had not found a way to silence his ambition, that deep-seated longing for recognition and praise, his loss of status and recognition, his failure to be known for what he himself knew he was, could have warped him into a bitterness incompatible with artistic productivity. It was in this internal struggle that Melville found the Pessimists a cheering section, assuring him that ambition was foolishness and fame worthless.

Melville had long realized that he was subject to the strong pull of ambition and that it was a pernicious and destructive force. He underlined in his copy of Alger's book: "It is not aspiration but ambition that is the mother of misery in man." Just below that sentence at the bottom of the page, he wrote in pencil: "H.M."[123] Though I believe it has not been widely argued, a substantial case could be made for ambition as the mainspring of Captain Vere's actions and thinking in *Billy Budd* and, consequently, as the cause of his misery. Toward the end of that work, Melville commented that although Vere never gained fame, as did Admiral Nelson, he "may yet have indulged in the most secret of all passions, ambition."[124] Melville's admiration of Montaigne derived at least partly from that writer's ability to avoid the "most secret of all passions" as he grew older. In a late poem, "Montaigne and His Kitten," Melville depicts Montaigne as having conquered ambition to such an extent that he identifies himself more with his carefree cat than with the poor "dizzards" who

> . . . strain and strive,
> Rave and slave, drudge and drive,
> Chasing ever, to and fro,
> After ends that seldom gain
> Scant exemption from life's pain.

Montaign considers the recognition that he has received in the past as nothing, and as for the future, he is of one mind with Blanche, his cat: "Ambition we let go."

Schopenhauer's attitude toward critics and the reading public—expressed frequently in many places in his essays—was that "the man who writes for fools is always sure of a large audience."[125] Though his ambition craved the large audience, Melville was no fool and could not write for fools. His experiences over the years with bad reviews and poor sales convinced him that Schopenhauer was correct. What Schopenhauer said, he had known for some time. When Melville wrote the poem "Immolated" is uncertain, but it looks back upon an event in the early 1860s, when he was getting ready to move from Pittsfield to New York City. At that time, he probably destroyed some manuscripts that he had on hand rather than see the critics attack them and have them thereafter assigned to public ridicule or neglect. In this act of authorial euthanasia, he feels that he has saved his work from

> . . . the drear
> Theft and ignoring which need be
> The triumph of the insincere
> Unanimous Mediocrity.[126]

Melville's quarrel with the critics was of course of long standing, but by the time he had reached the last fourteen years of his life, when his career was in retrospect one of his preoccupations, he had pretty much ceased to expect anything at all from them or from readers in general. When he read the section on Jesus in Alger's *The Solitudes of*

Nature and of Man, he marked only one sentence, Christ's admonition, "Cast not your pearls before swine, lest they trample them under their feet, and turn again and rend you."[127] No doubt one reason he was drawn to Schopenhauer and Thomson is that they echoed this pronouncement. Thomson's essay "Bumble, Bumbledom, Bumbleism" is in effect an inspired elaboration of Jesus' warning from the pen of a caustic but witty genius. Melville marked numerous parts of it and Salt's quotations from it. For example, Melville placed a check by Thomson's statement that "Bumble," here meaning the world of ordinary and respectable readers, "simply imposes death by starvation."[128]

The collection of poems called *Weeds and Wildings Chiefly: With a Rose or Two,* arranged and with a dedication to his wife and a table of contents but not published during his life, appears to be in large measure a tribute to Elizabeth, long a devotee of flowers of all sorts, written with her in mind and for the purpose of pleasing her. Such was one of Melville's aims, but even here he reveals at times the concern with self that is characteristic of his late life. In several poems, he praises the humbler flowers, those not cultivated but the ones that grow wild. His "democratic sense," as it has been called, may be at work in such poems, but it is also evident that when he speaks of such a wildflower, he is thinking of himself—largely unappreciated but glorious in its blooms. Of particular interest in this regard is his brief poem "The Avatar," where Melville indicates that when the "rose-god" came to earth, it took the humblest form of the rose, "Sweet-Briar, a wilding or weed." Unlike human beings, the "flower-gods" do not greatly value reputation. Melville's little religious allegory of the Incarnation also embodies thoughts about his own career. He is the Sweet-Briar, a wild rose, passed over and little valued, but a kind of avatar nevertheless.

Just as Melville's sensitivity to criticism intensified as he grew older, so did a lifelong trait all too seldom taken into account in biographies: his fear of disgrace. A determination to avoid shame motivated him strongly throughout his life and became one of his preoccupations as the years passed. His horror of public flogging expressed in several chapters of *White-Jacket* reveals his fear not of pain but of abasement. White Jacket states that he had spent nearly a year on the ship "making a hermit" of himself "in order to avoid the possibility of the scourge."

When an unforeseen event occurs and he is on the verge of being flogged, he seriously contemplates jumping overboard and taking the captain with him. The captain, he says, "was about to degrade me, and . . . I had taken an oath with my soul that he should not."[129] At the last moment, he is saved from the shame of flogging by shipmates who attest to his high sense of responsibility. A similar situation is at the heart of a much later work, "Bridegroom Dick," a poem in the *John Marr* collection. There a hardworking sailor, a giant Finn, has violated the Articles of War and is about to be flogged. Again Melville emphasizes the disgrace to be brought upon the victim, "abasement," a "grand champion shamed." Realizing that such abasement is a punishment that for this man goes far beyond the magnitude of the offense, the good captain sets the Finn free.

The connection between Melville's low threshold of pain inflicted by critics and his dread of shame is obvious. In the year he published *White-Jacket,* he wrote to Evert A. Duyckinck: "But I dont [sic] know but a book in a man's brain is better off than a book bound in calf—at any rate it is safer from criticism."[130] He had not felt at this point, however, the full scorn of the critics. By the time he was in the final fourteen years of his life, his every public act was influenced by his long experience in pain at the hands of reviewers. But it was not just criticism of his writings that he dreaded; his fear of disgrace pervaded every aspect of his late life. Elizabeth Melville was considering leaving him in 1869 during the crisis in their marriage documented in *The Endless, Winding Way in Melville.*[131] What brought on this situation still is not known, Melville's irritability and "mental cruelty," perhaps. At any rate, she did not break up the marriage. Besides the more obvious reasons—the children, her love for him, the memories of better moments together during a long marriage, and so forth—she feared the stigma of separation and divorce and knew the extent to which he did. Years later his brother-in-law John C. Hoadley wrote to an acquaintance in order to enhance Melville's security in the Customs Service. It was not that Melville wanted a better position or a more comfortable one: he was afraid of dismissal. The possibility seemed to haunt him. The care that he took to do his duty was not part of a plan for advancement. He was subject to the temptations of ambition but not involving government service. His conscientiousness as an inspector grew largely out of his abhorrence of being chastized. "He strives earnestly to so perform his duties," Hoadley wrote in his letter, "as to make the slighest censure, reprimand, or even reminder,—impossible from any superior."[132] He had come more and more to dread the disgrace that might accompany censure. To be "free from all despite," as he wrote in "Immolated," is far better than to be exposed to public ridicule. He composed a considerable body of writing after *Clarel* (which he originally intended to publish anonymously), but only two slim volumes found print before his death, both of those—*John Marr and Other Sailors* and *Timoleon*—printed at his own expense and in numbers sufficient only for his own personal distribution. These facts speak plainly of his ever-increasing fear of public ridicule as he pondered his career as it had been and as it yet was to be.

Given Melville's deeply ingrained abhorrence of shame, he must have read Schopenhauer's thoughts on the subject with more than a little interest. In a long section of *The Wisdom of Life*, Schopenhauer treats with sarcasm and humor people who are motivated by "honor" (especially chivalry) and by the desire to avoid disgrace. Nothing Schopenhauer wrote could eradicate Melville's fear of disgrace, but the German philosopher's treatment of the subject could and probably did have the effect of focusing Melville's attention on the negative aspects of this trait. In fact, Schopenhauer's use of a Latin word meaning "the feeling of shame" (*Vere*-cundia)[133] may have been a factor in Melville's choice of a name for his captain in *Billy Budd*, and Schopenhauer's discussion of the concepts of honor and shame possibly influenced the characterizations of Vere and Billy in the late stages of the novel.

According to Schopenhauer, persons in whom the desire for honor and the dread of shame are highly developed will go to almost any extreme to uphold their reputations, a motivation that he believes to be dangerous and misguided. He insists that codes of honor have no real moral basis, that they sometimes cause people to violate their basic nature, and that they can result in foolish and destructive behavior. The respect paid to a naval officer like Captain Vere and the determination of such a man to avoid tainting his reputation come under the category Schopenhauer terms "official honour," of which "military honour" is a part. The higher a person's rank, "the greater must be the degree of honour paid to him, expressed, as it is, in titles, orders and the generally subservient behavior of others towards him."[134] To maintain this situation of respect, artificial though it often may be, the official allows nothing whatsoever to violate his sense of duty, and he must always enforce "the legal penalty" for every breach of discipline. The military official, adds Schopenhauer, is bound to a code involving the defense of country requiring "courage, personal bravery and strength," and the willingness to defend one's country "to the death, and never under no circumstances desert the flag."[135] Captain Vere, who speaks in "an official tone" and who is addressed as "your honor," embodies all the principal qualities of Schopenhauer's man of official honor.[136] In his speech to the court, he stresses those aspects of the honorable military officer that Schopenhauer mentions. He links honor with avoidance of shame in discussing the repercussions of leniency for Billy: "Your clement sentence they [the ship's crew] would think pusillanimous. They would think that we flinch, that we are afraid of them—afraid of practicing a lawful rigor singularly demanded at this juncture, lest it should provoke new troubles. What shame to us such a conjecture on their part."[137]

Melville seems to have extended this motivation from Vere to Billy, for fear of shame is a factor in Claggart's murder. In his definition of *verecundia*, Schopenhauer writes that "it is this which brings a blush to his cheeks at the thought of having suddenly to fall in the estimation of others, even when he knows that he is innocent."[138] Billy explains his actions to the court by stating that Claggart defamed him "in the presence of my captain."[139] Schopenhauer indicates that "slander is the only weapon by which honour can be attacked from without; and the only way to repel the attack is to confute the slander."[140] Billy cannot with words "confute the slander," so he does it with a blow. Schopenhauer sarcastically comments in his section on knightly honor that if your honor has been impugned, "you can strike down your opponent on the spot.... This will restore your honor."[141] Billy does so, and in Vere's eyes his honor remains intact, but he kills a man and loses his life by that same code dictating his own actions, thus illustrating

Schopenhauer's main point that *verecundia* is not the highest and noblest guide for human behavior.

As Melville considered the broad area of his writing career, again and again he returned to the phenomenon of fame. Merton M. Sealts Jr. has shown how Melville began to distrust fame fairly early in his career; he wrote to Hawthorne in 1851: "All Fame is patronage. Let me be infamous."[142] Sealts points out that "he had thrown away the Biographico-Solicito Circulars from the compilers of dictionaries and encyclopedias, evidently little concerned with the accuracy or even the inclusion or omission of a biographical sketch of 'H.M. author of "Peedee" "Hullabaloo" & "Pog-Dog."'" Nevertheless, in Melville's "last years one detects a difference."[143] Fame becomes a major subject of his thinking in these years, as if he were struggling to reconcile himself emotionally to his lack of it while reminding himself, especially through his reading, of what he had always known intellectually—that fame is an untrustworthy gauge of greatness.

The Pessimists served him well with their reassurances on the subject. In this area as well as in others, Melville read Thomson and Schopenhauer with a sense of personal involvement. They were speaking directly to his concerns and in a way that uplifted and justified him. In *Essays and Phantasies,* for example, James Thomson wrote that many writers

> have been abject suppliants to fame, and have yearned and
> toiled and suffered for genuine and wide and enduring
> renown; yet the most genuine [renown] is so full of illusion
> and mockery, the most wide is so narrow and superficial,
> the most enduring is so infinitesimally brief, that for my own
> part I am quite unable to understand how any intelligent
> person can set a high value upon it. . . . The votaries of fame
> (that *last* infirmity of noble minds, in another sense than
> Milton's) exist on the paper money of heavy bills drawn on
> posterity. Posterity will ruthlessly dishonour nearly all these
> bills.[144]

The nobler and ultimately more sensible course for a writer, Thomson urges in many places, is to go against the popular current. Only the truly great, however, can disregard the pull of fame. In "Bumble, Bumbledom, Bumbleism," he comments: "In literature, there are always two or three really great writers living, who fling assured wealth and reputation to the winds, and dash their heads against Bumbledom."[145] They are rare exceptions, however. Melville drew a vertical line by a passage he read in Salt's biography of Thomson on that writer's uncompromising disregard of fame. Thomson, Salt concludes, "could not, and would not, write 'to order'; and poor though he was, he valued his own intellectual liberty above any prize the world could offer him. 'Luckily,' he says in one of his essays, 'I am an author thoroughly unknown, and writing for a periodical of the deepest disrepute.'"[146]

Schopenhauer's often repeated views on fame were, if anything, even more negative. The importance of renown was, in fact, one of the primary illusions, as Schopenhauer saw it, of that worldview to which the philosophy of disenchantment was most opposed. Ambition and the craving for repute were aspects of the will that had to be overcome before a person could be enlightened and free. Melville encountered this opinion, so congenial as it was with his own late thought about himself and his career, in numerous places in the several volumes of Schopenhauer that he read. He placed a check by a passage in *The Wisdom of Life* in which Schopenhauer quotes Tacitus: "Tacitus says, *The lust of fame is the last that a wise man shakes off.* The only way of putting an end to this universal folly is to see clearly that it is a folly; and this may be done by recognizing the fact that most of the opinions in men's heads are apt to be false, perverse, erroneous and absurd."[147] One can imagine Melville's delight increasing as Schopenhauer became more bitingly contemptuous of fame and those who offer it. Melville marked with checks and vertical lines such passages as the following from *The Wisdom of Life:* "And if ever we have had an opportunity of seeing how the greatest of men will meet with nothing but slight from half-a-dozen blockheads, we shall understand that to lay great value upon what other people say is to pay them too much honour."[148] An entire section of an essay in this volume is devoted to the subject of fame. Melville's markings indicate that he found it of particular interest, especially those parts arguing that great minds are never in tune with their time but with future generations, an idea that

Melville came to accept as he grew older. He penciled a line by Schopenhauer's statement that

> the more a man belongs to posterity, in other words, to humanity in general, the more of an alien he is to his contemporaries; since his work is not meant for them as such. . . . There is none of that familiar local colour about his productions which would appeal to them; and so what he does, fails of recognition because it is strange. People are more likely to appreciate the man who serves the circumstances of his own brief hour, or the temper of the moment—belonging to it, and living and dying with it.[149]

For a writer looking back on his career and feeling "alien to his contemporaries" yet knowing in his heart of his true greatness, these and other statements like them gave encouragement and support. In defending James Thomson against the charge of not having received fame, Melville sounds much like Thomson himself. To James Billson he wrote:

> As to his not acheiving [sic] "fame"—what of that? He is not the less, but so much the more. And it must have occurred to you as it has to me, that the further our civilization advances upon its present lines so much the cheaper sort of thing does "fame" become, especially of the literary sort. This species of "fame" a waggish acquaintance of mine says can be manufactured to order, and sometimes is so manufactured thro the agency of a certain house that has a correspondent in every one of the almost innumerable journals that enlighten our millions from the Lakes to the Gulf & from the Atlantic to the Pacific.—But this "vanity of vanities" has been inimitably touched upon by your friend [Thomson].[150]

The sharp and biting tone in which Melville described the nature of fame to Billson carries over into some of his verse of the later years on the subject. His "flowering" (or reflowering), he indicates in "The American Aloe on Exhibition," may have been long in coming because of "something retarding in the environment or soil." This poem in *Weeds and Wildings* develops an extended metaphor in which a century-plant, having not flowered for a long time, again blooms but with little or no appreciation from the public. Melville's own flowering in the period of his late poetry received the same reception, but the important thing is that he keeps deep within himself the secret of his worth while eschewing fame. "Ah, ye Roses that have passed," he concludes, "Accounting me a weed!"

Perhaps his most eloquent expression of the transiency of fame is "Thy Aim, Thy Aim?" an uncollected poem of his late years. In this work he warns that ambition or "yearning" may "be sequelled by shame" and that the external reward for great achievement

> . . . will be but a flower,
> Only a flower,
> The flower of repute,
> A flower cut down in an hour.

But even if more substantial fame is assured, even if the renown lives on into future ages,

> Again but a flower!
> Only a flower,
> A funeral flower,
> A blossom of Dis from Proserpine's bower—
> The belated funeral flower of fame.

In the second half of his bipartite poem on Luiz Vaz de Camoens, the Portuguese epic poet of the sixteenth century, Melville depicts the great writer dying in poverty and disease, now enlightened as to the meaninglessness of renown. He dies a forgotten man, a prey "to wile and guile ill understood" while others who can manipulate such deception retain high places. Once ardent in his ambition to receive the garlands of repute, Camoens, now disenchanted, speaks of the baseness of the world and the way in which the "noblest meet ignoble scorn."

If there is something of Melville himself in this depiction of the aged Camoens, his portrait of Timoleon is made up of even more thinly veiled thoughts about his career. Often considered a rumination on an old and painful notion, Melville's belief that his mother preferred his brother Gansevoort to himself, the poem is probably more directly a study from his experience of the vagaries of fame. Though modeled on the account of Timoleon in *Plutarch's Lives*, Melville's hero can be seen as any young aspirant to truth, one who "heeds the voice whose mandate calls, / Or seems to call, peremptory from the skies" as Melville himself did in his early decision not to pursue an easy course but to write as he must even if that be extremely risky. Such a decision brought him not glory but largely scorn, and he was in a sense exiled. From this point on, the poem becomes among other things a speculation on what he would do should he so distinguish himself in exile, write something of great power and magnificence, that those who had forgotten him would have to recognize him and welcome him back with more fame than he had ever received. His conclusion is that he would choose not to accept the world's acclaim, aware now of its emptiness, but to remain apart and in his own private world.

"Timoleon" suggests that Melville had committed himself to a quiet life apart, which he would not alter even if he should experience a surge of renown. During this period, he spent much time mulling over the subject of solitude. He obviously had the topic on his mind as early as 1867 when he marked in his copy of Camoens's poetry the following lines:

> My senses lost, misjudging men declare,
> And Reason banish'd from her mental throne,
> Because I shun the crowd, and dwell alone.[151]

By the time he had finished with *Clarel,* he was putting more and more into practice the art of shunning the crowd. So successful was he that what reputation he developed during these years was that of a hermit. Those few would-be biographers who tried after his death to capture the essence of the man faced a difficult task because he had dwelt apart from the multitude. As Merton M. Sealts Jr. has put it: "How to present as a man of their time this once-famous writer who had become a hermit, a recluse, in short an alien to his contemporaries—this was the problem confronting the biographers of the nineties that is unsolved in any of the early Lives of Melville."[152] What they did present was, to use the words of Robert Buchanan, a man who "loves to stay at home."[153] Edmund Clarence Stedman felt that even though Melville was "a sort of a recluse" at that time (1890), members of a new club to which Stedman belonged—the Authors Club—"might perhaps tempt him out."[154] Others seemed to know better, however. Stedman's son, Arthur, for example, wrote that "it is a well-known fact that his seclusion has been a matter of personal choice." He felt that Melville's "general refusal to enter into social life" was "chiefly due to natural disposition."[155] J. E. A. Smith, like all who knew him, was struck with Melville's isolation in New York City. After Melville died, Smith wrote a series of biographical articles about him for the *Pittsfield Evening Journal,* one of which quotes a writer for the *New York Times* (October 2, 1891): "When a visiting British writer a few years ago inquired at a gathering in New York of distinctively literary Americans what had become of Herman Melville, not only was there not one among them who was able to tell him, but there was scarcely one among them who had ever heard of the man concerning whom he inquired, albeit that man was then living within a half mile of the place of the conversation."[156]

Although Melville developed something of a "hermit's reputation" during these years, he was of course no hermit. He received visitors; he attended church; he frequented libraries and bookstores; he took walks; he wrote letters; until December 1885, when he retired from the Customs Service, he went to work every weekday except for his vacation period; and he engaged in numerous other activities that involved his family and the outside world. What we are dealing with here is not a thoroughgoing recluse but a man with growing reclusive tendencies, a person who was thinking more and more about the solitary life, reading about it, and in his own mind justifying it without ever intending to cut himself off completely from loved ones and society.

While it is a mistake to think of Melville as some kind of self-exiled misanthrope, at the same time it is clear that he was divorcing himself from many activities and gradually narrowing his circle of intimacy. He sought out no one, initiated no correspondence, usually answered the letters he received with brevity and politeness, cultivated or even tolerated no close friendships, and so on. It was almost as if he had thought through the problem of how far he could withdraw without damaging his psychological makeup beyond repair and without cruelly injuring his family. He tried not to go beyond that point, but reclusiveness was without doubt one of the subjects most on his mind in the period 1877–91.

Some of the reasons for his tendency to withdraw are not difficult to come by; others lie so deeply hidden in his heart that they may never be known. Considering the fact that Melville was always a proud man, it should surprise no one that he was somewhat ashamed of his job in the Customs Service and preferred that it not be widely known that he held, as Stanton Garner has said, "the lowest . . . position in the service, and [that] he never rose above it." Garner is unquestionably correct when he states that "the man who had wandered the archipelago of *Mardi* and had struggled with the white whale must have felt demeaned by it."[157]

After his retirement, he felt keenly the approach of old age with its debilitating loss of energy and decreased interest in worldly activities. As a younger man he had greatly valued geniality. Its appeal had drawn him into situations and relationships that made him appear to many as a highly sociable person. In the prose section of "John Marr," he comments on the disappearance of this motivating force as one grows older. The aging John Marr finds, as did Melville, that "something was lacking" now that at one time drew him out and made him seek companionship: "That something was geniality, the flower of life springing from some sense of joy in it, more or less." There is nothing unusual about the diminution of this certain joy in life, this "geniality," but when it is the principal reason for one's convivial associations with others, its loss results in a state conducive to reclusiveness. With just a few exceptions, Melville was not very successful in human relationships. He tried to cultivate a close friendship with Hawthorne but failed. He was either unable to or uninterested in sustaining lifelong friendships as some other notable writers did. In his final fourteen years, he had no circle of old and devoted friends to move away from. The truth is that Melville did not like many people, and he did not value superficial acquaintances and "contacts."

If a person with such traits is afflicted as he grows older with what can broadly be termed "nervousness," then he is even more likely to find pleasure in the contemplations of reclusiveness. So it was with Melville. That he suffered from this vague but understandable affliction is clear from his wife's accounts and from numerous other sources. When Hawthorne's son Julian visited him in 1883, the older man "seemed nervous, and every few minutes would rise to open and then shut again the window opening on the courtyard."[158] In Melville's uncollected poems of this era is one entitled "Give Me the Nerve," seemingly a plea for audacity in the face of life's dangers. Though he does mention courage in the poem, the word *nerve* seems to be used in the sense of "steadiness" or "coolness," a "lack of nervousness," as the second stanza makes clear:

> [When] tempests are over me scudding;
> > Give, give me the calm
> That is better than balm.

The desire for calm in a person in whom nervousness can be debilitating leads naturally to reclusiveness.

Arthur Stedman may have been more or less accurate when he attributed Melville's disinclination to socialize partly to his "very adverse critical reception."[159] Certainly such reception created in Melville a deep sense of resentment, which is quieter and less destructive than bitterness but which nevertheless is a powerful stimulus for withdrawal. He marked a passage in Alger that reveals Erasmus's resentment toward his fellows at Cambridge in 1515: "Here is one unbroken solitude. Many have left for fear of the plague; and yet when they are all here the solitude is much worse."[160]

In no area of his thinking during these last years did Melville find more enthusiastic support for his proclivities than in his concern with reclusiveness—and he discovered this support in his reading, particularly in the works of the Pessimists, who if they believed in anything, believed in the advantages of the solitary life. He read of Leopardi's love of solitude in Alger, where he is quoted: "In the company of others we are reminded of our rebuffs, our disappointments, our age. But in solitude the shames of memory are flung off, no fear of ridicule represses imagination."[161] The position of the Pessimists was grounded in the conviction that a superior person is by nature apart from the multitude and thus should do nothing to change that situation. Reclusiveness, they felt, is the way of life of the true genius. Thomson argues that there is "social comfort" in "always living among creatures whose thoughts and feelings are very similar to your own," but geniuses can never have that comfort because they do not have the qualities of a "commonplace wight."[162]

Melville's markings in his volumes of Schopenhauer reveal the extent to which very late in his life he had become occupied with the subject of reclusiveness. In his copy of *Studies in Pessimism*, he penciled a vertical line by Schopenhauer's remark that if a person "has a soul above the common, or if he is a man of genius, he will occasionally feel like some noble prisoner of state, condemned to work in the galleys with common criminals; and he will follow his example and try to isolate himself."[163] For Schopenhauer, the choice was fairly simple: "solitude on one side and vulgarity on the other."[164] Of particular interest to Melville was Schopenhauer's remarks on the growing tendency in the aging genius toward reclusiveness. He marked the following passage in *Religion: A Dialogue and Other Essays:* "In later years . . . the genius never feels himself at home in the common world of every day and the ordinary business of life."[165] Schopenhauer appeared fascinated with the connection between the aging process in the superior man and withdrawal from society. He dealt with it in another work Melville read, the essay called "The Ages of Life" in *Councils and Maxims*. The extraordinary person, he writes, becomes "gradually disappointed" as life goes on "to find that in the qualities of the head or in those of the heart—and usually in both—he reaches a level to which they [ordinary people] do not attain; so he gladly avoids having anything more to do with them."[166] He returns to the topic repeatedly, for he is convinced that it is the destiny of superior people to be alone, especially as they grow older.[167] He argues that the aging process in such intelligent and gifted people just about does away with any desire to be in the company of others: "From long experience of men, we cease to expect much from them; we find that, on the whole, people do not gain by a nearer acquaintance; and that—apart from a few rare and fortunate exceptions—we have come across none but defective specimens of human nature which it is advisable to leave in peace. . . . Finally, isolation—our own society—has become a habit, as it were a second nature with us . . . the element proper to our life, as water to a fish."[168] Such views constitute a major reason Melville read the Pessimists: what he found in them on subjects like solitude corresponded to a large extent to what he found in his own mind.

If the Pessimists agreed among themselves about the inevitability of self-absorption for the superior person, the emptiness of fame, and the advantages of reclusiveness, they wrote much as well about still another subject that Melville pondered in his late life, namely the value of leisure. At the beginning of the period considered in this book, Melville revealed a strong feeling about this in a letter to his cousin Kate Gansevoort. She apparently took a position popular at the time, one that stressed the importance of work in molding and maintaining character. If any one idea rivaled that of living for others as the highest virtue in Melville's America, it was that of the Protestant work ethic. It was an old value, going back to the very founding of the country, and it was more or less taken for granted. Therefore, when Melville used the expression "people of leisure" in a letter to his cousin, she responded with a disclaimer, reflecting the values of her time and place in glorifying work and fearing the corruption of leisure. Melville wrote back that by "people of leisure" he meant those "whose time is not subject to another." The lines that follow suggest that in her bantering, Kate had hit a nerve in Melville. She may have been lightheartedly voicing platitudes about the dangers of idleness (the "devil's workshop" as many people considered it), but Melville was too involved personally to let her remarks go unchallenged. There was not "merit," as he saw it, "in *not* being a person of leisure. Whoever is not in the possession of leisure can hardly be said to possess independence. They talk of the *dignity of work*. Bosh. True Work is the *necessity* of poor humanity's earthly condition. The dignity is in leisure. Besides, 99 hundreths of all the work done in the world is either foolish and unnecessary, or harmful and wicked."[169] With that he caught himself, realized that he was heatedly getting into a subject close to his heart and becoming entirely more serious than the occasion called for, and he ended the letter with a lighthearted apology. He had gone far enough, however, to reveal one of his great temptations during the coming years, the lure of leisure.

As in the other areas of thought reviewed here, he found his feeling about leisure echoed in the writings of the Pessimists. Leopardi's seminal statement on indolence Melville read in Thomson's work "Indolence: A Moral Essay": "Life is all idleness in every human condition, if it is proper to call idle such works and pursuits as are without worthy object, or can never obtain that object."[170] Thomson defends indolence, or leisure, as that state wherein a human being is most essentially human. Thoughts, not acts, he argues, manifest our highest achievements. The greatest minds "have learned that the very best acts are but rough and rude incarnations of thought: so they preserve a wise indifference, and do as little as possible. . . . [They] likewise know well that most if not all work is really idle." Those who are the opposites of the indolent, Thomson calls "the energetic," and selecting a quotation that fits his purposes, he charges that "it is industry who is the ally of sin."[171] Though there is no proof that Melville had this passage in mind when he wrote his poem "Fragments of a Lost Gnostic Poem of the 12th Century," the language and ideas of the one are remarkably close to those of the other. Certainly Melville was expressing a notion dear to Thomson (as well as to the Gnostics) and in Thomsonian language when he wrote: "Indolence is heaven's ally here, / And energy the child of hell."

Melville's markings indicate an interest in Thomson's discussion of this topic not only in the essay on indolence but also in "Per Contra," which is included in *Essays and Phantasies*. Melville penciled a vertical line by Thomson's remark that some people, not realizing the true value of leisure, still "wonder how Shakespeare in the maturity of his faculties, as soon as he had made a comfortable fortune, could renounce the sublime work of producing comedies and tragedies to settle down as a jolly burgess in his native place!"[172] Melville seemed particularly struck by Thomson's linking of genius with leisure. He placed a heavy line by the statement that a certain superior sort of idler resembles "men of genius who remain always obscure because they are all genius, having no vulgar profitable talents."[173] Thomson's stance on leisure is reflected in Melville's poem "Inscription" (*Weeds and Wildings*), in which he appears to be defying the popular notion about the sanctity of labor and usefulness:

> A weed grew here.—Exempt from use,
>   Weeds turn no wheel, nor run;
> Radiance pure or redolence
>   Some have, but this had none.
> And yet heaven gave it leave to live
>   And idle it in the sun.

Schopenhauer made frequent pronouncements about the life dedicated to what Thomson called "indolence." A truly wise person, he insists, strives not for material benefits but seeks leisure in order to be free from the annoying pettiness of ordinary existence. In *The Wisdom of Life*, he wrote that "leisure is the highest good, and everything else is unnecessary, nay, even burdensome."[174] What Melville read on leisure in this volume of Schopenhauer's work paralleled exactly the position he had taken in 1877 in his letter to Kate Gansevoort. "The greatest minds of all ages," said Schopenhauer, "have set the highest value upon undisturbed leisure, as worth exactly as much as the man himself."[175]

The watershed event of the period 1877–91 in Melville's life was his retirement from the Customs Service in December 1885. At that point his dream of leisure could become a reality, and he could experience relief from the frustration built up over the long nineteen years that he had been required to spend his days in unthinking and largely unrewarding labor. A series of events culminating in proceeds Elizabeth began to receive from her brother Lemuel's estate and in an inheritance Herman gained from his sister Frances's bequest (as well as in extra income from other sources, such as rent from the family farm in Gansevoort, New York) made it financially feasible for Melville to retire when he was sixty-six.[176] We have no statements in Melville's extant letters about the meaning he attached to this event. Apparently there was no celebrating, no festivities associated with it. He simply gave his ten-days' notice and slipped away. Leon Howard ends his brief explanation of Melville's leaving his employment with a mere statement of fact that is also a powerful understatement: "He was free from the customhouse and had leisure to use as he pleased."[177]

From what Melville heard and read of the Buddhists and Pessimists, their greatest appeal to him was their promise of release from illusion and their frank recognition of the darker aspects of existence. The problem with Optimism, as Melville made clear in poems like "Fruit and Flower Painter" and "Merry Ditty of the Sad Man," is that it pretends that human existence is largely a satisfactory affair, and this is false. The Buddhists and Pessimists found a kind of joy in their philosophy of disenchantment, stark as it is, and offered a realism that ultimately could be of use in coping with life. Melville was in tune with such a chord. William H. Shurr summarizes well this position in his statement about the theme of Melville's "Pebbles": "One can live in a terrifying universe by recognizing it as such, not by hoping and pretending that it is something else."[178] Unquestionably Melville was especially impressed with James Thomson and Arthur Schopenhauer, as his markings in copies of their books and echoes of their ideas in his own writings indicate. On the other hand, Herman Melville was Herman Melville: he never became the disciple of anyone, even a member of his own circle.

Three

THE WEAVER

*M*elville appeared to withdraw increasingly during his final fourteen years into a life of quiet simplicity. He denounced ambition and the hunger for fame, and in his self-absorption, he elevated solitude and leisure to the level of philosophical ideals. The disenchanted of his circle, those whose writings he read eagerly, seemed to cheer him on as these attitudes affected his thoughts and behavior.

Disenchantment is only part of the story of Melville's last years, however, for it was accompanied by an intensified awareness of the importance of the creative imagination to an aging writer. Pretty much taking his muse for granted when he was young, he began to cherish it and to fear its loss as he approached old age. His stoic reticence cannot hide the fact that old age was a crisis of tremendous proportions in his emotional life, a crisis brought on by a distressing drop in energy, a diminishment of interest, a leveling of emotions, a loss of enthusiasm, a disrelish of others' company, a dislike of noise and busy activities, a sense that nothing of importance could be accomplished, and a conviction that newness was merely the old in disguise. He began to feel these internal changes even before he was sixty. "You are young," he wrote to his brother-in-law John C. Hoadley, "but I am verging upon three-score, and at times a certain lassitude steals over one—in fact, a disinclination for doing anything except the indispensable."[1]

A conscious and concerted effort to keep his imagination working through reading, thinking, and writing and to dwell upon the spiritual value of art was Melville's way of dealing with the crisis of aging. Imagination was his stay against the numbness, boredom, and sense of futility that often mark this period of life. His determination to stimulate, nourish, and thus keep alive his imagination resembled a religious commitment. As he felt age taking its toll upon his body and mind, he became, in a sense, a born-again artist, accepting the imagination—that is, the power of artistic creativity—as his personal savior and promising to give it his highest allegiance. In one of his poems of this period, "The Weaver," he depicts himself as a kind of monastic devotee of art.

> For years within a mud-build room
> For Arva's shrine he weaves the shawl,
> Lone wight, and at a lonely loom,
> His busy shadow on the wall.
>
> The face is pinched, the form is bent,
> No pastime knows he nor the wine,
> Recluse he lives and abstinent
> Who weaves for Arva's shrine.[2]

"The Weaver" is an exaggerated but nonetheless revealing depiction of Melville's view of his own disengagement from the outer world and his intensified commitment to the inner world of the imagination. Without being aware of it, he was in large measure reenacting Emily Dickinson's drama of "white election," her decision to become wedded, nunlike, to her creative spirit, her "soul," as she called it, which she perceived as the closest semblance to God she would ever know.

Religious imagery is fused with references to art and the imagination repeatedly in Melville's poems of his late years. "The Enthusiast" is an ambiguous poem largely because the speaker sounds somewhat like the Pierre of Melville's novel (1852) proclaiming his destructive course in defiance of the world. The voice of this work, however, is not that of Pierre—who, admittedly, is called an "enthusiast" in the novel—but that of the older Melville confirming his determination to combat the dullness and mundaneness of age with his imagination even if it means sacrificing personal relationships. He concludes with these lines:

So put the torch to ties though dear,
> If ties but tempters be.
Nor cringe if come the night:
>> Walk through the cloud to meet the pall,
>> Though light forsake thee, never fall
> From fealty to light.

The aging artist has become an "enthusiast," a kind of religious fanatic, and he uses in the poem such words as "spirits," "worship," "sacred," and "faith." The "light," however, is not God except insofar as the creative spirit within may be of divine origin. The poem's epigraph is a line from Job: "Though he slay me yet will I trust in Him." In a sense, "The Enthusiast" is about a Job-like figure, an aging man who perseveres, who does not lose his belief amid pressure from the world's spokespersons to do so. He remains faithful through the terrible wakeful night. His fealty is to "light," to "youth," both synonyms for the creative imagination. Recognizing this inner source of the "sacred glow" and keeping it alive despite the ravages of age is the highest challenge. Fidelity to the creative impulse is akin to Job's faithfulness to God.

Such faithfulness is often but dimly understood by the world, and one who holds to it is frequently the subject of rebuke or worse. Melville had such a victim in mind when he composed "Lone Founts," a poem supposedly from the mouth of a rebel individualist, Giordano Bruno (1548–1600), an Italian monk who was deeply influenced by the ancient Greek philosophers and who refused to abandon his views though excommunicated and then condemned to death. The manuscript shows that Melville considered as titles "Giordano Bruno" and "Counsels." The poem is, indeed, counsel or advice offered by one who has largely given up on the present generation and who looks, as did Melville in his late years, admiringly backward to the Greeks and forward with hope to posterity, to those of a later time who may perceive with clearer vision and understand with deeper hearts his fidelity to light. The poem makes essentially the same point as "The Enthusiast," and since Bruno was an ecclesiastic, it treats faithfulness to artistic creativity in a religious context.

> Though fast youth's glorious fable flies,
> View not the world with worldling's eyes;
> Nor turn with weather of the time.
> Foreclose the coming of surprise:
> Stand where Posterity shall stand;
> Stand where the Ancients stood before,
> And, dipping in lone founts thy hand,
> Drink of the never-varying lore:
> Wise once, and wise thence evermore.

Physical youth is fleeting, and with its passing comes the temptation to become a "worldling." Resist this tendency, Melville-Bruno counsels. Preclude the surprises of life by dealing with them in advance through the function of the wondrous imagination, which flows from inside one's self, the source of all that resists the distressing dullness of age.

Melville's hymn to the imagination is his poem "Art," in which he again creates a religious context for exploring the function of the creative impulse.

> In placid hours well-pleased we dream
> Of many a brave unbodied scheme.
> But form to lend, pulsed life create,
> What unlike things must meet and mate:
> A flame to melt—a wind to freeze;
> Sad patience—joyous energies;
> Humility—yet pride and scorn
>
> Instinct and study; love and hate;
> Audacity—reverence. These must mate,
> And fuse with Jacob's mystic heart,
> To wrestle with the angel—Art.

Just as the angel of God wounded Jacob, who would not loosen his grip, so can a determination to hold on to the imagination in some ways injure and alienate, but the blessing to be gained is worth the price.

"One dripping trophy" brought up from the deep waters of the imagination, Melville insists, is worth far more than the world's gifts, even those offered by the church. He prefers a single hard-won cre-

ation of his imagination, he says in "In the Garret," to all the sumptu-
ousness of St. Sophia in Constantinople:

> Gems and jewels let them heap—
> Wax sumptuous as the Sophi:
> For me, to grapple from Art's deep
> One dripping trophy!

At times, Melville's treatment of artistic inspiration so resembles a
description of religious experience that the two are virtually indistin-
guishable. "Magian wine," as he called the imagination in another
poem of this period, "thrill[s] up from semblances divine." Wonders
and charms, rich beauty, and "Sibylline inklings" are experienced
through this extraordinary intoxicant. Drinking the Magian wine ad-
dicts one to a life apart from the masses (the "worldlings" who partake
only of the wine of the world) and calls for a commitment as single-
minded as that of a religious devotee. To become a weaver for the
shrine of art, one must reject what the ordinary world offers: "Recluse
he lives and abstinent." Devotion to the imagination is also the subject
of another late poem, "The Old Shipmaster and his Crazy Barn." The
speaker is an aging ship's captain, and his "Voice," that is, his creative
impulse, is in his "crazy barn," which others are urging him to tear
down. Knowing the importance of the spirit that communicates with
him from the barn, he refuses to do anything that would stop the
Voice:

> The site should I clear, and rebuild,
> Would that Voice reinhabit?—Self-willed,
> Says each pleasing thing
> Never Dives can buy,
> Let me keep where I cling!
> I am touchy as tinder
> Yea, quick to take wing,
> Nor return if I fly.

He valued the Voice above all else and fully recognized its fragility. He
would accept no advice, follow no philosophy, take no action that
threatened to silence it.

Melville's extensive reading in the works of Matthew Arnold and Honoré de Balzac as old age approached and engulfed him served to justify and strengthen his commitment to the life of the imagination. No two writers did he read more of or more about than these; they of all great authors would have been able to understand his particular stance on art and the imagination, and he read them for the encouragement that their words provided to a solitary weaver.

Melville's interest in Matthew Arnold spanned three decades. He purchased a copy of Arnold's *Poems* (1856) in 1862. Walter Bezanson suggests that in this collection of fifty-nine poems and a provocative preface, Melville found crucial support for his decision to become a poet.[3] Arnold was both a poet and an evangelist for poetry. "The future of poetry is immense," he wrote, "because in poetry, where it is worthy of its high destinies, our race, as time goes on, will find an ever surer and surer stay."[4] He often associated poetry with religion: "The strongest part of our religion to-day," he argued, "is its unconscious poetry."[5] Ruth apRoberts remarks that the "Arnoldian creed" posits a distinct "sense of the unity of religion and poetry."[6] The imagination filters and shapes thought, Arnold believed, and "the best poetry will be found to have a power of forming, sustaining, and delighting us, as nothing else can."[7]

Arnold's influence at the early stage of Melville's acquaintance with his work, however, was more general than specific, for even though Melville did, indeed, turn to the writing of poetry at least partly under Arnold's influence, his first collection, *Battle-Pieces and Aspects of the War* (1866), reveals little similarity to Arnold. As Bezanson puts it: "Melville's subject, the Civil War, was alien to the world of Arnold, and his prosody shows no marked indebtedness to the *Poems* [of Arnold]."[8] In 1871, Melville acquired Arnold's *Essays in Criticism* (1865) and *New Poems* (1867). The margins of his copies of both these volumes, especially the former, reveal Melville's keen interest in Arnold's ideas and artistic methods. Later, while Melville was in the planning stages of his long poetic work, *Clarel* (1877), he was, as Shirley M. Dettlaff says, clearly "fascinated with Matthew Arnold."[9] Bezanson and Dettlaff have traced the many echoes of Arnold in *Clarel*.

Melville may even have had Arnold in mind during the composition of one of his major poems, "After the Pleasure Party." Though it is not clear if or when he read Arnold's poem "Urania," the subject of that work bears a provocative resemblance to the woman Urania in Melville's poem. Probably written sometime in 1850, Arnold's poem describes a "remote and apparently cold and disdainful Urania,"[10] who has not yet met the right man to change her.

> Yet show her once, ye heavenly Powers,
> One of some worthier race than ours!
> One for whose sake she once might prove
> How deeply she who scorns can love.

When that time comes, she who has ignored or scorned men will reveal a deeply passionate side. To her, the eyes of such a man

> ... will be like the starry lights—
> His voice like sounds of summer nights—
> In all his lovely mien let pierce
> The magic of the universe!

> And she to him will reach her hand,
> And gazing in his eyes will stand,
> And know her friend, and weep for glee,
> And cry: *Long, long I've looked for thee.*

But until she has found such a man and reached that passionate state,

> Coldly she mocks the sons of men.
> Till then, her lovely eyes maintain
> Their pure, unwavering, deep disdain.

The focus of Melville's "After the Pleasure Party" is different from that of Arnold's "Urania," in which the scarcity of noble men is the point. Nevertheless, similarities in the descriptions of the two women suggest that Arnold may have been one of a number of influences on "After the Pleasure Party."

Arnold's impact on Melville was cumulative. He appeared to adopt to an increasing degree Arnold's conviction about the importance of knowing classical literature for its "steadying and composing effect"[11] and the appropriateness of the ancient world as a subject for poetry. How much he was originally impressed with Arnold's position is evidenced by his extensive marginal markings of the preface to Arnold's *Poems* (1856), where the British poet's views on the subject are forcefully stated: "I say, that in the sincere endeavour to learn and practise, amid the bewildering confusion of our times, what is sound and true in poetical art, I seemed to myself to find the only sure guidance, the only solid footing, among the ancients."[12] This influential preface, composed for the first edition of Arnold's *Poems* (1853), was not only reprinted in the American version of 1856 (Ticknor and Fields) that Melville owned, but it was also included in Melville's copy of *Mixed Essays, Irish Essays, and Others* (Macmillan, 1883) along with the preface to the second edition (1854) of *Poems*. Melville thus had double exposure, in the 1860s and later in the 1880s, to these prefaces embodying Arnold's provocative ideas about poetry. Wherever Melville found Arnold lauding the ancients, he was likely to indicate his interest and approval by leaving marginal markings. For example, he marked a passage in his copy of the essay "Equality" in *Mixed Essays, Irish Essays and Others* in which Arnold defined what ancient Greek civilization stood for: the synthesis of beauty and intellect.[13] In other places, Arnold called this distinctive synthesis "imaginative reason." Melville seems to have had something like Arnold's definition of it in mind when he composed the interview between the purser and the physician in *Billy Budd,* in which the former asks if the young sailor's death may not have been a form of euthanasia. One of Melville's narrow men of science and no Greek, the physician replies in disdain: "*Euthanasia* . . . is at once imaginative and metaphysical—in short, Greek."[14]

A longtime student of the ancients, Melville found stimulation in Arnold to devote more of his own writings to them. Many of his later poems, those in his collection *Timoleon* (1891), for example, deal with classical subjects. Bezanson has commented that "to both men [Arnold and Melville] the ancient world was a cornerstone of the imagination."[15] Whatever provoked the creative imagination was likely to grip Melville's attention.

Arnold intensified in Melville an already sharp interest in Aristotle. One cannot read Arnold's essays without being aware that he had, as one critic puts it, "absorbed Aristotle."[16] We should be guided, Arnold wrote, by "Aristotle's profound observation that the superiority of poetry over history consists in its possessing a higher truth and a higher seriousness."[17] It may well have been under Arnold's influence that Melville acquired late in his life copies of Aristotle's *Treatise on Rhetoric, The Poetic,* and *The Organan.* He marked in his copy of *The Poetic* Aristotle's distinction between history and poetry to which Arnold had referred: "Hence, poetry is more philosophic, and more deserving of attention, than history."[18] This follows a passage in which Aristotle tells why poetry is superior to history—it is the product of the creative imagination: "But they differ in this, that the one speaks of things which have happened [history], and the other of such as might have happened [imagination]."[19] If Melville were motivated by Arnold to look more deeply than he had before into Aristotle, what he found there on the theory of poetry could not but remind him of what he had read in Arnold. Thus he received two versions of the same ideas.

In between Melville's early and late acquisitions of Arnold's writings, a period of at least ten years intervened. Though he did not lose interest in Arnold during these several years, his interest was less pronounced. Then he purchased and read Arnold's great prose works *Literature and Dogma* (1881), *Culture and Anarchy . . . and Friendship's Garland* (1883), and *Mixed Essays, Irish Essays, and Others* (1883). Arnold was on his mind in December 1885 as he was about to begin his retirement from the customs service. In a letter to James Billson, Melville wrote about James Thomson's essays: "It would have been wonderful indeed had they hit the popular taste. They would have to be painstakingly diluted for that—diluted with that prudential worldly element, wherewithall Mr. Arnold has conciliated the conventionalists while at the same time showing the absurdity of Bumble."[20] Though some readers may take this statement as a criticism of Arnold, one need only refer to Melville's "Hawthorne and His Mosses" to see that the opposite is true. In that essay, Melville praised Hawthorne for his ability to do precisely what he attributes to Arnold—to fool the unsuspecting, to lull them into approval while writing dark truths about them and about human nature. Indeed, he was himself a master of literary camouflage. He was not condemning Arnold but praising him as he had Hawthorne years before for a quality he highly valued.

What rekindled his interest and motivated him to read these later books was probably Arnold's four-month tour of America from October 1883 to March 1884. Most likely Melville purchased the volumes of Arnold's late prose works about the time of this visit. The *New York Tribune* and other local papers easily available to Melville covered Arnold's reception and his lectures with the consistent thoroughness that only a controversial major figure commands. Arnold was controversial (in large measure because of statements he had made in print about America a short time before his arrival), but he was also a literary lion and worthy of respect. He was therefore received with open arms by such great and wealthy men as Andrew Carnegie, his host in New York City, but then often condemned in newspaper and magazine accounts for his attitudes and lecture style. In a letter of February 23, 1884, Mary L. Peebles, a close friend of Melville's Albany cousin Kate Gansevoort Lansing, wrote to Kate's husband, Abe, explaining why she declined his invitation to attend with them a lecture by Arnold on Ralph Waldo Emerson: "I confess to some curiosity in regard to Matthew Arnold, but am afraid I should have gone to sleep in the lecture, as they say most of his hearers always do. So perhaps it is best after all, for you might have been somewhat annoyed and mortified when I fell off the seat."[21] What Mary Peebles had heard of Arnold's lectures as he toured the United States in 1883–84 was not the universal opinion, but it was a view shared by many.[22] Melville no doubt heard it with sympathy and a feeling of personal connection to Arnold, for his own attempts at lecturing had sometimes brought forth such comments as "Let us yawn!"[23] Melville must have felt keen empathy as he read in the *New York Tribune* a scathing account of Arnold's first lecture in America, delivered to an overflow crowd in Chickering Hall on October 30, 1883:

> He has never been required to make great efforts to be heard.
> This style of speaking, too, begets a monotonous delivery,

especially when the lecture is not extempore. . . . He read his lecture. Slight shortsightedness compelled him to hold the manuscript close to his eyes, and the light at the desk was such that few could read it easily. A feeling of disappointment came over the audience when they discovered that Mr. Arnold's voice was scarcely audible half way down the hall.[24]

Present at this first lecture was General Ulysses S. Grant, who "was overheard to say after a few minutes, 'Well, wife, we have paid to see the British lion; we cannot hear him roar, so we had better go home.'"[25] In *Eccentricities of Genius,* Major Pond comments that "Matthew Arnold came to this country and gave one hundred lectures. Nobody ever heard any of them, not even those sitting in the front row."[26]

Pond exaggerated, for on other occasions Arnold did have success in being heard, and wherever he went, he was warmly received as a celebrity, but he was regularly taken to task for his views, chiefly on religion and Philistinism. Henry A. Beers sarcastically commented in an article in the *Century Magazine,* "Matthew Arnold in America," that "he will find the Philistine here in great rankness and luxuriance." But, continues Beers, "I think that we need not be overmuch disquieted by the presence of the Philistine among us, or by Mr. Arnold's discovery that he exists here in overwhelming numbers and in flagrant type."[27]

Though some of his family members and acquaintances went to hear Arnold, there is no record of Melville's attending a lecture. He would not have been eager to scramble for the hard-to-get tickets or to be among the hordes that packed the lecture hall, and he had no personal access to Arnold, who was moving strictly in the circles of the elite, "worldlings" that Melville had no desire or opportunity to associate with. He followed Arnold's visit from a distance, but follow it he did, for he could scarcely have done otherwise given the wide publicity it received.

Although many Americans resented Arnold's apparent distrust of what Melville had once called the "dead level of the masses," he himself realized anew why he had once heard in Arnold a voice that which echoed many of his own deepest convictions. Disapproval in the press of what Arnold said and of how he lectured could but have drawn

Melville, the onetime recipient of like criticisms, closer to him. Arnold never knew or probably even knew of one of his most ardent American admirers, a man living in obscurity just steps away from places like Delmonico's where Arnold was being lavishly entertained, a man then all but forgotten in his native land but who was destined to be thought of by posterity as perhaps the greatest American author of the time. When Melville read the recently published volumes of Arnold's splendidly articulate essays during or sometime shortly after Arnold's first lecture tour of America (he returned in 1886 for a second visit), he developed a heightened interest in the man who of all contemporary British authors would probably have most approved of his raising of the creative imagination to the level of a spiritual force. With the crisis of old age upon him, his rediscovery of the apostle of art and light was welcome support for his own rededication to the life of the imagination.

Melville sampled Balzac's fiction as early as December 1870, when he acquired a copy of *Eugénie Grandet*. It was not until just a few years before his death, however, when old age was making him keenly aware of the preciousness of his creative imagination that his interest in Balzac reached almost the intensity of an addiction. Balzac's "great and infinitely plastic imagination," as one critic has called it, was unquestionably good for Melville's imagination.[28] Edwin Preston Dargan comments that "major and minor evidences point to something that abides in the *Human Comedy,* something that grips its devotees for the remainder of their lives."[29] This something is the imaginary world that Balzac created and populated, the construct of what Somerset Maugham called Balzac's "fantastic imagination.[30] To read Balzac is to be transported to that wondrous place and to live in it. Perhaps no one has expressed better the imaginative appeal of Balzac than Oscar Wilde:

> After the *Comédie humaine* one begins to believe that the only real people are the people who have never existed. Lucien de Rubempré, le Père Goriot, Ursula Mirouet, Marguérite Claes, the Baron Hulot, Madame Marneffe, le Cousin Pons, De Marsay—all bring with them a kind of contagious illusion of life. They have a fierce vitality about them: their existence is

fervent and fiery-coloured; we not merely feel for them but we see them—they dominate our fancy and defy scepticism. A steady course of Balzac reduces our living friends to shadows, and our acquaintances to the shadows of shades. Who would care to go out to an evening party to meet Tomkins, the friend of one's boyhood, when one can sit at home with Lucien de Rubempré? It is pleasanter to have the entrée to Balzac's society than to receive cards from all the duchesses in Mayfair.[31]

Wilde's tendency to think of Balzac's characters as real people was shared by Balzac himself. Herbert J. Hunt has remarked that "it has indeed been maintained that Balzac's fictitious world was more real to him, or at any rate, more important, than the one he stepped into after his long wrestling bouts with the demon of inspiration. He could retire into it anew, as into a sure refuge, whenever financial and sentimental worries were too great; and not even Mme Hanska [his longtime love interest] could follow him there."[32] Such, precisely, was Melville's aim during this period of his life. To such minds, reality *is* the imagination. Geneviève Delattre observes that for Balzac, imagination

is the source of the intuitive vision that permits him to seize truth on the basis of just a sample. . . . Balzac invents reality as much as he observes it, and conversely . . . he observes the imaginary as much as he invents it. Invention and observation are, in his case, inseparable from each other. The two worlds from which the raw material of the *Comédie humaine* is extracted, the real and the imaginary, are too frequently mingled together for us to dare decide which, for Balzac, possesses the purest reality.[33]

Melville owned eighteen volumes written by or about Balzac. Only three of these have dates of acquisition inscribed in handwriting: *Eugénie Grandet* was acquired on December 1, 1870; Edgar Saltus's *Balzac* on August 1, 1885; and Balzac's *Correspondence* on August 1, 1899 (the last two gifts from Melville's wife, Elizabeth). It is unclear when Melville obtained H. H. Walker's *Comédie Humaine and Its Author* and Balzac's *Shorter Stories and Tales,* but all the rest of the volumes, thirteen of them, have publication dates ranging from 1885 to 1890 (American editions in a new translation), suggesting that Melville read them toward the end of his life. Jay Leyda enters in his *Melville Log* for 1890: "Before 1891 Melville buys, either as a set or in the individually issued volumes, a new translation of Balzac's works by Katherine Prescott Wormeley (Boston)."[34] In his copy of James Thomson's *Essays and Phantasies* (1881), which James Billson sent him in 1885, Melville underscored the following comment: "How many English writers of repute, earning good incomes by their writings, would have the courage, however pure and lofty their intent, to treat with the same freedom the same subjects we find treated in a work of Balzac." About a year before his death, Melville (or someone close to him) clipped and inserted into his copy of Balzac's *Correspondence* an article from the *Boston Transcript* on "Balzac's Burial," complete with the eulogy by Victor Hugo. In Melville's religion of the imagination, Balzac was a revered saint. He could not but admire an author who so clearly reflected his own views, as when Balzac responded to a criticism: "If you knew what it is to knead up ideas, to give them form and colour, you would not be so quick at criticism."[35] By these words Melville drew a vertical line to express his agreement and approval. When he read and marked passages like the following in the *Correspondence,* he was convinced that Balzac was the real thing: "You know that if I am sincere in anything, I am especially sincere in all that concerns Art."[36] In fact, the creative imagination was for Balzac, as he put it in another sentence that Melville marked, "that second religion."[37]

Melville shared with both Arnold and Balzac a resentment of the inevitable aging process. He marked a passage in the *Correspondence* where Balzac complained that "the old man is one who has dined and watches the others eat."[38] He read poem after poem in which Arnold speaks of the ravages of old age, such as "Growing Old," a few lines from which Melville partially bracketed:

> It is—last stage of all—
> When we are frozen up within, and quite
> The phantom of ourselves,

To hear the world applaud the hollow ghost
Which blamed the living man.[39]

By the time Melville read Arnold's volume *Mixed Essays, Irish Essays and Others* (1883), he was old enough to understand keenly the yearning for youth reflected in a passage he marked in "The French Play in London": "But there is a new generation growing up amonst us,—and to this young and stirring generation who of us would not gladly belong, even at the price of having to catch some of its illusions and to pass through them."[40] Melville was reacting in a similar vein when in "Old Age in His Ailing" he reminded himself that as he grew older he should not take a jaundiced view of youthfulness:

Old Age in his ailing
At you will be railing.
It scorns youth's regaling
Pooh-pooh it does, silly dream;
But me, the fool, save
From waxing so grave
As, reduced to skimmed milk, to slander the cream.

Melville also realized that Arnold connected, as he himself did, the term *youth* not only with the transient early stage of life but also with an internal faculty, the creative impulse, which does not necessarily die as does one's physical youth. It was the "buried self," to use Arnold's term. He has his character Empedocles say when he is espousing Buddhist metempsychosis that we return to this life "To see if we will now at last be true / To our only true, deep-buried selves." The phrasing is similar to the epigraph Melville pasted to his portable writing desk: "Keep true to the dreams of thy youth." Another parallel to this epigraph occurs in an essay where Arnold quotes the French critic Edmond Henri Adolphe Scherer on Milton: "When the day shall arrive when he [Milton] can at last realise the dreams of his youth, and bestow on his country an epic poem, he will compose it of two elements, gold and clay."[41] By this passage Melville penciled a check mark.

Arnold called "youth" in this broad sense "richness of soul," and he referred to its opposite as "a dead barren negative callosity."[42] He recorded in his *Note-Books* for 1879 a quotation from Goethe: "One must continually change oneself, renew, become young, in order not to stultify."[43] Balzac thought of this place of youthful renewal as, in the words of George Frederic Parsons, "the interior region of the mind, the permanent, enduring part."[44]

It was that permanent and enduring part of his being to which Melville pledged his devotion. Consequently, in his late poems, he declares that the aging process must not be allowed to destroy inner youth as it does the outer. He was determined that like Rip Van Winkle's lilac in his poem, his imagination would remain a source of creative bloom despite an aging trunk:

> Rip's Lilac to its youth still true.
> Despite its slant ungainly trunk
> Atwist and black like strands in junk,
> Annual yet it flowered aloft
> In juvenile pink, complexion soft.[45]

In 1888 Melville made his last sea journey, a steamship voyage to St. Augustine, Florida, and Bermuda. Though he was sixty-eight, he listed his age as thirty-seven.[46] Apparently a mere mischievous jest, this incident was in reality a telling action, for it masked a deep longing for what was lost, but it also declared a sort of psychological victory, a boasting, as it were, that he, indeed, may be old physically but creatively was still in his thirties. Losing one form of youth, he would hold on tenaciously to the other, work hard at keeping it vital, and cherish its powers. An epigraph, a quotation from Hawthorne, that he chose for his posthumously published *Weeds and Wildings Chiefly: With a Rose or Two,* is revealing for its labeling an imperishable inner quality "youth," which Melville associated with the imagination: "Youth is the proper, permanent, and genuine condition of man." *Weeds and Wildings* begins on this note sounded by Hawthorne and ends on a similar one in the poem "L'Envoi," where Melville stirringly proclaims that the antidote to that "dull tranquilizer," age, is to be "young at core," that is, to exercise "at three-score" the creative imagination and thus to become "Boys in gray wigs" who can shake out the "moths [that] infest your mantle Tyrian."

Melville returned repeatedly in his later years to the subject of youth. The novel on which he was putting the finishing touches when he died is about a youth, who represents among other things the power, magic, and beauty of the imagination. Originally intending Billy Budd to be an older sailor guilty of mutiny, Melville apparently changed his mind somewhere in the process of composing the work and depicted him in terms that suggest both male and female qualities—androgyny. How much this change may have owed to Balzac is not clear, but Billy Budd as he was finally conceived is remarkably similar to Balzac's androgynous youth in a novel Melville read late in his life, *Seraphita*.[47] The great masculine strength combined with the pronounced feminine beauty of Balzac's character ("hair, curled by a fairy's hand and waving to the breeze") results in a portrait much like that Melville created.[48] Seraphitus (as he is called when viewed as a male) is, like Billy Budd, a "moral phenomenon."[49] His face is marked by "perfect regularity" and expresses "strength and peace," and yet his "slender feet which hung at the side of the couch were those of a woman."[50] Nevertheless, it was "impossible not to note how the forehead and the outlines of the head gave evidence of power brought to its highest pitch."[51] Balzac, like Melville, focuses on "innocence of which that of children is a symbol."[52] They are not mere children, however, for they possess great power. When a minister of God wishes to baptize Seraphitus, he is told, "your ministrations are superfluous."[53] Balzac writes: "You must not baptize in the waters of an earthly Church one who has just been immersed in the fires of Heaven."[54] The chaplain aboard the *Bellipotent* comes to the same realization about Billy Budd. The death of the androgynous youth comes at the end of both novels, and in both the character is seemingly caught up in the heavens, in Balzac's work to be a seraphim. Whether or not Melville was as deeply influenced by *Seraphita* as it appears, he must have been thinking of himself and *Billy Budd* when he marked Balzac's comment in his *Correspondence:* "It is thus that I make my enemies say with rage, 'At the moment when people thought he had written himself out, he publishes a master-piece.'"[55]

Almost with religious fervor, Melville held steadily to the belief that by losing his physical youth, he had come to value and appreciate his inner youth as never possible before. A crippling or dulling of the imagination he considered the most terrible of fates. The imperiled imagination is the subject of another late poem "Madam Mirror" in which the speaker is an old looking glass now completely cut off from the outside world and "stranded" in a garret. No longer able to image forth because it no longer sees images, the mirror-imagination looks back upon what it once reflected and concentrates on trouble and suffering. A degree of contentment has emerged as it has ceased to strive and reflect, but it no longer functions as it was intended:

> Tho' lone in a loft I must languish
> Far from closet and parlor at strife,
> Content I escape from the anguish
> Of the Real and the Seeming in life.

Melville was concerned that he not store away his creative spirit in some attic of his inner self in an effort to gain contentment. Age is not the only threat to the imagination, however, as he suggests in the companion poem, "The Wise Virgins to Madam Mirror." The speakers are young, and much of what they say about the limitations of Madam Mirror's opinions are true, but the youth that they manifest is simply chronological and not to be confused with the quality Melville had in mind when he wrote of the old lilac's being true to its "youth." They are "virgins" and espouse a view of life strikingly like that of the optimists who were writing in Melville's time. Their blindness endangers the creative impulse in a different fashion but imperils it nonetheless.

Nowhere has Melville presented a more melancholy picture of what it is like to grow old and lose the creative impulse than in his poem about the plight of an aging writer in whom the imagination is dead, "C———'s Lament." When the speaker of the poem uses the term *youth*, he refers not just to his earlier time of life but to his lost imaginative faculty.

> How lovely was the light of heaven,
> What angels leaned from out the sky
> In years when youth was more than wine
> And man and nature seemed divine

Ere yet I felt that youth must die.

     Ere yet I felt that youth must die
How insubstantial looked the earth,
Alladin-land! in each advance,
Or here or there, a new romance;
I never dreamed would come a dearth.
     And nothing then but had its worth,
Even pain, Yes, pleasure still and pain
In quick reaction made of life
A lover's quarrel, happy strife
In youth that never comes again.
     But will youth never come again?
Even to his grave-bed has he gone,
And left me lone to wake by night
With heavy heart that erst was light?
O, lay it at his head—a stone!

This was Melville's stark reminder to himself of what old age can be without an active imagination that functions vitally when one reads and creates.[56] It is a poem about what he feared, not what he became.

The creative imagination, Melville recognized, faces a constant challenge from lassitude, which cries out not for the hard work of literary weaving but for quietness and rest. In "The Garden of Metrodorus," he presents a speaker tempted by an existence of peace disengaged from the life of the imagination:

The Athenians mark the moss-grown gate
And hedge untrimmed that hides the haven green
     And who keeps here his quiet state?
     And shares he sad or happy fate
Where never foot-path to the gate is seen?
Here none come forth, here none go in,
Here silence strange, and dumb seclusion dwell:
     Content from loneness who may win?
     And is this stillness peace or sin
Which noteless thus apart can keep its dell?

Critics have been busy trying to identify which Metrodorus Melville had in mind, since several Greek philosophers held that name.[57] This is not a poem about Metrodorus, however, but about a "garden," a quiet and peaceful place where there is no activity of the imagination, where there is but "dumb" silence. Although such an inner life may be peaceful, the choice to extinguish the vital activity of the imagination may be a "sin."

Often Melville's metaphor for the condition most dangerous to the functioning imagination is sleep. The aging Admiral of "The Haglets," one of two poems in *John Marr and Other Sailors* that Melville composed about a tragic shipwreck, is destroyed because he sleeps. After leading his English sailors in victory over the Spanish, he returns home, weary in triumph and yearning for rest.

> He feels the touch of ocean lone;
> Then turns, in frame part undermined,
> Nor notes the shadowing wings that fan behind.

These "shadowing wings" are the unfathomable sea-fowl, haglets, that followed the Spanish ship before its destruction and that now pursue the victor as it runs aground, betrayed by a faulty compass that is the direct cause of the tragedy. By implication, however, the Admiral is culpable, for he is asleep when the needle trembles and changes its reading erroneously.

> Belted he sits in drowsy light,
> And, hatted, nods—the Admiral of the White.
>   He dozes, aged with watches passed—
> Years, years of pacing to and fro;
> He dozes, nor attends the stir
> In bullioned standards rustling low,
> Nor minds the blades whose secret thrill
> Perverts overhead the magnet's Polar will.[58]

Surrendering to the sleepiness of old age, benumbed to unusual possibilities, and wanting only peace and rest, he dozes and becomes insensitive to the direction his ship is taking because he is not aware of what is going on—he is operating with a faulty compass. The ship sinks and

"Forever he sinks deeper in / Unfathomable sleep." Thus ends one of Melville's little allegories of the self.

He decided that he would not go down as did the Admiral of the White. It was better, he felt, to be a restless insomniac with an active imagination than a contented sleeper. He projected these options in a work in the *Timoleon* collection, a poem that he once intended to call "Insomnia or the Bench of Boors." These are the two options: to experience insomnia *or* to be like boors. Later he deleted the first two words from the title. While he is in bed, sleepless, his imagination vividly pictures for him a painting that he had seen by the seventeenth-century Flemish artist David Teniers the Younger in which Dutch peasants doze in a tavern. The poem is highly effective in its poignant contrast between what the speaker is doing and what the subjects in the painting are doing. His imagination is working; it is recreating marvelously a scene of stupor. Any subject becomes wondrous through the office of the imagination, even drunken peasants. But if one has no imagination or has allowed it to sleep and perish, then he is but a dozing boor himself.

> Within low doors the slugs of boors
> Laze and yawn and doze again.
> In dreams they doze, the drowsy boors,
> Their hazy hovel warm and small:
> > Thought's ampler bound
> > But chill is found:
> Within low doors the basking boors
> Snugly hug the ember-mound.
> Sleepless, I see the slumberous boors
> Their blurred eyes blink, their eyelids fall:
> > Thought's eager sight
> > Aches—overbright!
> Within low doors the boozy boors
> Cat-naps take in pipe-bowl light.

Melville underscores the contrast between slumber and imagination (which he calls "thought") through the arrangement of the poem on the page. References to imaginative activity are indented as if not only subordinated to sleep but engulfed by it.

While the slugs of the world rest peacefully and doze, the imaginative insomniac weaves. But there is no doubt that even in sensitive and imaginative people, a tired body demands calm. Nevertheless, as Arnold wrote in "Youth and Calm,"

> Calm's not life's crown, though calm is well.
> 'Tis all perhaps which man acquires,
> But 'tis not what our youth desires.

"Youth," in the sense of the creative spirit, desires commitment to the imagination and to the work of manifesting it in art. How to follow through on the commitment, how to avoid or conquer whatever threatens the commitment and active engagement with the life of the imagination, became the preoccupation of Melville's final years. In his solitary contemplation of these issues, he arrived, as he always did, at his own solution, but Arnold and Balzac were the catalysts.

Arnold's formula for sustaining the creative spirit echoes throughout his writings. It was, in a nutshell, Socrates's "Know thyself." Arnold consistently emphasizes the necessity of getting in touch with one's core of being and of remaining in harmony with it. A remarkable affinity becomes apparent here between Arnold and Melville, whose novels from *Moby-Dick* through *Billy Budd* explore and develop precisely the same subject. Melville's concept of the calm and inviolate inner self finds expression in Arnold's poem "Palladium":

> So, in its lovely moonlight, lives the soul.
> Mountains surround it, and sweet virgin air;
> Cold plashing, past it, crystal waters roll;
> We visit it by moments, ah, too rare!

This cool center of the self Melville described in *Moby-Dick*: "Oh, man! admire and model thyself after the whale! . . . Do thou, too, live in this world without being of it. Be cool at the equator. . . . Retain, O man! in all seasons a temperature of thine own."[59] Arnold referred to it again in his poem "Self-Dependence," where stars rather than whales supply the metaphor:

> Unaffrighted by the silence round them,
> Undistracted by the sights they see,
> These demand not that the things without them
> Yield them love, amusement, sympathy.
>
> . . . .
>
> For self-poised they live, nor pine with noting
> All the fever of some differing soul.
>
> . . . .
>
> These attain the mighty life you see.

The "notion of a self withdrawn from the struggle of warring impulses," observes Kenneth Allott, "occurs frequently in Arnold's poetry and prose."[60] The same could be said of Melville. In another place, Arnold remarked: "Our remotest self must abide in its remoteness awful and unchanged, presiding at the tumult of the rest of our being, changing thoughts contending desires etc. as the moon over the agitations of the Sea."[61] The gravest of human error consists, Arnold and Melville believed, in not knowing or "visiting" this remote essential self. Melville marked with double lines in the margin a stanza making this point in Arnold's "A Southern Night":

> And [we] see all sights from pole to pole,
>   And glance, and nod, and bustle by;
> And never once possess our soul
>   Before we die.

The search for self-knowledge, Arnold makes clear in "Self-Deception," is fraught with difficulty:

> And on earth we wander, groping, reeling; .
> Powers stir in us, stir and disappear.
> Ah! and he, who placed our master-feeling,
> Failed to place that master-feeling clear.

Nevertheless, he insists in "The Buried Life" that we must probe and explore within ourselves:

> Into the mystery of this heart which beats
> So wild, so deep in us—to know
> Whence our lives come and where they go.

In his final work of fiction, Melville pursued this theme in his portrayal of Captain Vere, who fails to understand the mystery of his heart.[62] The concluding stanza of "Self-Dependence" serves as a summary of all Arnold had to say in his poetry on this subject:

> O air-born voice! long since, severely clear,
> A cry like thine in mine own heart I hear:
> "Resolve to be thyself; and know that he,
> Who finds himself, loses his misery!"

Melville encountered the same ideas in Arnold's later writings. As he read the essays in *Culture and Anarchy,* he must have felt that he was reviewing his own convictions formed through a lifetime of thought and experience. No one could have agreed more with Arnold that the goal of life is "to win peace by self-conquest."[63] Nothing that Arnold had to say either in his poetry or in his late prose about the better self and about self-knowledge would have been new or startling to Melville. On this topic, Arnold was but preaching to the choir. But when Arnold connected the failure of self-knowledge in a sensitive person to disillusionment and bitterness and that in turn to the loss of the imagination, he was sounding a warning Melville very much needed to hear.

It was the warning of culpability. The cause of crippling disillusionment and bitterness is often within, not without, Arnold insists. His honesty about self-responsibility is not only ingenuous but redemptive, for it "helps to vitalize his prose, and keeps him from resting with any one doctrine, any one world outlook, any one set, fixed answer to social problems."[64] "Empedocles on Aetna" is Arnold's most poignant depiction of the culpable hero, a creative man in whom the imagination will no longer function: "Something has impair'd" his "spirit's strength / And dried its self-sufficing fount of joy." Yet Empedocles appears tragically unaware of the source of his problem. Lionel Trilling has commented that "the ancient world, sunlit and warm and mysterious, is a world the weary Empedocles cannot believe in; imagination is quite dead for him."[65] If not dead, it is dying. Melville placed a vertical line by a passage in which Empedocles contemplates his suicide:

Before the soul lose all her solemn joys,
And awe be dead, and hope impossible,
And the soul's deep eternal night come on,—
Receive me, hide me, quench me, take me home!

The trouble with Empedocles is Empedocles. Arnold directly connects his loss of "awe" or the imagination with his lack of self-examination and thus with his failure to accept his culpability:

Once read thy own breast right,
And thou hast done with fears;
Man gets no other light,
Search he a thousand years.
Sink in thyself! there ask what ails thee, at that shrine!

The disillusioned, however, tend to blame the world or even God for their bitterness. Melville was so impressed with the following five lines from "Empedocles on Aetna" that he placed double vertical lines by them:

So, loath to suffer mute,
We, peopling the void air,
Make Gods to whom to impute
The ills we ought to bear;
With God and Fate to rail at, suffering easily.

Arnold's poetic drama features a sympathetic tragic figure whose flaw is self-ignorance. Melville was unquestionably drawn to Empedocles, but he was at the same time struck with Arnold's insistence that by blaming the sophists and others for his disillusionment, Empedocles became embittered and that bitterness destroyed the one facility that made life worth living—the imagination. Recognizing the Empedocles strain in himself, Melville marked Arnold's pointed placing of the culpability:

'Tis not the times, 'tis not the sophists vex him;
There is some root of suffering in himself,
Some secret and unfollow'd vein of woe,
Which makes the time look black and sad to him.

Arnold's own conduct, according to Lionel Trilling, was often designed "to preserve imagination" so that "he might still be a poet."[66] Though he maintained a longtime interest in Étienne Pivert de Senancour (1770–1846), an interest that fascinated Melville,[67] he recognized that the source of the French author's discontent was, like that of Empedocles, interior; Senancour was himself responsible, not his world: "But a root of failure, powerlessness, and ennui, there certainly was in the constitution of Senancour's own nature; so that, unfavourable as may have been his time, we should err in attributing to any outward circumstances the whole of the discouragement by which he is pervaded."[68] Whenever Arnold encountered the woe that kills awe, he did not fail to find the sufferer himself at least partly culpable. His admiration for the Swiss philosophical essayist Henri Frédéric Amiel (1821–81), whose journal he read with great interest, was tempered by his recognition of that writer's creative impotence brought on by a crippling of his imagination. Amiel's "disgust with life, despair, pessimism," as he himself referred to it, a "mournful old age, a slow agony, a death in the desert"—this "melancholy outlook on all sides"—was the result, Arnold writes, of a paralyzing preoccupation with abstract ideas. His imagination stifled, he became "impotent and miserable."[69]

One of Amiel's gravest mistakes, Arnold felt, was his surrender to Buddhism. Like Melville, Arnold possessed a profound respect for Buddhism. In *Literature and Dogma*, he called Buddhism "a religion to be saluted with respect, indeed; for it has not only the sense for righteousness; it has, even, it has the secret of Jesus" by which he meant self-sacrifice.[70] Yet he saw in Buddhism a threat to the creative imagination. Amiel's "bedazzlement with the infinite," as he himself termed it, "intoxicates him," Arnold states, "until the thought of absorption and extinction, the Nirvana of Buddhism, becomes his thought of refuge."[71] At that point, the imagination becomes engulfed in the yearning for nothingness and literary production is impossible: "With this bedazzlement with the infinite and this drift towards Buddhism comes the impatience with all production, with even poetry and art themselves."[72] Amiel thus found himself, as he wrote in his diary, unable to "fuse together material and ideas."[73] He could no longer master form nor see the need for it.

Melville's thinking about Buddhism paralleled Arnold's to a remarkable degree. Strongly drawn to it, he recognized as did Arnold that it posed a danger to the creative imagination. In his poem "Buddha," he implies that the goal of a Buddhist is to "swim to less and less," aspiring "to nothingness!" To give up all striving, all desire to create, would be to denounce art. A weaver must not stop weaving. As clearly as Melville understood the tenets of Buddhism and the centrality of nirvana in its belief, he did not even mention the concept in another work on Buddhism, "Rammon." Left unpublished at his death and (in some parts) in his most difficult handwriting, "Rammon" has offered a worthy challenge to those few scholars and critics who have attempted to decipher it.

"Rammon" probably belongs to the period in which *John Marr and Other Sailors* was completed and published, 1887–88.[74] In Melville's handwriting, it consists of 276 lines chiefly in prose. Melville begins by admitting that he has taken liberty with chronology, for he has set his work in Jerusalem in the tenth century B.C., and he has depicted his main character as being introduced to the teachings of Buddha, who did not live until the sixth century B.C. He realizes that he is playing free and loose with history, but he says that "in historical matters the romancer and poet have generously been accorded a certain license, elastic in proportion to the remoteness of the period embraced."[75]

The protagonist of this work, "not mentioned in canonic Scripture," is an "unrobust child of Solomon's old age" and half brother of Rehoboam, who assumed rule upon Solomon's death and unwisely refused an alliance with Jereboam. Rammon advises his brother not to reject the high-spirited and proud Jereboam, who is capable of stirring up much mischief, but Rehoboam is attracted to "flatterers of his own age" and manifests the "arrogance of ignorance." Seeing the futility of trying to change the tragic course of events, Rammon is confirmed "in his natural bias for a life within" and pursues his search for truth, which leads him to Buddhism. As a firm believer in Solomon's teachings, Rammon is confused by the Buddhist belief in metempsychosis though he readily accepts the pessimistic view of human existence and is strongly attracted to the figure of Buddha himself. He hears that a sophisticated and well-traveled man is in Jerusalem, so he invites this man of the world to visit him, hoping to learn more about Buddhism, especially about the idea that bothers him most—transmigration of souls. He is conditioned to reject the thought of any form of immortality; being reborn is abhorrent to him since all worlds are the same— chiefly rotten. His guest has little to offer except a stale optimism. He knows nothing of Buddha and his beliefs, and he is not worried by questions that trouble Rammon's heart. Therefore, Rammon quickly changes the subject and asks his visitor to recite a pleasant poem.

At this point, "Rammon" ends. The best available evidence, however, suggests that a poem was at one time meant to be included. Melville probably composed the poem "The Enviable Isles" first, wrote the mostly prose "Rammon" to precede it, and then removed "The Enviable Isles" for inclusion in *John Marr and Other Sailors*,[76] where he entitled it "The Enviable Isles (From 'Rammon')." Since the two works were once one, Eleanor Tilton restores the poem to its original position at the end in her edition of the text, concluding with good reason that "Rammon" and "The Enviable Isles" cohere as a single work.

If Melville initially intended "The Enviable Isles" to be the poem that Rammon's guest recites, why did he sever it from its context and publish it in *John Marr and Other Sailors*? Did he decide that the two works did not logically fit together, that "The Enviable Isles" conflicted thematically with "Rammon"? So it has been argued.[77] It may well be, however, that when he was gathering poems together for *John Marr*, he decided to include "The Enviable Isles" because it could stand on its own as a unit and because he did not consider the rest of "Rammon" yet ready for publication. This argument appears probable because there is no proof that Melville rejected the introductory material; he simply never got around to putting it into finished form. Furthermore, the theme of "The Enviable Isles" is not actually in conflict with that of "Rammon" but a completing element of it. The theme is that no doctrine is adequate to answer all the questions raised by life's complexity, even a system of thought emerging from so pure a soul as Buddha.

Melville's principal method of projecting this idea in "Rammon" (including "The Enviable Isles") is irony, the most apparent level of which develops from the fact that the young prince is disturbed that

Buddhism does not teach cessation of being when in truth that is precisely what it does teach. Indeed, in Buddhism cessation of being is that which is most to be desired. Rammon hears erroneously that Buddha believed only in an eternal cycle of metempsychosis. Since he is not attuned to any form of eternal life, this concept deeply disturbs him. Had he only known that Buddhists do not associate reincarnation with heaven but with a kind of hell and that rebirths are merely steps on the way to the real goal, nirvana, and had he known that nirvana *is* cessation of being, he might have been spared frustration and despondency, and he could have embraced Buddhism as embodying all that he was searching for.

Irony underlies irony in this work, however, for real Buddhism probably would not have satisfied Rammon either. The poem that originally concluded "Rammon" suggests that the Buddhist aspiration to nothingness and the practice of Buddhist meditation actually deaden its followers to the wonders of the world around them, their imaginations asleep. "The Enviable Isles" is very much about Buddhism but not about the Buddhist concept of the afterlife.[78] The people in the poem are not dead but deadened. They are deeply involved in what they regard as "the trance of God." They have found a form of escape, the Buddhist trance, similar to that of Tennyson's lotus eaters. The comparison is appropriate, for the inhabitants of the Enviable Isles are just as surely drugged to life, nature, and their own inner selves as are Ulysses' men after eating the lotus fruit.[79] The natural setting they inhabit may be enviable, but they certainly are not, for they have lost their individuality and creativity. The rhythms and beauty of creation are all around them, but they are totally unaware of them:

> . . . inland, where the sleep that folds the hills
> A dreamier sleep, the trance of God, instills—
> On uplands hazed, in wandering airs aswoon,
> Slow-swaying palms salute love's cypress tree
> Adown in vale where pebbly runlets croon
> A song to lull all sorrow and all glee.
> Sweet-fern and moss in many a glade are here,

Where, strown in flocks, what cheek-flushed myriads lie
Dimpling in dream—unconscious slumberers mere,
While billows endless round the beaches die.

Though Melville was familiar with the Buddhist concept of nirvana, he did not mention it in "Rammon" because its very absence contributes largely to the work's irony. Nirvana is conspicuous by its absence. Anyone with even a rudimentary knowledge of Buddhism will be struck with the fact that nirvana is the ingredient the young prince is seeking. The irony is thus already pronounced, but it is made even more intense by the concluding poem, which vividly depicts the results of a life given over to Buddhism—removal from the vitality of the imagination for a sleepy contentment. "Rammon" presents, therefore, both what Melville liked about Buddhism and what he disliked about it. The Prince, like Melville, is understandably drawn to Siddhartha, a saintly figure of great tenderness and goodness. Though Rammon does not realize it and fails to find it out, Buddhism actually teaches what he thinks he is looking for. Despite that fact, however, Buddhism would not ultimately suffice for Rammon any more than it would for Melville, who realized as did Matthew Arnold that a drift toward it could bring death to literary creativity. It is probably no coincidence that the name *Rammon* (with the accent on the first syllable) closely resembles *Herman*.

The basic subject of "Rammon," therefore, appears to be not the nature of evil or immortality, as some critics have argued,[80] but Buddhism, its attractiveness and its unattractiveness, and by extension, the inadequacy of any formula, any dogma, no matter how appealing its founder or compelling his teachings. All "transcendent teaching," Melville charges, is "alike unprovable and irrefutable."[81]

Still, Melville seemed to find most aspects of Buddhism attractive. What frightened him most was what he calls in "The Enviable Isles" the "trance of God." As Willliam H. Shurr has pointed out, Melville was here referring to Buddhist meditative practice, and the phrase "trance of God" appears "to have been the core from which Melville developed first the poem and then the introductory *Rammon*."[82] Repeating hypnotically a mantra (a word that comes from Sanskrit meaning "spell"), the Buddhist is transported to a transcendent state. The recitation of a mantra is thus a chant that leads to what is commonly thought of as a trance.[83]

As much as Melville experienced lassitude and longed for a peaceful escape from the misery of old age, his creative imagination remained too commanding to permit its demise. Consequently, whenever Melville refers to or merely suggests the mantra or the Buddhist trance, the context is that of a temptation. The extent to which he intended to make tempting the situation he pictured in "The Enviable Isles" is indicated by his original title for that poem: "The Tahiti Islands." This is significant because of what he associated with Tahiti. Though it has been assumed that he originally chose "The Tahiti Islands" as a title merely because of the exotic attractiveness of that Edenic locale, it should be remembered that in *Omoo*, he created a situation in which the narrator has to overcome the temptation represented by Tahiti and its hypnotic indolence.[84] In Melville's mind, Tahiti and the nearby Imeeo came to be associated not only with innocence and pristine beauty but also with the seductive temptation to surrender one's self-conceived identity for a life of half-conscious contentment. At the broadest level, "Rammon" repeats the theme of *Omoo* using Buddhism instead of Tahiti as the temptation.

Remarkable and, as far as I can determine, hitherto unrecognized is Melville's creation in some of his later poems of an approximation of the Buddhist chant, presented as seductive and hypnotic and by implication dangerous to the artistic impulse. The repetition of certain sounds or syllables and the monotonous and heavy rhythms imitate the sounds of a Buddhist chanting a mantra. "Buddha" begins: "Swooning swim to less and less, / Aspirant to nothingness." Here Melville wanted not only to write about Buddhism but to convey sensuously its compelling call to rest, to give up cares and ambitions and strivings of all sorts, to float into unworldliness. With its soothing repetition of *s*'s, its regular trochaic meter, and the ease with which it lends itself to a hypnotic monotonal reading, this passage is extraordinarily onomatopoeic. Yet it furnishes an additional ingredient not found in the Buddhist chant: rhyme. While imitating the liquid and somewhat ritualistic quality (as of one reciting mechanically) of the

Buddhist chant, Melville creates a rhyming pattern that gives the lines something of the effect of an incantation as in black magic. Thus the lines combine an earnest prayer with a witch's verbal formula. The two-sidedness of Buddhism then becomes evident. The first word of the poem manifests in and of itself this duality: *swooning* can mean being carried away with pleasure, experiencing rapture, but it also suggests fainting, undergoing an unwanted loss of consciousness. The Buddhist trance (or "swoon"), therefore, is presented as temptingly peaceful but privative.

Closely related to "The Enviable Isles" and to "Buddha" is "Lamia's Song," one of the poems in the volume *Timoleon*. The voice of the poem is that of a siren inviting all those who hear to join the throng "dimpling in dream—unconscious" on the enviable isles. Lamia was not merely a siren, however. In Greek myths and later, she was a vampire who seduced young men so that she could drink their very lifeblood. From the title, therefore, it is clear that the appeal of the song is dangerously seductive. Listeners who accept the compelling invitation will lose their life-giving force. The similarity of settings (mountains and lowland) and of the nature of the rewards offered naturally link "Lamia's Song" with "The Enviable Isles," but a further parallel can be seen in the idea of giving up striving to float on a "downward way," a surrender of the high terrain in order to be, as Melville puts it in "The Enviable Isles," "adown in vale." "Lamia's Song" shares with "Buddha" a strong sensuous appeal; the entire poem is an incantation:

> Descend, descend!
> Pleasant the downward way—
> From your lonely Alp
> With the wintry scalp
> To our myrtles in valleys of May.
> Wend then, wend:
> Mountaineer, descend!
> And more than a wreath shall repay.
> Come, ah come!
> With the cataracts come,

That hymn as they roam
How pleasant the downward way!

In general, "Lamia's Song" is in sound and sense an invitation to give up the struggle. The poem's imagery hints that Melville may have had in mind especially the inward struggle, the striving for self-conquest, for the "lonely Alp" recalls other passages where the inner terrain is suggested in like metaphors.[85] He may also have had in mind the creator of art as the "mountaineer," who is tempted to give up the arduous attempts to create and win the "wreath." The poem's several similarities to "Buddha" and "The Enviable Isles" suggest that it is specifically about Buddhism. Like the opening of "Buddha," it invites a monotonal reading that is spellbinding. One of Melville's most effective poems, it is hauntingly hypnotic. Though the philosophical basis of the poem is broad—the appeal of rest, the reward of a life free of struggle—it projects this theme in terms that point to Buddhist beliefs, especially the one represented by Rammon's question: "Why strive?"

A reviewer of Arthur Lillie's *Buddha and Early Buddhism* commented in the *Atlantic Monthly* in 1881 that a true Buddhist "must neither deny, nor yet believe in, the existence of God, a future, or a soul."[86] Besides describing a true Buddhist, this statement may also apply to Melville, who was "neither believer nor infidel" but a man who was something of both.[87] His doubts and intuitions; his vision of suffering; his discomfort with Western religions and their concepts of God, evil, and heaven; his desire for rest and quietness as he grew older—all these characteristics and others drew him to Buddhist beliefs. But the goal of Buddhism is to make this life resemble as much as possible the cessation of being that is nirvana. When one sets out utterly to extinguish all desire, to "achieve an absolute indifference to everything," death of the creative imagination and artistic production seem likely to follow.[88] Melville suffered from lassitude, and he craved peace as he grew older, but he could not tolerate the thought of killing the artist in him. In his delightful satirization of easy answers to universal problems, "Herba Santa," he facetiously offers tobacco and, by implication, Buddhism, as cures for the world's ills. His humor has a sharp edge, however, for surrender to opiates, though pleasant, results in inner death. In the final stanza, he speaks of finding an "Eastern chamber" where he can undergo an experience that rehearses the "long release," a slightly cloaked reference to nirvana:

> Forebear, my soul! and in thine Eastern chamber
> > Rehearse the dream that brings the long release:
> Through jasmine sweet and talismanic amber
> > Inhaling Herba Santa in the passive Pipe of Peace.

Whether or not Melville was thinking of Buddhism when he wrote "In a Bye-Canal" is largely a matter of conjecture, but the language of the poem directly links it to "The Enviable Isles" and "Buddha," and a siren figure resembles the vampire in "Lamia's Song." The opening lines suggest that the speaker is spellbound, and the specific words "a swoon" and "a trance" closely parallel those used in "Buddha" ("Swooning swim to less and less") and in "The Enviable Isles" ("A dreamier sleep, the trance of God, instills"). The woman summoning the speaker has a "basilisk glance of conjuration" and is referred to as a "true" siren, certainly terms that are also applicable to Lamia.[89]

"In a Bye-Canal" differs from these other poems, however, in that it is lighthearted on the surface. Published in *Timoleon* in 1891, it was probably written, at least in part, at some earlier date. It depicts the speaker's narrow escape from a strange woman as he glides along in a gondola enjoying the magic of Venice. The point is highly serious, however, and the situation allegorical. As in the other poems, Melville is expressing his belief that a siren awaits him, a dangerous siren that will rob him of his desire to create and the imaginative energy to do so. If he is not alert to this peril, if he sleeps, he may be lost. The opening stanza sets the stage with references both to the charms of sleep and to betrayal:

> A swoon of noon, a trance of tide,
> The hushed siesta brooding wide
> > Like calms far off Peru;
> No floating wayfarer in sight,

> Dumb noon, and haunted like the night
> When Jael the wiled one slew.

In this setting of quietude, the speaker is attracted to the eyes of a woman summoning him from behind a lattice. Though some readers have found in this situation a sign of Melville's fear of women or of normal sexuality, it is more likely an allegorical representation of the dangers of losing one's alert imagination, of becoming dull and sleepy.

> A languid impulse from the oar
> Plied by my indolent gondolier
> Tinkles against a palace hoar,
>> And, hark, responses I hear!
> A lattice clicks; and lo, I see
> Between the slats, mute summoning me,
> What loveliest eyes of scintillation,
> What basilisk glance of conjuration!

The speaker remarks humorously that he has been through mighty perils in his time, but none has confounded him more than this sweet pernicious invitation; therefore, he alerts his gondolier, and himself, with a "Wake up!" and escapes the temptress waiting to lull and seduce him into a life he does not want to live:

> Fronted I have, part taken the span
> Of portents in nature and peril in man.
> I have swum—I have been
> Twixt the whale's black flukes and the white shark's fin;
> The enemy's desert have wandered in,
> And there have turned, have turned and scanned,
> Following me how noiselessly,
> Envy and Slander, lepers hand in hand.
> All this. But at the latticed eye—
> "Hey! Gondolier, you sleep, my man;
> Wake up!" And, shooting by, we ran;
> The while I mused, this, surely now,

> Confutes the Naturalists, allow!
> Sirens, true sirens verily be,
> Sirens, waylayers in the sea.

Sirens appear not only in myth but in real life, the "waylayers" of the sea. The poem ends with an ostensibly lighthearted admonition to flee the "deadly misses," but Melville is describing more than a brush he may have had with a loose woman or prostitute when he was abroad. He is indulging in a bit of self-revelation about dangers to the imagination and to artistic productivity. Sirens are always there to lure one off course to destruction as they tried to draw Ulysses from his course:

> Well, wooed by these same deadly misses,
> Is it shame to run?
> No! flee them did divine Ulysses,
> Brave, wise, and Venus' son.[90]

Melville thus found no religious thought, including Buddhism, attractive beyond the point that it seemed to threaten the vitality of the imagination. It was for this reason that he seemed attracted to what Arnold had to say about religion in *Literature and Dogma*. Arnold's was a brand of Christianity tailor-made, not acquired from others; it followed the dogma of no denomination. He was in this area, as in several others, as Archibald L. Bouton has stressed, a "liberator."[91] Melville marked with triple checks Arnold's poem "Religious Isolation," which reads in part: "To its own impulse every creature stirs. / Live by thy light, and earth twill live by hers!" When Arnold wrote in "Stanzas from the Grande Chartreuse" of a Greek who was "Wandering between two worlds, one dead, / The other powerless to be born," he was not only describing himself but also unwittingly expressing Melville's situation as "neither believer nor infidel," a situation Hawthorne referred to when he wrote in his notebooks of Melville: "He can neither believe, nor be comfortable in his unbelief; and he is too honest and courageous not to try to do one or the other."[92]

Of course, Arnold's particular and peculiar form of Christianity was not appreciated by the orthodox. James Main Dixon, for example, devoted an entire book to proving that Arnold was not a Christian of any sort but a "Sadducee": "The theology in Arnold's prose and poetry is essentially the same. . . . The theology in both is extraordinarily warped and defective."[93] William E. Gladstone was kinder but made essentially the same point in observing that Arnold "combined a sincere devotion to the Christian religion with a faculty for presenting it in such a form as to be recognisable neither by friend nor foe."[94] According to Herbert W. Paul, if Arnold had not alienated just about every Christian denomination before the publication of *Literature and Dogma,* he certainly did thereafter: "With this book he severed himself from orthodox Christianity, and even from Unitarianism as commonly understood."[95] The effect of reading *Literature and Dogma* upon the average Bible-reading Christian, Paul writes, was "like suddenly swallowing a fish-bone."[96]

Reading it was not like swallowing a fishbone to Melville, though he was nominally a Unitarian. If he found anything shocking or offensive in *Literature and Dogma,* he did not record it in the margins of his copy. In fact, there was much for him to admire in it. Arnold was, like Melville, a God-seeker to whom "all creeds were anathema. He could not away with them. The Apostles' was as bad as the Nicene, and the Nicene no better than the Athanasian."[97] Melville would have recognized as few others did that Arnold did not write *Literature and Dogma* for "those who were satisfied with the popular theology. He wrote for those who were not. His object was not to disturb any one's faith, but to convince those who could not believe in the performance of miracles, or the fulfillment of prophecies, that they need not therefore become materialists."[98]

Above all, Arnold's brand of religious thought did not appear to threaten the life of the imagination or to discourage devotion to art. On the other hand, Melville found in his reading of Thomson and Schopenhauer a complete rejection of Western civilization's concept of a personal God in favor of a Buddhist-like view of ultimate reality, which does not posit a Creator or Supreme Being. To some extent, the Pessimists echoed the Buddhist admonition against "striving," and that included, in theory anyway, artistic production. Melville agreed with much that Thomson said about art and its relationship to life in "Per Contra," but he could not accept the Pessimist's conclusion that

"Artistry, then, as the absolute devotion to Art in and of itself, is, I repeat, a symptom of weakness," and "to be weak is in itself to be miserable."[99] Melville read in H. S. Salt that "Thomson's views on art and literature were pervaded by the same tinge of melancholy and despondence." Thomson regarded art merely as a "substitute and makeshift."[100] Schopenhauer differed in his attitude toward art with Thomson (as he did in several other areas), but his conclusions were equally unacceptable to Melville. Schopenhauer's theory of literature is based mainly upon what it does for the reader rather than on what it does or does not do for the artist. Melville read in the "Translator's Preface" to *The Wisdom of Life* the following description of Schopenhauer's thoughts on the function of art: "In the apprehension of Art we are raised out of our bondage, contemplating objects of thought as they are in themselves, apart from their relations to our own ephemeral existence, and free from any taint of the will."[101] In his summary, the translator goes on to point out, however, that Schopenhauer believed one's "highest ethical duty, and consequently the supreme endeavour after happiness, is to withdraw from the struggle of life, and so obtain release from the misery which that struggle imposes upon all." This would presumably include withdrawing from the struggle to produce art.[102] Perceptively, a contemporary of Melville, the critic W. L. Courtney, wrote that Pessimism cuts "at the very root of the artistic impulse."[103]

Like Melville, Arnold admired much in the writings of the Pessimists. Also like Melville, he was open to the appeal of Buddhism, which so influenced the thought of the Pessimists.[104] In fact, he was often thought of as part of that group. Gamaliel Bradford revealed a widespread attitude when he linked Arnold with them in an entry dated February 29, 1924, in his *Journal:* "Nothing has comforted and helped me more than the most pessimistic of writers, Senancour and Leopardi and the poetry of Arnold."[105] Yet Arnold wanted to be considered as neither Pessimist nor Buddhist. He was probably familiar with the explanation Leopardi gave for his own profound sadness: he said that it resulted from, as Lionel Trilling puts it, "the shrivelling of the imagination."[106] During his first lecture tour of America, Arnold was greatly irritated when he was confused with Sir Edwin Arnold,

British purveyor of Buddhism and author of the popular *The Light of Asia.* When he read a German writer exhalting Schopenhauer "at the expense of Jesus," he reacted sharply. He resented the implication that "Schopenhauer faced the pessimism" that is the apparent truth of life whereas "Jesus sought to escape from it by the dream of a paradise to come." Jesus taught that the Kingdom of God is *now,* Arnold points out. He quotes the German writer's version of Schopenhauer's message: "In abstinence from the further propagation of mankind is salvation. This would gradually bring about the extinction of our species, and with our extinction, that of the universe."[107] The idea is but a variation of the Buddhist concept of salvation through the ending of striving, and that includes artistic striving. Apologizing to his readers "for whom Schopenhauer is just now in fashion," Arnold concludes that such a view of life is "absurd."[108] He predicts that "Christianity, however, will find the ways for its own future. What is certain is that it will not disappear."[109]

Melville was attracted to Arnold's theological pronouncements because they involved little dogma, espoused only a few basic principles, and posed no threat to the life of the imagination. As unorthodox as it was, Arnold's religious thought always reflected profound admiration for the figure of Jesus Christ, an admiration that Melville shared. Among the miscellaneous poems left unpublished at Melville's death is one entitled "Honor," a work powerful in its insistence that Christianity be valued over materialism and by implication that it be considered on an equal footing with the popular and dazzling wisdom arriving with its exotic trappings from the East:

> With jeweled tusks and damask housings
> August the elephants appear:
> Grandees, trumpets, banners, soldiers—
> One flame from van to rear!
>
> Bid by India's King they travel
> In solemn embassage to-day,
> To meet the Diamond from Golconda,
> The Great Find of Cathay.

O the honor, O the homage!
But, methinks, 'twere nice,
Would they say but *How-de-do*?
To the Little Pearl of Price.

He could value the Pearl of Price, but he was not one of those people who could believe what most Christians, even his wife, accepted on faith. In fact, Elizabeth's long-suffering and unquestioning acceptance of the beliefs of her church and her pastors probably had the opposite effect on her husband of what she hoped and intended. The more she humbly accepted without reservation or question, the more he resisted and questioned and the more he was irritated by what he considered her simple and unthinking piety. Her patience with his unorthodoxy sometimes appeared to his overly sensitive temperament as condescending pity. Husband and wife therefore silently (and perhaps sometimes not so silently) disturbed and challenged each other. At least some of the friction evident in their relationship derived from this source. Had he not been married to such an ostensibly pious woman, he may have been less frequently agitated.[110] Marriages may be made in heaven, but if so, some of them proclaim the existence of divine irony. When troubles came, Elizabeth would sometimes seek advice from her pastor; Melville felt about preachers as he did about most doctors. He marked emphatic vertical lines on both sides of the following stanzas from Arnold's poem "A Wish":

Nor bring, to see me cease to live,
Some doctor full of phrase and fame,
To shake his sapient head and give
The ill he cannot cure a name.

Nor fetch, to take the accustomed toll
Of the poor sinner bound for death,
His brother doctor of the soul,
To canvass with official breath.

The situation in the Melville household never became intolerable, however. In fact, Herman remained in his late years a member, with

Elizabeth, of the All Souls Unitarian Church in New York City. Together they attended worship services fairly regularly to hear the prominent Dr. Henry Bellows preach and later the Reverend Theodore Chickering Williams. Melville did what he had to do, but his allegiance during these years was not so much to church and family as to the life of the imagination and art. He was, in essence, a stoic during this period. What Van Wyck Brooks said of Matthew Arnold could be applied to Melville as well: "The rôle he chose was that of the Stoic, who wraps his mantle about him, patiently, wearily, without bitterness and without expectancy, and stands up nobly egotistical before fate."[111] With only three years separating them at each end of their lives, Melville and Arnold were children of the same era. Both were longtime servants of the government and to varying extents suffered under that burden. They led different lives, to be sure, Arnold during his final years a literary lion basking in the glow of fame and traveling in the circles of the influential and famous and Melville quietly living out his final days in relative obscurity. Nevertheless, they were intellectual and spiritual brothers with many of the same affinities. Melville probably did not know but would not have been surprised to learn that Arnold also cherished and grew roses.

Balzac, like Arnold, was a kindred soul, and that is the primary reason Melville spent so much time reading him. Judging from Melville's marginal responses in his copies of Balzac's works, he recognized close parallels between his own thought and experience and that of the great French writer. In areas that particularly interested him, he could not miss the links tying Balzac to Arnold and to himself. For example, though he had not worked long years for the government as had Melville and Arnold, Balzac wrote about those in government service with such penetrating truth that Melville's pencil was kept busy marking passages in several works.

Melville knew true drudgery as a district inspector for the New York Custom House, a branch of government service in which "corruption was the order of the day."[112] Stanton Garner suggests that "Melville observed much to disgust him" and that "the corruption touched him personally."[113] From this subordinate position, Melville was never elevated. In the year *Clarel* was published, he suffered a temporary decrease in his salary of four dollars a day, a subsistence that was never increased beyond that amount in all the nineteen years he was employed. He was somewhat like Balzac's Xavier Rabourdin of the novel *Bureaucracy,* an honest and talented man among corrupt climbers and petty tyrants. Melville underlined, checked, and marginally marked numerous passages in his copy of *Bureaucracy* that deal with Balzac's observations on government employment. Though Melville did not read this novel until 1889 or later, years after he had retired from his job with the Customs Service, he was clearly struck with how accurately Balzac depicted what he called in the novel "the high comedy of government." Melville marked this phrase as well as the following passage: "To worship the fool who succeeds, and not to grieve over the fall of an able man is the result of our melancholy education, of our manners and customs which drive men of intellect into disgust, and genius to despair."[114] As a man of intellect and imagination himself, Melville was driven to disgust while in government employment, and as a genius, he was doubtlessly close to despair. His situation must have been nearly intolerable. Perhaps the greatest triumph of his life was his emerging without whining from these nineteen years in a situation where unfairness, pettiness, corruption, and stupidity were rife. He came through with his honesty and his imagination intact and without the bitterness that can cripple or even destroy.

Resignation somehow sustained him during those years in the crucible of government service. He marked the following passage in Balzac's *Seraphita:* "At the zeneth of all virtue is Resignation,—to be an exile and not lament."[115] Perhaps he realized then the truth of what he later read and underlined in *Bureaucracy:* "You cannot prevent the buying and selling of influence, the collusions of self-interest."[116] Yet he never forgot what he had witnessed, and his reading of Balzac's novel brought it poigantly again before his eyes. He placed double lines of emphasis beside a passage that treats the subtle evil that is rampant in the offices of the government: "Moralists usually employ their weapons against obtrusive abominations. In their eyes, crime belongs to the assizes or the police-courts; but the socially refined evils escape their ken; the adroitness that triumphs under shield of the Code is above them or beneath them; they have neither eye-glass nor telescope; they want good stout horrors easily visible. With their eyes fixed on the carnivora, they pay no attention to the reptiles."[117] Marking such sections with the interest of remembered melancholy, Melville reviewed his past and marveled that he had recently discovered another man, and a Frenchman at that, so like himself.

Melville also observed that Balzac shared Arnold's views about a best self and the importance of self-knowledge. He read George Frederic Parsons's statement in the introduction to *Louis Lambert* that Balzac thoroughly believed what "Browning has put into the mouth of his Paracelsus":

> Truth is within ourselves, it takes not rise
> From outward things, whate'er you may believe:
> There is an inmost centre in us all,
> Where truth abides in fulness; and around,
> Wall upon wall, the gross flesh hems it in,
> This perfect, clear perception—which is truth;
> A baffling and perverting carnel mesh
> Blinds it, and makes all error; and, "*to know*"
> Rather consists in opening out a way
> Whence the imprisoned splendor may escape,
> Than in effecting entry for a light
> Supposed to be without.[118]

There is no doubt that Melville fervently believed the same thing. Balzac wrote in *Eugénie Grandet* a passage that expresses the need for self-understanding and for assuming responsibility for one's deepest motives: "It often happens that certain actions of human life seem, literally speaking, improbable, though actual. Is not this because we constantly omit to turn the stream of psychological light upon our impulsive determinations, and fail to explain the subtile reasons, mysteriously conceived in our minds, which impelled them?"[119] In reading Balzac's *The Duchesse de Langeais*, Melville encountered a situation in which a woman, not realizing her own passionate nature, scorns a man until her repressed emotions ambush her, but too late for a satisfactory relationship. This theme—the destructiveness of self-ignorance—was Melville's focus in "After the Pleasure Party."

Like Arnold, Balzac created for himself a patchwork religion, if, indeed, one can call it a religion. He found it impossible to accept the dogma of the Catholic Church. In a letter to Madam Hanska, he stated: "I am by no means orthodox, and I do not go to the Roman Church."[120] Harry Levin has commented that to Balzac, "Catholicism was too formal, too political, too terrestrial to satisfy his need for a personal theology."[121] His "Christianity," writes Michel Butor, "had less and less to do with that of the Church."[122] So he created what one critic has termed a "hodgepodge."[123] To a considerably thinned base of Christianity, he added a touch of Buddhism, a sampling of alchemy, a bit of Swedenborgism, a smattering of Rosicrucianism, and a little of this and that until he found the flavor acceptable and took a few gulps of the mixture. J. B. Priestly referred to Balzac's theology as "heavy occult hocus-pocus."[124]

A strange mixture it indeed was, vague enough not to tie him to any single system of dogma but close enough to being a religion to afford him respectability. He reacted strongly when accused of having no religion at all. Melville marked a passage in a letter in which Balzac complained with resentment to Madame Hanska: "You write severely, as if I believed in nothing, and as if you would send me to the Grande Chartreuse to be converted."[125]

There was nothing vague about his antimaterialism, however. He simply could not by nature be a materialist. His short novel *Melmoth Absolved* is a powerful statement about the emptiness of worldly power and pleasure—even when experienced to the ultimate degree—and the horrible agony that is the result of a total separation from any spiritual dimension.

That he found this spiritual dimension in the religion-philosophy he espoused, one heavily laced with mysticism and occultism, is doubtful. He even warned Madame Hanska against mysticism in a letter that caught Melville's attention: "I am sorry to see that you are reading the Mystics: believe me, this sort of reading . . . is an intoxicating narcotic. . . . This kind of reading, believe me, is pernicious." He goes on to write: "I have myself gone through this, and I speak from experience."[126] Balzac picked the ingredients that made up his philosophical and theological beliefs like he selected the various exotic beans for his evening coffee. When an ingredient failed to enhance creative inspiration, he made substitutions. Once strongly attracted to mysticism, he discovered that it was "pernicious." If forms of mysticism no longer seemed to fit into his particular religious or philosphical brew, it was because they threatened in some way his creative vitality. They acted as a "narcotic," and he could not tolerate drugs like opium that dull rather than stimulate the senses and that bring on sleep or stupor. He clearly mirrored the sentiment of the insomniac Melville, who wrote poem after poem in his later years about the threat of sleep and who rejected any aspect of religion or philosophy that seemed detrimental to the creative imagination.

Balzac's principal way of transcending materiality was through his writing. When he wrote that art was "that second religion," he was revealing not that art was second in his priorities to religion but that it was another kind of religion. He was convinced that he possessed supernatural powers of observation, that he was gifted with a rare ability to look into the lives of others and see what was happening there. The power of the imagination that one of his characters claims to possess was in actuality Balzac's own: "To quit my own life, to become some other individual ... and to play this game at will, such was the recreation of my studious hours. To what have I owed this gift? Was it second sight? Is it one of those qualities the abuse of which leads to insanity? I have never sought to discover the causes of this power. I possess it, and I use it; that is enough for me."[127]

By using it, Balzac was indulging in creation, an activity that brought him in his own mind close to divinity. A man gifted with a phenomenal imagination who clearly rejects materialism as an end but who cannot piously devote himself to God through a simple but profound faith manifested in the ways readily recognized by the orthodox—such a man may have another antimaterialist alternative, "that second religion," art. On his deathbed, Balzac did not call upon God to save him but asked for a physician he had himself created for the *Human Comedy:* "Balzac is reported to have said before he finally lost consciousness, 'Only Bianchon can save me.'"[128] This is not to claim that Balzac did not have a strong and genuine spiritual drive. He certainly did, but it was his artistic creativity that fueled the drive rather than the reverse.

What Melville discovered in Balzac, then, from reading his novels, short stories, correspondence, and works about him was the example par excellence of a weaver, a man exceptionally devoted to art. From the *Correspondence,* Melville became aware of one of the most peculiar but important ingredients in Balzac's life: coffee. Melville never failed to mark allusions to it. He placed a vertical line in the margin by Balzac's remarks in a letter to a close friend Madame Zulma Carraud: "I have the gratitude still fresh in my heart of the time when you showed yourself so sweet and indulgent towards the foolish irritation caused in me by the use of coffee."[129] In the same letter, Melville marked another reference to Balzac's coffee nerves: "It has personally cost me a thousand francs for corrections, of which the arbitrators have taken no account whatever. I say nothing of my nights and days of work, of my health undermined by the abuse of coffee."[130]

It soon became clear to Melville that Balzac was not drinking coffee socially or because he simply liked it. He drank it to keep him awake during periods when his imagination was active, usually late in the evenings. He consumed large quantities of it despite his awareness that it was detrimental to his health, despite the warnings of his doctors. Melville marked a passage in a letter Balzac wrote to his sister in which he indicates the value of coffee in prolonging inspiration, his need to take ever-increasing amounts of it, and the dire physical consequences: "The time which the inspiration caused by coffee formerly lasted has now diminished; it only gives a fortnight's excitement to the brain—a fatal excitement, for it causes me horrible pains in the stomach."[131] What better example could Melville find of an artist so devoted to the life of the imagination that he would sacrifice his very material existence to it?

Like Melville, Balzac saw sleep as the enemy. From everything he read by or about Balzac, Melville pieced together a portrait of the ideal weaver. Though socially inclined, Balzac prescribed through example a life for the artist of limited social engagement, a solitary life. Melville marked a passage in one of Balzac's letters where he refers to a certain painter: "It would be better for him to struggle for two years with light and shade in a corner, like Rembrandt, who never left his own house, than to run about America, and to come back cruelly disenchanted, as he surely would be, in his political ideas."[132] Balzac "withdrew to the country," comments Frederick Wedmore, "to labour, as other men withdraw to it to rest."[133]

Melville revealed interest through his marginal markings wherever Balzac mentioned the necessity of solitude for a person devoted to the life of the imagination. When chastised by his friend Madame Hanska for his allowing other people to take advantage of him, Balzac responded: "Whilst my strength and faculties are night and day at their full stretch to invent, to write, to execute, to recollect, to describe— whilst with slow and painful, often wounded wings, I am traversing the moral fields of literary creation, how can I at the same time be occupied with material things?"[134] He clearly realizes that his commitment to art is destroying his personal relationships "because no one either loves or serves a man who works night and day, and who does not lay himself out for the advantage or amusement of others; who stays at home, and who must be visited if he is to be seen; whose genius, if genius he has, will not bear fruit under twenty years; it is because this man has identified his personality with his own works, and because all personality is odious when it is not accompanied by power to give or bestow."[135]

Nevertheless, he continued to live the life of a monastic devotee until his body failed from the long hours of weaving for Arva's shrine, no longer able to tolerate the rich strong coffee that kept him awake and inspired. Gretchen R. Besser comments that "Balzac prescribes for himself the . . . relentless rule of isolation from the world and its pleasures, which he loved so well. Time and again in his correspondence, he refers to the monastic seclusion in which he is living. When he takes refuge at Sache in order to write undisturbed, he views the chateau as a monastic retreat. For long periods of time, he shuts himself up in what he terms his 'monk's cell,' emerging only to attend to urgent business, and otherwise leading the life of a Trappist."[136] To the "idlers and the strollers on the boulevards" of Paris, according to Stefan Zweig,

"Balzac was invisible" during "the twenty-three hours of his creative solitude." Although many "jeered at him for his extravagance, he was an industrious ascetic with the steadfact, persevering patience of an anchorite."[137]

After a few hours sleep early in the evening, he rose sometime after midnight and assumed the costume that symbolized his total devotion to the creative spirit of art. He wrote—intensely, hour after hour—while wearing the robe of a monk with a cord or gold chain tied loosely around his waist. At intervals during the long solitary hours of the night and morning—eight, ten, sometimes twelve—he would refill his cup with the special coffee that he himself had purchased and prepared so that it was as strong as possible. "Coffee was the black oil that started the engine running again; for Balzac it was more important than eating or sleeping."[138] He thought that he needed it in order to stimulate his imagination and to keep it going. It has been estimated that he consumed during his composition of the works in the *Comédie humaine* fifty thousand cups of fiercely strong (and ultimately poisonous) coffee for self-induced insomnia.[139]

In his final years, Melville was not as driven as Balzac, but the difference was one of degree rather than kind. He saw in Balzac a man of great creative genius whose devotion to art made him a member of the same monastic order as himself. No one could have understood more clearly Balzac's determination to live in the world of his imagination nor sympathized more deeply with Balzac's frustrations, the inevitable frustrations of a great writer. He marked numerous passages in the *Correspondence* where Balzac complains about his creative uncertainties and failures. He was especially interested in anything Balzac wrote in his letters about his inability to compose, such as the following comment to Madame Hanska:

> I have been home a week, and during the whole week I have been vainly trying to take up my work; my head refuses all intellectual effort. I feel it is filled with ideas which cannot be expressed; I am incapable of fixing my fancy, or of constraining it to consider a subject on all sides, or of deciding upon any form of treatment. I know not when this imbecility

will cease, perhaps I am out of practice. When a workman leaves his tools for any length of time his hand stiffens, he is, so to speak, divorced from his tool; he must again begin, little by little, to restore that brotherhood between himself and his work, which is due to habitual use, and which unites the hand to the tool, as much as the tool to the hand.[140]

Melville could have had no doubt about the great French author's tenacious weaving for the shrine of art, for he repeatedly noted Balzac's comments about exhaustion from work. "I have not been out of the house for twenty days," Balzac wrote to Madame Hanska. "Literally I am living in the stupefaction which so much hard work has brought on."[141] Melville placed a check by Balzac's comment to Madame Hanska: "I have no wish to go into the world; on the contrary, I have a horror of it; celebrity is irksome."[142]

The works of Balzac were possibly Melville's coffee during this late period when the desire for rest and sleep was naturally strong. His own imagination soared as he consumed the products of another's imagination. When he read the two volumes of Balzac's *Correspondence*, however, he not only took heart from the example he discovered there of a writer who devoted himself to art as he himself had determined to do, but he was carried back to a period in his life when he was deeply engaged in the profession of authorship. In 1889, when Elizabeth presented him with the *Correspondence*, he had not been involved with commercial publishers for some time. As he went through these two volumes, he was forcefully reminded of what it means to be a busy writer, not just writing and publishing a poem here and there or having volumes privately printed but dealing with all the knotty problems and experiencing all the excitement of an author writing for a hungry public and for demanding publishers. In his letters, Balzac covered the spectrum of all the frustrations and satisfactions inherent in the life of a creative writer turning out one work after another. A partial list of the subjects Melville found Balzac addressing includes the following: pain and resentment from bad and unfair reviews; speculation on how to make his works more accessible; his reluctance to consider a work finished; new ideas for novels and stories and hopes for the future; discouragement; sense of failure; a desire to be read and admired; concerns about royalty income and about debt; the "torments of an author's life" (a phrase Melville underlined); hard, constant, frenzied creative activity; inspiration; the slow development of one's craft as artist; isolation from the world at large; art as a kind of religion; total devotion to art; lost manuscripts and parts of them; the pain as well as the exhilaration of writing; the necessity of letting other matters go as one writes; opinions of other authors; literary lawsuits; the pain of proofreading; the headaches from dealing with publishers; the frantic attempts to meet deadlines; the more than occasional inability to create and invent; the public's power to inflict pain; the strange workings of the creative imagination; the agony of having works rejected; good and bad critics; and fear of being a has-been.

If Matthew Arnold was responsible, or at least influential, in turning Melville toward the writing of poetry, Balzac was perhaps instrumental in turning him back to fiction. It may well have been under Balzac's influence that Melville changed his work about a young sailor, Billy Budd, from a poem to a short novel. Balzac awakened in him an old interest in the imaginative possiblities of fiction, and reminded him poignantly of how varied and exciting the profession of authorship can be.

His reading of Sir Walter Scott and William Dean Howells served only to confirm these feelings. It is doubtful that Scott would have been on Melville's late-in-life short list of authors to read had not he found in Balzac so much glowing praise for him.[143] Indeed, Scott not only impressed Balzac but actually influenced his thinking and fictive techniques. Melville found Balzac's discussions of Scott in several places. In *Modeste Mignon*, the character Canalis explains that one of the "prime characteristics" of the "man of genius" is "inventiveness," and "Walter Scott was an inventor," a genius "above all else."[144] In the preface of the edition of *Père Goriot* that Melville owned, Balzac bemoans the fact that Scott, whom he so profoundly cherished, was forced to depict women as entirely too pure and passionless because of the false "ideas of a public essentially hypocritical."[145] Melville placed a vertical line by Balzac's praise of Scott in a letter to Madame Hanska: "What you write now about Walter Scott, I have said for the last twelve years. Byron is nothing to him, or next to nothing."[146] He could not have offered a more flattering estimate in view of his admiration for Byron. In a later paragraph of the same letter, he continues: "You are right; Scott will grow in greatness when Byron is forgotten. I speak of Byron translated; for the original poet will endure, if only by his powerful inspiration and intense personality. Byron's brains never bore any more than the impress of his own personality; while the whole world sat to the creative genius of Scott, and, so to speak, saw itself reflected by him."[147]

Though Melville had early a passing acquaintance with the works of Sir Walter Scott, he probably became interested in him only after reading Balzac.[148] In June 1890, he borrowed from the New York Society Library copies of Scott's *Quentin Durwood* and *Peveril of the Peak.* These two long novels, romantic and often far-fetched as they are, nevertheless abound in sheer fictive energy. Once involved in the compelling characterizations and intricate plots, Melville experienced anew and forcefully the unique possibilities of the novel.[149]

Scott rivaled Balzac in the art of storytelling and in the rare ability to make history come alive. After reading many of Balzac's works and then two lengthy novels by Scott, Melville was saturated with the richness of character delineation, historical detail, and intricate plotting. In some measure, then, Scott simply reinforced what impressed him in Balzac. Himself drawn to secrecy and intrigue, he encountered these motifs repeatedly in both authors. Schemes and intrigues underlie schemes and intrigues. Both writers were masters at depicting shady, colorful people. Numerous characters in the two Scott novels must have reminded him of Balzac's creations. For example, Edward Christian of *Peveril of the Peak,* a cunning, selfish, hypocritical but skillful confidence-man who ostensibly wishes to avenge his brother's death but actually is a self-serving opportunist, is strikingly Balzacian. Perhaps Melville thought of himself and the possibility of reactivating his long-dormant fictive talent when he read what Scott has one of his characters say about great men: "It must be a noble sight . . . to behold the slumbering energies of a great mind awakened into energy, and to see it assume the authority which is its due over spirits more meanly endowed."[150]

In 1890, William Dean Howells was at the peak of his American reputation and at the center of a controversy over Realism. Many praised him glowingly; others condemned him for his choice of subject matter that was beneath the dignity of art. But almost no literate person was unaware of him. Edward Marshall wrote in 1894: "The remark of a critic to me a few weeks ago was: 'There is no middle ground with Howells—people think him either a master or an ass.' That is literally true. . . . Everybody that reads in America knows about Howells, and likes or dislikes him. There is none to whom he is unknown."[151] Perhaps it was for this reason—the controversy swirling around the notorious Howells—that Melville decided to take a look at his novels. More than likely, however, he was attracted because Howells was widely known as "the American Balzac." In his "Editor's Easy Chair" column for *Harper's Monthly,* George W. Curtis wrote in January 1890, that in *A Hazard of New Fortunes,* Howells revealed himself to be "like Balzac," that is, "a student of life."[152] The prominent French philosopher and critic Hippolyte Taine paid Howells the highest compliment when he praised him as the American novelist "most like Balzac."[153] Henry James predicted that his friend Howells "will be the American Balzac."[154]

Howells followed Balzac in his "attempt to create a self-contained fictional world, peopled with recurring characters."[155] Significantly, the two novels that Melville checked out from the New York Society Library in May and June of 1890, *A Hazard of New Fortunes* and *The Shadow of a Dream,* are among those with recurring characters, Basil March and his wife, Isabel. But there was much more in Howells to remind Melville of Balzac. One critic has commented that "just as the royalist Balzac had populated his *Comédie Humaine* with the crass representatives of a triumphant *bourgeoisie,* so the elitist Republican Howells would write . . . about . . . social crudities."[156] Both also wrote about social injustice. Melville found in Howells a talent for amassing detail reminiscent of Balzac. "The drawing room of Mrs. Green's apartment in *A Hazard of New Fortunes,*" as George C. Carrington Jr. observes, "is presented with such great richness that the incautious reader might be reminded of Madame Vauquer's parlor in *Père Goriot.*"[157] As Melville read *The Shadow of a Dream,* he may well have been reminded of his own thematic concerns of *Pierre* as Howells pleads for an understanding of one's true self and a surrender of romantic nonsense about the nobility of self-sacrifice. A Frenchman, a Scot, and a fellow American led Melville late in his life to a renewed awareness that fiction is a high form of art with a compelling and unique attractiveness not possible in other genres.

Whether Melville would have continued to compose fiction had he lived after writing *Billy Budd* is of course a moot question. What is clear is that he would have continued to follow wherever his imagination led. These were trying times for him, but he would follow no course except that of the weaver. On a page that he marked in his copy of Alger's *The Solitudes of Nature and of Man* appears a statement about Beethoven: "If he suffered hunger, loneliness, the misunderstanding of the vulgar and conventional, he kept himself free, and felt himself supreme in his sphere."[158] This is a fitting description of Herman Melville in the final fourteen years of his life as he faced crises and as he pondered his own nature, his past career, and the wisest mode of behavior for his remaining years. Though disenchanted, perhaps he would have said, as did Beethoven when explaining why he refused to take his own life, "Art held me back."[159]

Four

ASSOCIATING

WITH THE ROSE

*M*elville's circle in these late years was diverse enough to accomodate both a "sublime old infidel," as he affectionately referred to the twelfth-century Persian poet Omar Khayyám, and a contemporary Anglican clergyman, Samuel Reynolds Hole. It included as well Omar's English translator, Edward FitzGerald, and an American artist, Elihu Vedder, whose drawings for FitzGerald's version of the *Rubáiyát* Melville greatly admired. He could embrace both the minister—Hole—and the infidel—Omar (and his translator FitzGerald)—because he discerned that they were not opposites but complements. Together with Vedder, they manifested collectively a coherent vision that Melville perceived as a variation on his own religiouslike set of convictions about art and the imagination, the emblem of which became the rose.

Though Melville mentions the rose in a few of his earlier writings (notably *Mardi, Moby-Dick,* and "Jimmy Rose"), not until the later stages of his life did it take on for him a deeply personal significance.[1] In his copy of Sadi's *The Gulistan, or Rose-Garden,* which he acquired in 1868, he marked with triple parallel lines in the margin a passage dealing with the power of the rose to raise those who keep company with it above the baseness of life: "One day, in the bath, a piece of perfumed clay came to me from the hand of a friend. I said to it, 'Art thou musk, or an artificial compound of sweets, for I am charmed with thy delightful odour?' It answered, 'I am a worthless piece of clay, but having for a season associated with the rose, the virtue of my companion was communicated to me; otherwise I am the same identical earth that I was at first."[2]

Associating with the rose thus both ennobles and inspires. In this thirteenth-century book of proverbs and stories embodying the wisdom of the ages, Sadi, perhaps the most famous of all ancient Persian writers and thinkers, links the rose with the intoxication of religious experience, fleeting to be sure but precious beyond expression. He tells the story of a man who experienced such an inspiration: "When he came back to himself from that state, one of his companions sportively asked him—'From that flower-garden where thou wast, what miraculous gift hast thou brought for us?' He replied, 'I intended to fill my lap as soon as I should reach the rose-trees, and bring presents for my companions. When I arrived there the fragrance of the roses so intoxicated me that the skirt of my robe slipped from my hands.'"[3]

Melville himself began associating with roses in the 1880s, that is, he began about that time to grow them. Leon Howard conjectures that Melville waited until he was relatively sure that his wife was not allergic to roses ("rose cold" as it was called in those days) before he began to cultivate them.[4] In the postscript of a letter of October 5, 1885, to his wife's cousin Mrs. Ellen Marett Gifford, he wrote: "You see the rose-leaves have not yet given out. I shall always try and have a rose-leaf reserved for you, be the season what it may."[5]

In August of that same year, on her husband's sixty-fifth birthday, Elizabeth presented him with a copy of Samuel Reynolds Hole's *A Book About Roses,* which he read with careful attention, marking numerous passages.[6] At the time Melville acquired and read *A Book About Roses,* Hole was Curate and Vicar of Caunton, but he was soon to be appointed Dean of Rochester (1887). The author of several books, including *A Little Tour in America* (1895), Hole was a man of unusual wit, learning, and common sense who wrote not with the superiority of piousness that one might expect of a man of the cloth who became a high official of the Church of England but with a humane urbanity reflecting an unusual degree of understanding of his fellow creatures combined with a compelling genuineness. Seldom do any overt religious pronouncements find their way into *A Book About Roses,* but neither is his work merely a book about roses. From the

"Omar's Emblem" by Elihu Vedder, 1886. From *Rubáiyát of Omar Khayyám the Astronomer-Poet of Persia Rendered into English Verse by Edward FitzGerald with an Accompaniment of Drawings by Elihu Vedder.*

first page, it is clear that roses are deeply metaphorical to Hole, and that fact accounts at least in part for the obvious interest that Melville showed in the book, an interest that goes far beyond what he would have manifested in an instruction guide.

Not much reading between the lines is necessary to see that *A Book About Roses* is about the urge to create. It repeatedly refers to the cultivation of roses as an art and stresses that in order to succeed at it, one must possess the right motivation and a capacity for complete dedication. In the most undidactic way possible, it connects roses with the religious impulse. Its advice about growing roses is frequently interspersed with an almost angry impatience with charlatan gardeners and superficial and half-committed admirers of the rose. It speaks of manure and soil in terms that lift them above the mundane into the realm of art. If your neighbors disapprove of your wasting good manure on mere flowers, Hole writes, in a passage beside which Melville placed double vertical lines, "quote for their edification those true words of Victor Hugo in 'Les Miserables': "*The beautiful is as useful as the useful, perhaps more so.*"[7] Condemning falseness and pretention, particularly the "pseudo-Rosist" (10), and praising humble devotion to the rose, Hole fills his book with incidents and stories that are never digressive or random; they all point in the same direction, to the necessity of sincere commitment if one aspires to bring forth beautiful roses. Melville marked a passage in the first chapter ("The Causes of Failure") in which Hole's words apply not only to the scarcity of beautiful roses in comparison to the great number of bushes but also to the rarity of great art works despite the profusion of writers: "But now comes a most important question: Have we beautiful Roses in proportion to this great multiplication of Rose-trees? The printer will oblige me by selecting a brace of his biggest and blackest capitals, with which I may reply emphatically, NO" (5).

If the principal reason for the dearth of beautiful roses is the absence of the grower's commitment, another major problem—as Hole bluntly charges—is a lack of aptitude for gardening. Talent is required for both growing roses and artistic endeavor. Melville was struck and no doubt amused by an anecdote Hole recounts illustrating this point: "As a rule, the amateur Rosarian has made about as much progress as George III. with his fiddle. After two years' tuition, the King asked his tutor, Viotti, what he thought of his pupil: 'Sire,' replied the professor, 'there are three classes of violinists; those who cannot play at all, those who play badly, and those who play well. Your Majesty is now *commencing to enter* upon the second of these classes'" (10).[8]

As Hole enumerates with an enthusiasm that reaches into passion the attributes of a true rosarian, Melville would have realized that he was also describing the qualities of him who weaves for the shrine of art. Practical advice about such matters as the best place to locate one's rosarium frequently broadens in scope and then soars poetically into the realm of suggestiveness. Melville was impressed with the following passage—beside which he placed a vertical line—because Hole's description of the ideal rosarium probably reminded him of his own concept of the calm and inviolate inner self, that "one insular Tahiti, full of peace and joy, but encompassed by all the horrors of the half known life" that he referred to in *Moby-Dick:*[9] "The centre must be clear and open, around it the protecting screen. It must be a fold wherein the sun shines warmly on the sheep, and the wind is tempered to the shorn lamb; a haven in which the soft breeze flutters the sails, but over which the tempest roars, and against whose piers the billow hurls itself, in vain" (56).

More than likely, Melville had such a passage, and Hole himself, in mind when he wrote "The New Rosicrucians," one in a group of poems about roses that he included in *Weeds and Wildings,* left unpublished at his death.

> To us, disciples of the Order
> > Whose rose-vine twines the Cross,
> Who have drained the rose's chalice
> > Never heeding gain or loss;
> For all the preacher's din
> There is no mortal sin—
> > No none to us but Malice!
>
> Exempt from that, in blest recline
> > We let life's billows toss;
> If sorrow come, anew we twine
> > The rose-Vine round the Cross.

Melville makes it clear in the title with the word *New* that he is not writing about the secret fraternal order founded in the fifteenth century by Christian Rosenkreuz, who professed to have discovered in his travels in Arab countries certain keys to unlocking the essential mysteries of the universe, secrets that adepts passed down through the ages from ancient times. The members of the "Order" Melville mentions in his poem with deceptive lightheartedness are followers not of Christian Rosenkreuz but of Samuel Reynolds Hole. The New Rosicrucians are Rosarians. In *A Book About Roses,* Hole refers to himself not only as a "Rosarian" but on occasion as a "Rosicrucian." Melville placed a check beside a sentence in which Hole, remarking on how well he had been treated by an admirable group of humble rose growers, writes: "I had been enthroned as Grand Master of a Rosicrucian Lodge" (24). The New Rosicrucians are not as secretive or as esoteric as the old ones, but they, too, have found in the rose a representation of one's spiritual center. Hole makes it clear that malice is the greatest sin because he emphasizes throughout his book that its opposite, love—love of the rose especially—is the greatest virtue. Not an ordinary preacher, he resembled Christian Rosenkreuz in his ability to harmonize an ancient pagan emblem, the rose, with the Christian symbol of the cross. The speaker in the poem has become a "disciple," and like other members of the "Order" has found the calm center, the rosarium, where "We let life's billows toss," a line that recalls Hole's statement that the rosarium is a place where "the billow hurls itself, in vain." Despite its playful tone, "The New Rosicrucians" is serious evidence of Melville's commitment to certain attitudes and values espoused by the man who has been called "the greatest champion of the rose Britain has ever known."[10] The antithesis of the rosy cross in "The New Rosicrucians" is the slashed cross of Melville's late sketch "Daniel Orme." The one represents a kind of alternative (rather than an opposition) to Christianity; the other suggests the negation of Christianity altogether. One is the badge of love and creativity; the other, of war and destruction.

"Disciples of the Order" of the rose are those who not only appreciate its beauty and are uplifted by it but who also understand and accept its message, who follow what may be called a kind of rose religion. Jack Gentian, who narrates "Naples in the Time of Bomba," hears the rose speaking to him:

> You wear an Order, me, the Rose,
> To whom the favoring fates allot
> A term that shall not bloom outlast;

No future's mine, nor mine a past.
Yet I'm the Rose, the flower of flowers.
Ah, let time's present time suffice,
No Past pertains to Paradise.

But Jack Gentian does not accept this message to the extent that he becomes, as it were, converted. When the flower he carries loses its petals, he "rings down the curtain on the Rose." He is like the rich young ruler in the Bible who is attracted to Jesus and hears his words but who nevertheless sadly remains lost in the labyrinth of his mind. Jack Gentian thus cannot become a disciple of the Order; his emblem is not the rose but the badge of the Cincinnati. Neither can Jack's contrasting counterpart, Daniel Orme, be a member of the Order, for though he once had a cross tattooed on his chest and though after his death, wild roses (eglantine) grow over his grave, his emblem is not the rose but the cross with a telling scar of war running through it.

Precisely when Meville composed the episode in "Naples in the Time of Bomba" in which Jack Gentian receives a rose from a street vendor is difficult to determine.[11] Its striking similarity to a passage in *A Book About Roses* suggests that he may have written it after he read Hole. On a visit to Naples, Gentian takes a carriage to see the city. Stopping momentarily, he encounters a young woman who pins a rose to his lapel and receives from him a few coins. The flower seems to exert a strong and favorable influence on him, but its spell does not last. In *A Book About Roses,* Melville read Hole's account of how "once upon a time, hard on fifty summers since," he visited London, "rode in the Park" in a carriage, and then

> to enliven my scenery, I bought a Rose. Only a common Rose, one from a hundred which a ragged girl was hawking in the streets.... Only a twopenny Rose; but as I carried it in my coat, and gazed on it, ... it seemed as though they [his own roses] had sent to me a messenger, whom they knew I loved, to bid me "come home, come home." ... And I arose, reflecting; and though I had taken my lodgings and arranged my plans for three more days in London, I went home that morning with the Rosebud in my coat. (174–76)

This simple reminiscence is shot through with suggestiveness that Melville would not have missed, especially the power of the rose to bring the devotee "home," away from the glittering materiality of the world into the rosarium of one's best and deepest inner self. Nor would Hole's punning be lost on Melville. In the single word *arose*, he conjoined the rose with the cross.

Melville's rose poems reflect his own genius and distinctive thought, but echoes here and there of *A Book About Roses* attest to his careful and responsive reading of that work. The initial poem in the first part of "A Rose or Two" is often considered a sort of love letter to his wife. The title of this poem, "Amoroso," suggests love, but Melville may also have been comparing the woman of his poem to a certain rose that Hole describes in his chapter "Garden Roses," the Armosa rose: "Armosa is a charming little Rose, neat in form and bright pink in complexion" (196). Melville wished to remember in this way his wife Elizabeth, to whom he dedicated *Weeds and Wildings* just as Hole dedicated *A Book About Roses* to his wife.

The subject for the preacher in the poem "Rose Window" is from "Solomon's Song," consisting of "Four words for text with mystery rife— / *The Rose of Sharon*." Recounting the importance of the rose in holy scripture, Hole comments in a passage that Melville marked with a vertical line: "In the Song of Songs the Church compares herself unto 'the Rose of Sharon'" (36). To be sure, Melville did not need anyone to remind him of the Rose of Sharon (though Hole may have), but he appears more definitely to have had *A Book About Roses* in mind when he composed "The Devotion of the Flowers to Their Lady," which carries the second title, "To Our Queen." The poem's two principal concepts, the rose as queen and love of the rosarium as a subconscious longing for the lost Eden, reflect Melville's reading of Hole. Chapter 3 of *A Book About Roses* is entitled "Our Queen of Beauty" and argues why "florists," as Hole calls growers, "should admire and honor pre-eminently the Queen of Flowers. First of all, because she is Queen. . . . Her monarchy is the most absolute, and her throne the most ancient and the most secure of all, because founded in her people's heart. Her supremacy has been acknowledged, like Truth itself, *semper, ubique, ab omnibus*—always, everywhere, by all"

(35–36). By these particular lines Melville placed a check. He encountered similar language in various other places of the book, where Hole speaks of the rose as "Queen of Summer," as "her Majesty," and as "Queen Rosa" (206, 221). The rose is "that queen who brooks no rival near, much less upon, her throne" (9). Melville begins his poem with "O Queen, we are loyal." The true rosarian is not only loyal to the rose as queen of beauty, however, but also realizes that love for it reflects a longing for Eden, from which all human beings are exiled.

> . . . shall sad ones forget?
> We are natives of Eden--
> Sharing its memory with you, and your handmaidens yet.

As rosarians live in exile, they "Languish with the secret desire for the garden of God." They are "Banished, yet blessed in banishment," for they have the rose. In similar terms, Hole explained rosarians' love of their flowers: "What is our love of flowers, our calm happiness in our gardens, but a dim recollection of our first home in paradise, and a yearning for the Land of Promise!" (105).

Hole's shadow also hovers over one of Melville's most tasking poems, "The Rose Farmer," which with "L'Envoi" makes up the second part of "A Rose or Two" in *Weeds and Wildings*. The poem is troublingly ambiguous because its speaker, who has inherited a rose-farm, decides to follow a course of action that on the surface would seem to violate the kind of deep-diving that Melville found noble earlier in his life. He is torn between the example of a prosperous rose grower, who sells and gives away his roses when they are at their greatest beauty, and a Parsee, who with great difficulty attains the precious attar from all the roses he grows. Expressing his dilemma, he asks: "Shall I make me heaps of posies, / Or some crystal drops of Attar?" Since the rose grower he speaks with seems a successful materialist and the Parsee a searcher after the essence of things, the speaker's decision to follow the former may appear to dissociate him from the author. Yet details of the speaker's background closely parallel those of Melville's life; he seems to be Melville in every way except in the choice he makes concerning his roses.[12]

Indeed, the speaker in all likelihood is the author himself, but he is a somewhat lighthearted—at times even impish—Melville. With some serious points to make, the poem is nevertheless essentially comic in tone rather than ponderously philosophical. Puns and humorous rhymes aside (*whistles/ thistles, scrambles/ brambles,* and so on), the very situation is almost farcical: the narrator prepared, of all things, "a chowder" for the Rhamadan feast of "a corpulent grandee of the East," who in gratitude remembered him in his will, passing along the "brave bequest" of a large track of land near Damascus on which thousands of roses are cultivated. Its description is a comic version of Coleridge's Xanadu:

> And laved by streams that sacred are,
> Pharpar and twin-born Abana,
> Which last the pleasure-ground incloses,
> At least winds half-way roundabout—
> That garden to caress, no doubt.
> But, ah, the stewardship it poses![13]

The speaker humorously complains that his inheritance is something of a burden: "Indigence is a plain estate: / Riches imply the complicate." What to do, what to do, he puzzles, "to smell or sell."

Melville's delineation of the man who gives him advice, a "rose-farmer, long versed / In roses husbanded by him," is almost certainly a good-natured, fun-poking portrayal of Samuel Reynolds Hole. The "downright man" of the poem closely resembles Hole, who claims that he proposed to write a book about roses that would be "*sans* humbug" and, "it will suffice to say, without dictionaries or high-falutenation" (37). The speaker in the poem calls him "a sort of gentleman-rose-farmer," a description that echoes Hole's admonitions in *A Book About Roses* in a passage that Melville marked that "he who knows and reverences the gardener's art (and I would admit no other to our club) must be a gentleman" (212–13). Though a "downright man," Melville's rose farmer, like Hole, is capable of poetic flights of fancy when he lovingly describes the "Celestial" charms of his roses, charms that more than "Eve's fair daughters" enticed and "lured the sons of God below."

Melville apparently enjoyed certain incongruities in Hole's position—a devout man of God who sometimes seemed to worship the rose; a modest curate whose book on roses had gone through numerous editions and made him a good deal of money. More with the patient amusement with which a sensitive observer chides a good friend than with the snarl and bite of disapproving satire, Melville suggests how these qualities are mixed in Hole's character as he finds him

> On knees beside his garden-gate
> Telling his beads, just like a palmer.
> Beads? coins, I meant. Each golden one
> Upon a wire of silver run;
> And every time a coin he told
> His brow he raised and eyes he rolled
> Devout in grateful orison.

The speaker's turning late in his life to this "gentleman-rose-farmer," this "pious man," for advice about roses corresponds to Melville's coming unto his roses late, that is, his cultivation of roses in his last years and to his reading of the advice-filled *A Book About Roses*.[14] Numerous hints throughout the poem link the rose farmer to Hole. After the speaker calls him "the pious man," he writes: "A florist, too." In various places throughout *A Book About Roses*, Hole calls himself a "florist," and writes that he is part of a "brotherhood," a "club," of "florists" (272, 212). Melville may have also had Hole in mind when he describes the face of the rose grower as "ruddy." According to Hole, this is an appropriate complexion for the rosarian: "a rich, glowing, gipsy brown is that one touch from Nature's paint-brush which makes the whole world of florists kin, which . . . unites all of us, heart and hand" (15–16). Though the "pious florist" of the poem conjectures that the speaker may be even older than himself, he is probably about the same age; he is "elderly," his mien "Tinged doubly by warm flushings thrown / From sunset's roses and his own." Melville probably made the two men of the poem elderly and of about the same age because he and Hole were the same age; indeed, they were born in the same year. The rose grower's initial irritation, which sounds much like the testy impatience that Hole manifests in some of his anecdotes, disappears when the speaker appeals to him in terms of the unaging core of youth they both possess: "down in heart youth never dies." From that point onward, the rose farmer is generous with his advice:

Meseemed his purs'd eyes grateful twinkled
Hearing of veteran youth unwrinkled,
Himself being old.

Now they are members of the same circle.

The narrator speaks with amusement in his voice of the way that the old "florist" seems to woo his roses, which are described as "like ladies," who turn their heads when "they hear themselves discussed by men." The farm is a "rose-seraglio," and the rosarian comments about his flowers: "My darlings cluster to caress me." Melville read much the same sort of language in *A Book About Roses,* where roses are often described as women. Hole stresses on the very first page the necessity of wooing the rose if one desires to cultivate it successfully:

> To win, he must woo, as Jacob wooed Laban's daughter, though drought and frost consume. He must have not only the glowing admiration, the enthusiasm, and the passion, but the tenderness, the thoughtfulness, the reverence, the watchfulness of love. With no ephemeral caprice, like the fair young knight's, who loves and who rides away when his sudden fire is gone from the cold white ashes, the cavalier of the Rose has *semper fidelis* upon his crest and shield. He is loyal and devoted ever. . . . As with smitten bachelor or steadfast mate the lady of his love is lovely ever, so to the true Rose-grower must the Rose-tree be always a thing of beauty.
> (1–2)

Later in the book Hole warns that "for the flirt, for the faint-hearted, for the coxcomb, who thinks that upon his first sentimental sigh she [the rose] will rush into his arms and weep, she has nothing but sublime disdain" (62). He associates the rose with Venus and Helen of Troy and a field of roses with a gathering of women whose "beauty which you see will be real—no false foliage, no somebody-else's ringlets, no rouge, no pastes, no powders, no perfumes but their own" (45). In his own pursuit of this beautiful but demanding woman, Hole says: "I labored to discover her favorite dish as earnestly as the alchemist to realise the Philosopher's Stone," and he claims that he found it—

a certain form of fertilizer (86). His rose-women even seem to speak to him on occasion, as they convey to him which ones of them he should write about first (126).

The pious and devout Samuel Reynolds Hole may not have been unaware that his intense enjoyment of the fleeting beauty of roses and his treatment of them as lovely and sensuous women somewhat resembled the pronouncements of that "sublime old infidel," Omar Khayyám. In fact, Hole begins one of his chapters with an admission that "every gardener must be an infidel—I am, and I glory in the fact" (104). Melville recognized this strange similarity with amused admiration and projected it in the advice that the rose farmer, Hole, gives the narrator of the poem, Melville himself. With cheerful irony, Melville has made the English clergyman what he really seemed in sense to be—a "Persian," that is, one who is at heart a kinsman of Omar Khayyám.

The rose farmer's strong preference for the rose over the attar results from his realization that "this evansecence is the charm!" His foil is the Parsee, who is ungenerous and "lean as a rake with his distilling" of the rose into attar. Distilling produces essence, but attar is no more the essence of the rose than ambergris is the essence of the whale. "I am for roses," concludes Hole-Omar, "*sink* the Attar!" The speaker learns his lesson well:

> Discreet, in second thought's immersion
> I wended from this prosperous Persian
> Who, verily, seemed in life rewarded
> For sapient prudence not amiss,
> Nor transcendental essence hoarded
> In hope of quintessential bliss:
> No, never with painstaking throes
> Essays to crystallize the rose.

What Melville puts into the mouth of the "prosperous Persian" is identical to what he read in the *Rubáiyát:*

> Some for the Glories of This World; and some
> Sigh for the Prophet's Paradise to come;

> Ah, take the Cash, and let the Credit go,
>
> Nor heed the rumble of a distant Drum! (13)[15]

The debate between the rose farmer and the Parsee involves two ways of living and of looking at life and death, options that are represented in the poem by the metaphors of sight and smell. The rosarian's motivation is "to please the sight," as the "prosperous Persian" indicates. The Parsee, on the other hand, gives up this pleasure of the moment for future rewards, "in hope of quintessential bliss." Attar, however, is but the scent of what has passed rather than the esssence of what is or will be. If the rose's beauty quickly fades for the rose farmer, he revels in what he terms "the brief delight." He believes in the image, the moment, the rush of the imagination, rather than in sweet-smelling transcendental crystallizations.

Melville dealt with the same contrast in his poem "The Vial of Attar," where the speaker first attempts to follow the way of the Parsee of "The Rose Farmer" but finally admits that he is a devotee of the bloom. He finds that his vial of attar does not satisfy but merely serves to remind him of what he has lost. Here again Melville echoes some of the phrases and ideas that he encountered in *A Book About Roses*. When the speaker in the poem calls himself "the Rose's lover," he sounds much like Hole, who says that he is "a lover of the Rose" (10). "There *is* nothing like the bloom," comments the narrator, echoing Hole's statement that he heard someone say, "There is nothing, after all, like the Rose" (203).

Doubtlessly, what impressed Melville most about Hole was his unwavering devotion to the rose. Probably no emotion or concept is evoked more in *A Book About Roses* than love. Since Hole insists that gardening is an art and that the drive to create beauty is the rosarian's strongest urge, it was easy for Melville to read into passage after passage his own commitment to art and the creative imagination. He placed double parallel lines in the margin beside a passage in *A Book About Roses* in which Hole quotes Izaak Walton on the art of fly-fishing: "*Have but a love of it, and I'll warrant you*" (35).

If Hole emphasized love, that sublime old infidel, Omar Khayyám, emphasized death.[16] Together, these strange bedfellows of Melville's later circle addressed in ways appealing to him two of the most compelling areas of human existence. Hole insisted that the creative urge demands nothing short of complete devotion, whether one is engaged in the art of growing roses or of writing poetry. Omar focused obsessively not on love but on death. What Melville found "sublime" in him was his inspired honesty about human destiny. It worked paradoxically not to support nihilism but to enhance the value of art and justify a commitment to the creative imagination. Omar faced squarely the terrible truth of extinction and provided a psychological solution for dealing with the potentially paralyzing fear of death. Self-absorbed as he was in these late years, Melville may not have experienced sharp and prolonged pangs of bereavement when those around him passed on, but he had to deal nevertheless with recurrent anxieties about his own mortality. If he did not derive his manner of coping with them from Omar, he at least found in the Persian a fellow, one worthy to be a member of his circle, one in whom he discovered an emotional stance similar to his own.

Of course, the Omar that Melville knew was Edward FitzGerald's version of him. Melville was acquainted with FitzGerald even before he owned a copy of the *Rubáiyát*. In 1875 he acquired FitzGerald's *Polonius,* a collection of "Aphorism and Apophthegms." Death is a recurrent subject in the much admired preface of this volume, which Melville read with care and annotated.[17] One of FitzGerald's major points is that death is the greatest teacher of what he calls "the grand Truisms of life."[18] He turns to Sir Walter Raleigh for proof of this theory: "It is Death, says Sir Walter Raleigh, 'that puts into a man all the wisdom of the world without saying a word.' Only when we have to part with a thing do we feel its value—unless indeed *after* we have parted with it—a very serious consideration."[19] True realization of death, in other words, is the catalyst of insight. Sir Walter Scott, writes FitzGerald, perceived this "truism" with clarity as he approached his own end. Melville checked a passage in the preface in which FitzGerald makes the same point in connection with Samuel Johnson: "'You knew all this,' wrote Johnson to Mrs. Thrale, rallying for a little while from his final attack—'You knew all this, and I thought that I knew it too: but I know it now with a new conviction.'"[20]

Among the greatest follies of humankind, FitzGerald argues, is the failure to face squarely the reality of extermination: "Death itself was no Truism to Adam and Eve, nor to many of their successors, I suppose; nay, some of their very latest descendants, it is said, have doubted if it be an inevitable necessity of life: others, with more probability, whether a man can fully comprehend its inevitableness till life itself be half over; beginning to believe he must Die about the same time he begins to believe he is a Fool."[21] Melville marked FitzGerald's comic example from Shakespeare of one who simply could not "fully comprehend" the inevitability of death though he could speak in platitudes about it: "Old Shallow was not very sensible of Death even when moralizing about old Double's—'Certain, 'tis very certain, Death, as the Psalmist saith, is certain to all—all shall die—How good a yoke of bullocks at Stamford fair?'"[22]

In another place, Melville penciled a check by a footnote in which FitzGerald relates a humorous episode in order to stress the willful blindness most people exhibit in regard to the reality of death:

> A party of us were looking one autumn afternoon at a country church. Over the western door was a clock with, "THE HOUR COMETH," written in gold, upon it. Polonius proceeded to explain, rather lengthily, what a good inscription it was. "But not very apposite," said Rosencrantz, "seeing the clock had stopped." The sun was indeed setting, and the hands of the clock, glittering full in his face, pointed up to noon. Osric, however, with a slight lisp, said the inscription was all the more apt, "for the hour *would* come to the clock, instead of the clock following the hour." On which Horatio, taking out his watch, (which he informed us was just then more correct than the sun,) told us that unless we set off home directly we should be late for dinner. That was one way of considering an Inscription.[23]

Melville's marginal markings in the preface to *Polonius* suggest that he was impressed with FitzGerald's conviction that an honest and courageous admission of the inevitability and finality of death is prerequisite to wisdom and insight. That he sustained an interest in FitzGerald beyond his reading of *Polonius* is indicated by the fact that he owned three different copies of the Englishman's translation of the *Rubáiyát* and that as late as April 1890 he borrowed from the New York Society Library a two-volume edition of FitzGerald's collected works (Boston: Houghton Mifflin, 1887). In 1889, he clipped from *The Evening Post* a review of the *Letters and Literary Remains of Edward FitzGerald* and placed it in one of the copies he owned of the *Rubáiyát*.[24] He was prone to save clippings dealing with members of his circle.

The centrality of death in FitzGerald's personal weltanschauung directed in large measure his selection and treatment of quatrains to be included in his version of the *Rubáiyát*. *Version* is perhaps a more accurate term than *translation*, for the Persian *Rubáiyát* is a different work from FitzGerald's. Iran B. Hassani Jewett notes that "Omar's quatrains are not confined to the themes of doubt of a future life and the advocacy of enjoyment in this one."[25] While Omar "struck off at intervals during his life" the "epigrams" that make up the original *Ruyáiyát,* and "attempted no consistency of belief, no continuity of thought," observes Joanna Richardson, FitzGerald, concentrating on the dark shadow of death, "imposed consistency, indeed dramatic unity upon them."[26] The result was not really a translation at all, as FitzGerald himself readily admitted, but an English poem inspired by and based on a Persian one. It "might fairly be called," as one critic has put it, "an improvisation on Omar's quatrains, rather than a transla- tion."[27] The principal difference is the extent to which Fitzgerald's version focuses unrelentingly on death. With a forceful, almost cruel, shake, it wakes the slumberer from the sleep of insensitivity or fantasy or vain hope, points with compelling truth to the terrible specter of death, and then proffers its sad but beautiful music as the antidote of the creative imagination to the fear of personal extinction. Fitz- Gerald's intent, according to A. C. Benson, is to "set a garland of roses in the very shrine of death."[28]

Though FitzGerald's version of the *Rubáiyát* has been widely cele- brated for the value it places on life in the face of death's inevitability, it actually stresses the insignificance of life. Its way of diminishing the importance of death is to diminish the importance of an individual's life. We think that we are unique, it argues, but our existence is but like that of countless others, and when we are gone, countless others like us will follow. We are but bubbles and pebbles:

> And fear not lest Existence closing your
> Account and mine, should know the like no more;
> > The Eternal Saki from that Bowl has pour'd
> Millions of Bubbles like us, and will pour.

> When You and I behind the Veil are past,
> Oh, but the long, long while the World shall last,
> > Which of our Coming and Departure heeds
> As the Sev'n Seas should heed a pebble-cast.
> > > (46–47)

The argument results in a kind of happy futility: if life is inconsequential, why worry so much about the end of it?

The *Rubáiyát* appeals especially to those who continually stuggle to find answers to the great questions of human existence, questions that deal with the purpose of life, the existence of God, the possibility of an afterlife, the nature of fate, and so forth. It is not addressed to those with deep and unshakable religious faith or to confirmed atheists. Nor is it for mere creatures of the appetites who are never worried with thoughts of human destiny. Contrary to popular belief, the *Rubáiyát* was not written for the hedonist but for the deep-diving doubter. For that person, Omar has especial sympathy and recurrently offers his advice: cease being frustrated because answers will not come. He seems to know what it is to yearn for these answers as if he had himself long searched and doubted. Accept doubt as a natural state of mind, he implies, and end the futile and perplexing pursuit of answers to the unanswerable.

> Perplex no more with Human or Divine,
> To-morrow's tangle to the winds resign,
> > And lose your fingers in the tresses of
> The Cypress-slender Minister of Wine.
> > > (41)

Omar's brand of futility is happy not only because it furnishes a psychological method (albeit somewhat drastic) to overcome the fear of dying and offers rest to the weary seeker of certitude but also because it reveals how death can be *used*. A guiding purpose of Fitz-Gerald's version of the *Rubáiyát* is to reveal the message that death is the mother of beauty. Life and death may be inconsequential, but beauty is not. It is all we have, and the awareness of the brevity of life but intensifies its appeal. To the author of "Magian Wine," the counsel to embrace the "Minister of Wine" suggested devotion to art and the creative impulse. Another way of saying that death is the mother of beauty is that "Decay is often a gardener," one of the epigraphs Melville chose (or created) for *Weeds and Wildings*.[29] He marked lines in the *Rubáiyát* in which death is linked with beauty, the rose: "I sometimes think that never blows so red / The Rose as where some buried Caesar bled" (19). Melville's poems about roses in *Weeds and Wildings* frequently associate the rose with death. "To set a garland of roses in the very shrine of death," as A. C. Benson described FitzGerald's aim in the *Rubáiyát,* is precisely Melville's purpose in his poem "Under the Ground":

> Between a garden and old tomb
> Disused, a foot-path threads the clover;
> And there I met the gardener's boy
> Bearing some dewy chaplets over.
>
> I marvelled, for I just had passed
> The charnel vault and shunned its gloom:
> "Stay, whither wend you, laden thus;
> Roses! you would not these inhume?"
>
> "Yea, for against the bridal hour
> My master fain would keep their bloom;
> A charm in the dank o' the vault there is,
> Yea, we the rose entomb."

Carrying roses to the "charnel vault" is a way of heightening their bloom, of pointing up that death is the mother of beauty. Not by fearing death, as does the speaker in "Under the Ground," but by using it does the gardener intensify the beauty of his roses.

Melville may also have had the *Rubáiyát* in mind when he composed "Hearth-Roses," a term he uses for the odorous embers of sugar-maple wood dying gloriously in his fireplace. The poem concludes with a quatrain:

> Ah, Love, when life closes,
> Dying the death of the just,
> May we vie with Hearth-Roses,
> Smelling sweet in our dust.

The sweet smell of death is an unusual subject, one that Melville found in two quatrains of the *Rubáiyát:*

> Ah, with the Grape my fading Life provide,
> And wash the Body whence the Life has died,
>   And lay me, shrouded in the living Leaf,
> By some not unfrequented Garden-side.
>
> That ev'n my buried Ashes such a snare
> Of Vintage shall fling up into the Air
>   As not a True-believer passing by
> But shall be overtaken unaware.
>
> (91–92)

The association of the rose with death is even present in "Amorosa," which appears to be a rather simple love lyric.[30] The setting of the poem, however, is winter, a metaphor for death, when "icicles despond / Chill drooping from the fane!" Wooing the rose in winter and thereby finding its beauty intensified by the setting is closely akin to experiencing a heightened love of roses that have been placed in a tomb.

In a dream the speaker of "Rose Window" has while sleeping in church, an angel carrying a rose enters a sepulchre. The rose illuminates, throwing colored lights upon the dead:

> I saw an Angel with a Rose
> Come out of Morning's garden-gate,

And lamp-like hold the Rose aloft,
He entered a sepulchral Strait.
I followed. And I saw the Rose
Shed dappled down upon the dead;
The shrouds and mort-cloths all were lit
To plaids and chequered tartans red.[31]

The rose and death are symbiotic partners: death intensifies the beauty of the rose, and the rose casts its light even upon death. By implication Melville connects the power of the rose to infuse beauty into the terrible to the power of the creative imagination to transform even ordinary human experience into art. In fact, the final stanza of the poem depicts the imagination at work:

I woke, the great Rose-Window high,
A mullioned wheel in gable set,
Suffused with rich and soft in dye
Where Iris and Aurora met;
Aslant in sheaf of rays it threw
From all its foliate round of panes
Transfiguring light on dingy stains,
While danced the motes in dusty pew.

The creative imagination is that which can throw "transfiguring light on dingy stains" and can cause motes to dance in dusty pews. In "Rosary Beads," Melville's most direct treatment of his rose religion, the marvelous power of the rose (and by implication, of the imagination) is described in terms suggestive of Transubstantiation:

But live up to the Rose's light,
Thy meat shall turn to roses red,
Thy bread to roses white.[32]

"Rosary Beads" is a fusion of Christianity and New Rosicrucianism, the treatment of the latter sounding distinct echoes of both Samuel Reynolds Hole's *A Book About Roses* and Edward FitzGerald's the *Rubáiyát* of Omar Khayyám. The idea of referring to a rose garden as a "rosary" probably came from Hole, who frequently does so. Christian implications are obvious from the title of the work, from the three-part division recalling that the Roman Catholic rosary traditionally consists of three parts, from the references in the first section to 2 Corinthians 6:2 ("The Accepted Time")[33] and in the second part (titled "Without Price") to the biblical pearl of great price (Matthew 13:46), from the use of terms like *fane, censers,* and *priests,* and from the suggestion of Transubstantiation mentioned above. The urgency of the first line—"Adore the Roses; nor delay"—and of the fourth—"Today!"—resembles the admonition of the *Rubáiyát:* "Oh, make haste!" (48). The final section of the poem, "Grain by Grain," reflects Melville's reading and appreciation of both *A Book About Roses* and the *Rubáiyát:*

> Grain by grain the Desert drifts
> Against the Garden-Land:
> Hedge well thy Roses, head the stealth
> Of ever-creeping Land.

This haven of a garden land in the midst of the desert is much like Hole's ideal rosary or rosarium, but it also recalls the *Rubáiyát,* wherein another ideal spot is described, "the strip of Herbage strown / That just divides the desert from the sown" (11). Indeed, this is the very setting for the most famous quatrain in the work:

> A Book of Verses underneath the Bough,
> A jug of Wine, a Loaf of Bread—and Thou
> > Beside me singing in the Wilderness—
> Oh, Wilderness were Paradise enow!
> > > (12)

Melville's purpose in "Rosary Beads" was not to attack Christianity, for there was much in Christianity that he continued to cherish. But there was also much in it that continued to trouble and vex him, taxing his belief beyond its limits. His solution was neither to try to accept all the doctrines of Christianity on blind faith and pray for blessed assurance as did his wife, Elizabeth, nor to reject it in toto but to hang on to what appealed to him in it, to quit fretting over the deeply troubling aspects since they would remain unknowable, and to place a new emphasis upon growing roses—that is, cultivating the artistic imagination as the strongest and most creative power available to him. Thus his rose religion, which he came to late, was not in his view anti-Christian although it was in some ways non-Christian. To develop it, he could profit from the teachings of an English curate as well as a Persian infidel, both of whom loved the rose.

Several of Melville's rose poems convey an underlying sense of discovery, of waking up to a surprising and important truth, which the speaker relates sometimes with an almost evangelical enthusiasm. This is the effect produced by his insistence that he came unto his roses late. It took him a long time, he implies, but he finally found the rose. Having found it, he relishes it, and it in turn wards off the paralytic numbness of old age and the unbearable dread of death. All of these attitudes are reflected in the last poem of the section "A Rose or Two" in *Weeds and Wildings*, "L'Envoi":

> Rosy dawns the morning Syrian,
>> Youthful as in years of Noah:
>> Why then aging at three-score?
> Do moths infest your mantle Tyrian?
>> Shake it out where the sun-beams pour!
> Time, Amigo, does but masque us—
>> Boys in gray wigs, young at core.
> Look, what damsels of Damascus,
>> Roses, lure the Pharpar's shore!
> Sign not—Age, dull tranquilizer,
>> And arid years that filed before,
> For flowers unfit us. Nay, be wiser:
>> Wiser in relish, if sedate
>> Come gray-beards to their roses late.

In "L'Envoi," Melville seems to be addressing directly and admonishing just such a person as he characterizes in a late prose sketch, "Under the Rose." In that work an English ambassador to Persia, a man preoccupied with his "aging at three score" (he is sixty-three, to be exact) becomes fixated on a vase of amber with small insects caught in the substance, a prized possession of a Persian Azem. He recognizes the rarity and value of the vase, and he attempts diplomatically to talk the Azem into making a gift of it to him. Its owner will not part with it, however, and instead gives the ambassador a "vellum book," which is "rich with jewelled clasps, and writ by some famous scribe in the fair Persian text.[34] This book contains verses by "their great poet, one Sugar-Lips," who once viewed this very vase and wrote a poem about it. A Greek "renegado" translates the poem (after being duly lubricated with the grape) for the ambassador:

> Specks, tiny specks, in this translucent amber,
> Your leave, bride-roses, may one pry and see?
> How odd! a dainty little skeleton chamber;
> And—odder yet—sealed walls but windows be!
> Death's open secret.—Well, we are;
> And here comes the jolly angel with the jar!
>
> (344)

These lines cause the amabassador to become highly agitated and "sadly distraught" as he withdraws to his chamber. His servant Geoffry, who narrates the sketch, attributes his master's distress to his fear of death, which the poem brings to the surface. The narrator explains that the ambassador is "in privy fear, as I knew who long was near him, of a certain sudden malady whereof his father and grandfather before him had died about that [his] age" (345). The "angel with the jar" refers to a figure in "a round device of sculpture" on the vase. Geoffry describes the scene that makes up the sculpture as follows: "The figure of an angel with a spade under arm like a gardener, and bearing roses in a pot; and a like angel-figure, clad like a cellarer, and with a wine-jar on his shoulder; and these two angels, side by side, pacing toward a meagre wight, very doleful and Job-like, squatted hard by a sepulchre, and meditating thereon; and all done very lively in small" (340). The angel carrying a rose is perhaps the same as that in "Rose Window." The other one is the angel of death whose jar contains crushings from the black grape, a figure probably inspired by Melville's reading of a quatrain in the *Rubáiyát:*

So when the Angel of the darker Drink
At last shall find you by the river-brink,
    And, offering his Cup, invite your Soul
Forth to your Lips to quaff, you shall not shrink.

$$(43)^{35}$$

The ambassador, however, does shrink and at the mere thought of the "Angel of the darker Drink." In so doing, he reveals that although he is acutely aware of the closeness of his own death, as Omar insists we should be, he has no way to deal with that inevitability, no way to alleviate the fear—if not panic—that accompanies the thoughts of his mortality. He is sensitive to the reality of death, but insensitive to what the *Rubáiyát* offers as the antidote to the dread of annhilation. He desperately wishes to escape the inescapable.

If human beings are all "Job-like" wights, as the narrator of "Under the Rose" describes the squatting figure in the vase's sculpture, and if the angel "with a wine-jar on his shoulder," Omar's Angel of Death, comes to all of us, so does the other angel, the "gardener" with the rose. The idea is not to shrink from either but to welcome and accept both. At least part of the reason that the ambassador cannot accept the Angel of Death is that he does not accept the Angel of the Rose, which offers a way of coping with the dread of death.

In the terms of "The Rose Farmer," the ambassador has opted for the attar over the bloom; he ignores the rose. Though the vase is filled at one time with beautiful roses, he scarcely notices them. He is concerned only with what is "under the rose," that is, the vase, amber. The attar of "The Rose Farmer" becomes the amber of this sketch. The ambassador considers it "exceeding precious" and esteems it beyond measure. To him it is a quintessential substance as is attar to the Parsee in "The Rose Farmer." The speaker of "The Rose Farmer" decides in favor of the bloom; he declares against trying to hoard "transcendental essence," against attempting "to crystallize the rose." In contrast, the ambassador in "Under the Rose" is obsessed with the amber, which is described as like "crystallised honey" with "bees glued up therein" (341). The description is reminiscent of a passage in *Moby-Dick*, where Ishmael comments on the "death of an Ohio-hunter, who seeking honey in the crotch of a hollow tree, found such exceeding store of it, that leaning too far over, it sucked him in, so that he died embalmed."[36] The insects in the amber of the Azem's vase suffered the same fate.

The attar of "The Rose Farmer" and the amber of "Under the Rose" are both greatly prized as containing precious essence by those who seek them, but in actuality each is merely a memento mori. The poem by Sugar-Lips deeply disturbs the ambassador because it points to the amber as a "skeleton-chamber." The speaker in "The Vial of Attar" seeks solace in attar, but instead of comforting him, the attar poignantly reminds him of death, of "the bloom that's passed away."

The narrator of "Under the Rose," Geoffry, is—like the masses depicted in the *Rubáiyát*—simply oblivious to the closeness of his own death. He resembles Old Shallow, whom FitzGerald describes as "not very sensible of Death" even when commenting on another's demise. Geoffry thinks it "a mighty weakness" in the ambassador to allow the verse of Sugar-Lips to upset him. After all, this poem about the amber is but "the ribald wit of a vain ballader, and he a heathen." As far as he is concerned, the poem is rather pleasing in a way that "the profane capering of a mountebank at Bartholomew's Fair by Thames" would be. However, in the spirit of what he no doubt considers compassionate humanity, he adds that if he were as old as his master and subject to the same inherited malady, he, too, might have been made somewhat "sorrowful" by the poem. That statement is followed by an abrupt and significant *but*, immediately breaking the spell of any unpleasantness he might feel at a mention of the "black grape": "But now no more hereof" (345). Even a thoughtful reading of the *Rubáiyát* probably would not wake Geoffry from his complacency and make him truly see that life is brief and that death—his death—is certain and much closer than he knows. He is but a version of FitzGerald's version of Old Shallow.

"Under the Rose," then, is a kind of counterwork of "The Rose Farmer." The former depicts characters who are not members of the "Order" of the rose, the latter those who are (with the exception of the Parsee). Both works raise the same question involving the wisdom of devoting oneself to the rose or the attar, that is, whether to be a celebrator of the live rose or a seeker after what Melville in "The Rose Farmer" calls a "mummified quintessence," whether to be a Rosarian or a Parsee. Melville's reading of FitzGerald's introduction to the *Rubáiyát* provided him with this precise dichotomy in regard to Omar Khayyám himself. Was he a devotee of the rose or of the attar? The question arises, according to FitzGerald, because another edition of the *Rubáiyát* published while his was in preparation claims that Omar was not "the material Epicurean" that FitzGerald depicted but "a Mystic, shadowing the Deity under the figure of Wine. . . . In short, a Sufi Poet like Hafiz and the rest."[37] FitzGerald insists, however, that Omar's outlook was not that of a mystic. In other words, he was not after the attar so much as an appreciation of the living rose. In a passage that Melville partially underlined, FitzGerald writes that Omar's thought was "probably the very original Irreligion of thinking men from the first; and very likely to be the spontaneous growth of a Philosopher living in an Age of social and political barbarism, under sanction of one of the Two and Seventy Religions supposed to divide the world."[38] The personalities of the authors of sufi poetry, FitzGerald argues, seem submerged in their work and abstract, but Omar is what he appears to be, not a mystic, but a real flesh and blood man "with all his Humours and Passions, as frankly before us as if we were really at Table with him, after the Wine had gone round."[39] Melville apparently agreed, for he placed a check in the margin beside these lines.

FitzGerald's introduction to the *Rubáiyát* may also have been the source for a detail in "The Rose Farmer." The narrator of that poem indicates that prior to the gift of the rose garden, he had little. Thanks to the bequest of "a corpulent grandee of the East," however, he is now secure for the rest of his life, though such "riches," entail "stewardship." In other words, an old friend is responsible for his being able to come unto his roses. FitzGerald describes a similar occurrence in the life of Omar Khayyám, who was able to live a comfortable and independent existence in a quiet "corner" because of the generosity of another "grandee of the East," a certain Vizier named Nizam-ul-Mulk, whom Omar had known years before: Omar's "Takhallus or poetical name (Khayyám) signifies a Tent-maker, and he is said to have at one time exercised that trade, perhaps before Nizam-ul-Mulk's generosity raised him to independence."[40] As the beneficiary of the Vizier's largesse, Omar was able to cultivate his roses, as it were. Toward the end of his life, according to FitzGerald, he said: "My tomb shall be a spot, where the north wind may scatter roses over it." In 1894 cuttings from the rose bushes that grew upon Omar's grave in Naishapur were sent to England where some of them were planted on the grave of Edward FitzGerald. The *Kew Gardens Bulletin* reported in 1894 that these roses had bloomed "for the first time": "The plant proves to be a form of *Rosa centifolia,* the sweetest of all the roses, from which the cabbage rose, the moss rose, and the pompon are derived. The native country of the plant is not known with certainty. . . . Omar Khayyám's plant has fully double flowers and evidently belongs to a long cultivated race."[41] Melville could not have seen this suggestive notice, but had he read it, he no doubt would have marked it, perhaps with those three interlocking checks he occasionally penciled in the margins of books and essays by and about members of his private circle.

The edition of the *Rubáiyát* that Melville most greatly admired was that of Elihu Vedder, which he acquired probably in 1886 or shortly thereafter. Never had Melville seen anything like this volume. From the very beginning of the project when Vedder proposed it to Houghton Mifflin and Company to its publication, he had complete control over it, determining every aspect of its contents and design including format, kind of paper, and binding.[42] It was not simply an illustrated version of FitzGerald's translation but a new and exciting combination of art forms. The book was, as Will H. Low stated in 1908, "Vedder's monument, and quite unlike any other [book] issued from an American publishing house."[43] Low believed that Vedder's volume "opened an era in the history of American art publishing and its success opened the way for all other 'de luxe' editions to appear in America from that time on."[44] But Vedder's *Rubáiyát* was not merely the first of the deluxe art books that were to pour from American presses and occupy countless coffee tables across the land. It was and still is a uniquely original accomplishment, the magnitude of which few people realized as poignantly as did Herman Melville. Hershel Parker has written that Melville "cherished the Vedder edition, poring over the words and the illustrations for long sessions during the years he was working on *Billy Budd*."[45]

Vedder did not execute his fifty-odd drawings, however, as "illustrations" of FitzGerald's words. Many of them do not follow at all the imagery of the quatrains with which they appear. Vedder thought of his art not as illustration but as "accompaniment" to the poetry, and he so indicates on the title page. He wrote in a letter of June 28, 1883: "I do not intend the drawings to be clear illustrations of the text—except when they naturally happen to be so—they are an accompaniment to the verses, parallel but not identical in thought."[46] In fact, he did not even pretend to represent a Persian setting. His drawings "speak more of Vedder and his pictorial world than of the Near East" as Jane Dillenberger observes.[47] They are classical in nature rather than Eastern. As one views the large oversized pages of the volume, the drawings do not seem to serve the text but the other way around. FitzGerald's words are placed in boxes within the drawings; that is, the pictoral scene surrounds and dominates the text. Sometimes a single quatrain, almost as if incidental, is enclosed in a small box within the larger scene. Indeed, the drawings are not so much illustrations for the quatrains as the quatrains are captions for the drawings. Furthermore, the lines of verse are not in type. The text is in Vedder's own hand, not printer's type. Calligraphy (if Vedder's strange and ornately beautiful hand printing can be called that) becomes a part of the total artistic endeavor; the text does not contrast with the drawings or even stand out dramatically from them. Thus Vedder further integrated the text into his own elaborate artistic scheme. To its credit, Houghton Mifflin Company indulged Vedder in his desire to create a book that would offer a rare and integrated aesthetic experience.[48] In a letter to a friend, he said: "I have planned the whole thing page by page." He wrote that the book "will be the most important record I shall ever leave of myself."[49]

Significantly, Vedder did not follow precisely the arrangement of any one of FitzGerald's editions of the *Rubáiyát* (FitzGerald himself did not always arrange in the same order the one hundred and one quatrains he chose to be included). Melville would have noticed that in the Vedder version, quatrains thirty-one through seventy-seven are not the same as in the third edition of the FitzGerald *Rubáiyát* (which he owned). Vedder rearranged nearly 47 percent of the quatrains. Precisely what it was he wished to underscore through this rearrangement is difficult to conclude, but one critic argues that he wanted "to emphasize the delimma of life," that is, the desire to have faith but not being able to, a yearning to find religious assurance but being prevented from doing so because of persistent questionings.[50] He was, in this sense, another Herman Melville.

It is not surprising, then, that Melville was drawn to Elihu Vedder. The more he experienced Vedder's art and read about him, the more he seemed to identify with him. He had found Vedder's portrait "Formerly a Slave" impressive and moving many years before and had written a poem for *Battle-Pieces* based on it. It is a mistake, however, to assume that Melville dedicated his volume of poems *Timoleon* to Vedder because of a painting he had admired twenty-five years earlier.[51] His dedication was the result of his profound admiration for the Vedder who produced that extraordinary edition of the *Rubáiyát*. Chances are that Melville had kept up his interest in Vedder during the intervening years between *Battle-Pieces* and *Timoleon*. During the late 1870s and throughout the late 1880s, Melville would have encountered occasional articles about him in the journals he read and scanned. For example, S. G. W. Benjamin included Vedder in his discussion of "Fifty Years of American Art, 1828–1858" published in *Harper's New Monthly Magazine* in September 1879. Benjamin found Vedder's art "full of deep suggestions and weird attempts at psychology in color. Outward nature with him is but a means for more effectively conveying the impressions of humanity, and his faces are full of vague, mystic, far-off searching after the infinite, and the why and the wherefore of this existence below."[52] If Melville read this article, he would have learned that Vedder had become by choice an exile from America, that he had taken up "his residence permanently in Italy," and that he had lately produced some "remarkable" paintings such as "Lair of the Sea-Serpent."[53] Almost as soon as Vedder's edition of the *Rubáiyát* appeared in 1884, articles began appearing that offered background material on him, analyzed his accomplishment, and lavished praise on him. One of the most detailed was that in the *Century Magazine*.

H. E. Scudder wrote a sensitive and intelligent commentary on Vedder's achievement: "An American artist has joined the Persian poet and the English translator, and the result is a trio which presents the original strain in a richer, profounder harmony."[54]

How much Melville knew about Vedder is unclear, but he learned enough to provoke the identification with him suggested by his dedication in *Timoleon:* "To my countryman Elihu Vedder." Though some seventeen years Melville's junior, Vedder had much in common with his fellow American. Both were born in New York City and were of Dutch background. Like Melville, Vedder married a woman whose first name was Elizabeth and who was the daughter of a judge.[55] Her family was from Glens Falls, New York, a place Melville knew well and visited fairly often. Vedder himself spent time painting there in the late 1860s. During his lifetime, Vedder, like Melville, lost two sons and was attracted to aspects of Buddhism. He studied and loved classical art and literature. He was a genial companion who was also in certain important ways a loner. He was a lifelong doubter who was drawn to Christianity but troubled by persistent questions about it. FitzGerald's version of the *Rubáiyát* attracted him long before he created his own version of it. As one critic puts it: "From the 1870s until his death, FitzGerald's Omar was Vedder's constant companion, a presence that fed his imagination."[56]

It was probably Vedder's devotion to his imagination and to art that most evoked Melville's admiration. When he wrote in his dedication that Vedder was his "countryman," he meant far more than that they were both Americans. They were Americans of similar backgrounds, but they were also both expatriates in a sense, Vedder literally by living abroad in Italy, Melville by a kind of self-exile though residing in New York City. Their native land was America, but they had become citizens of another kind of country. Joshua C. Taylor makes the point precisely with regard to Vedder: "Living most of his life in Italy, Vedder was in many ways a truly expatriate artist; he realized early that art itself provided a homeland and to it he was a loyal citizen."[57] Thus Melville probably had more than "American" in mind when he used the word *countryman* in his dedication: he meant the homeland of art. He saw Vedder as a member of his circle. In his copy of Vedder's *Rubáiyát,* he placed a portrait of this artist he so highly esteemed. The degree of his sympathetic identification with Vedder is suggested by the fact that he dedicated no other book to a person whom he did not know either personally or through correspondence. It was highly appropriate that he dedicate *Timolean* to Vedder because its primary subject is devotion to art. As Leon Howard succinctly expresses it: "the most consistent theme running through the poems in *Timoleon* was that of devotion to 'Art'—often with the implication that the devotion required and received a voluntary sacrifice of worldly success."[58]

Several years after Melville's death, his wife, Elizabeth, wrote to Vedder, sending him a copy of *Timolean* and explaining that her husband made the dedication "in admiration of your genius." Only her vivid memory of Melville's enthusiasm for Vedder would have motivated the highly reserved and dignified Elizabeth to wax so eloquent in her praise: "It will give you pleasure to know that a spirit, so appreciative as my husband's estimated your artistic rendering of the profound and mysterious 'quatrains' of the poet (of which he never tired) in the manner which appealed so powerfully to his own imagination and enlisted his sympathy with the artist. He was 'proud to call you his countryman' he would say after an absorbed study of your work."[59] By "sympathy with the artist," Elizabeth Melville clearly meant "sympathetic identification with the artist."

Vedder's imaginative work inspired Melville's own imagination and thus linked and endeared the artist to him. What "absorbed" him were drawings like the one Vedder called "The Blowing Rose" (for quatrains 13–16). Here a human skull occupies the lower left corner of the drawing. Partially covering the top of this image of death and as if growing out of it, a rose bush rises and makes its way over to the other side of the page and upward to climb closely beside the figure of a beautiful woman in the full bloom of youth, the personification in this work of the rose.

The drawing that most imspired Melville, however, was perhaps "Omar's Emblem," which Vedder described in a note as "A bird singing on a skull, while the rose of yesterday is floating away on the stream."[60] Present with the symbols of the rose, skull, and bird is Vedder's frequently depicted swirl ("the stream"), which in another note he commented on as follows: "The swirl which appears here, and is an ever-recurring feature in the work, represents the gradual concentration of the elements that combine to form life; the sudden pause through the reverse of the movement which marks the instant of life, and then the gradual, ever-widening dispersion again of these elements into space." Against this background of universal and indifferent energy, the rose and death are brought together, the one intensified by the other. The bloom will not stay, but triumphantly perched on the very face of death, a nightingale sings as the petals of the rose swirl upward around and about it. Thus the rose is connected not only with the skull but also with the bird, which is, in fact, an aspect of the rose. What the nightingale sings is the song of the rose. This song is, in the most immediate sense, the *Rubáiyát*, but in a broader sense, art itself.

Vedder's drawing of "Omar's Emblem" is a dramatic representation of an unarticulated but suggested and underlying motif in the *Rubáiyát*. Death (the skull) is in the center of the drawing as it is in the verse, but Vedder gives expression to what is only implied in the text, namely that singing is the best revenge, that imaginative creation is the noblest response to mortality. Amid the death's head and the rose and caught in the swirl of time, the nightingale sings, and that bird is Omar Khayyám and Edward FitzGerald and Elihu Vedder and Herman Melville—in a word, the artist. In the *Rubáiyát*, Omar recommends wine, not writing or painting, but while doing that, he is in the very act of artistic creation: his poem as poem, not as philsophy, is Omar's ultimate answer to the stark and terrible realities of human existence.

Vedder's purpose was to make the *Rubáiyát* more effective as poetry, that is, to make the work more concrete, more appealing to the senses. To him the senses constituted the gateway to the imagination. Though the several nudes included in the drawings shocked many in Vedder's contemporary audience, they appeared (along with everything else in the work) to delight Melville. He no doubt grasped Vedder's calculated purpose: to shock not with pruriency but with directness and honesty, to emphasize not only the value of beauty wherever it is found but also the importance of admitting openly what it is that appeals to the senses and why. Vedder admired greatly the honesty of the *Rubáiyát*. It speaks directly to the human heart of the human dilemma; it offers no sophisticated inventions to disguise the awful truth of fate.

Thus hypocrisy, especially in regard to the senses, is not only one of Omar's (and FitzGerald's) main targets in the text but also one of Vedder's in his accompanying drawings. He wrote the following note in connection with the drawing called "Spring" to accompany quatrains 93–95 (in his own arrangement): "It is useless and even pernicious, if one wishes to combat the seductiveness of the pleasures of the senses, utterly to ignore them. They exist as much as man's other faculties, and have their proper uses and place. Examine and dissect them, and one will be enabled to give them their proper weight. This is the aim of the poet against an overwhelming pressure in the other direction leading only to hypocrisy, a thing which Omar most of all detests."

This note in his edition of Vedder's *Rubáiyát* must have been of profound interest to Melville, for it embodies precisely the same message as "After the Pleasure Party" and along with passages that Melville encountered in Schopenhauer could well have been an inspiration for that poem. Vedder's words from the note also echo throughout "The Ambuscade," a poem Melville included with his rose poems in *Weeds and Wildings:*

> Meek crossing of the bosom's lawn
> Averted revery veil-like drawn,
> Well beseem thee, nor obtrude
> The cloister of thy virginhood.
> And yet, white nun, that seemly dress
> Of purity pale passionless,
> A May-snow is; for fleeting term,
> Custodian of love's slumbering germ—
> Nay, nurtures it, till time disclose
> How frost fed Armor's burning rose.

Vedder's drawing "Spring" is perhaps the most sensual of all those in his edition of the *Rubáiyát.* It depicts a voluptuous nude woman appearing to a dreamy man poring over books. Rose petals blow in a swirl around them. The quatrain that Vedder was mainly respond-

ing to suggests, as does Melville's poem "The Ambuscade," that religious good intentions ("Repentance," "Penitence") cannot stave off
the strong appeal of the senses, especially when that compulsion
comes on unexpectedly:

> Indeed, indeed, Repentance oft before
> I swore—but was I sober when I swore?
> And then and then came Spring, and Rose-in-hand
> My thread-bare Penitence apieces tore.

(94)

Although Melville's victim of the senses is a woman in both "The
Ambuscade" and "After the Pleasure Party," he created situations in
both those poems that reflect his admiration for the *Rubáiyát* and
for Vedder's drawing "Spring" (with the artist's accompanying note).
The woman in "After the Pleasure Party" is a scholar-scientist as is
perhaps the male figure of "Spring," and the woman in "The Ambuscade" has attempted to devote herself to religion, as Omar says he once
tried to do in his quatrain 94. "Spring" with "rose-in-hand" of the
Rubáiyát becomes May's "burning rose" in "The Ambuscade."

The history of Melville's involvement with Vedder, Fitz-
Gerald, Omar Khayyám, Buddhist writings, James Thomson, Schopenhauer, Balzac, Matthew Arnold, Scott, and (to a lesser extent)
Howells is in a sense the story of a persistent imagination in the face of
old age and all the losses that go with it. With the help of a few friends,
Melville kept his creative imagination alive to the end, and his devotion to art but deepened with time.

Herman Melville, who associated with the roses, died at age
seventy-two in the very early hours of September 28, 1891. His death
certificate indicates that he died from "cardiac dilatation, mitral regur-
gitation" with "contributory asthenia."[61] Elizabeth simplified the matter and said that her husband died of "enlargement of the heart."[62]
His funeral was held in his home at 104 East Twenty-Sixth Street, New
York City, on September 29 with the current pastor of his church, All
Souls Unitarian Church, officiating. The Reverend Theodore Chicker-

ing Williams delivered "a short address."[63] Besides a few family members and friends of the family, three men attended who were not friends at all but merely admirers of Melville's writings.[64] Interestingly, they were all members of a New York club, the Century, and they had wished Melville to join their circle, but that was not to be. He already had a circle. The soul selects its own society.

Notes

One: The Soul Selects Its Own Society

1. Quoted in Jay Leyda, *The Melville Log: A Documentary Life of Herman Melville, 1819–1891* (New York: Gordian Press, 1969), 2:836–37.

2. Melville Society *Extracts*, no. 53 (February 1983): 2.

3. *Herman Melville* (New York: Literary Guild of America, 1929), 326.

4. "'The Adjustment of Screens': Putative Narrators, Authors, and Editors in Melville's Unfinished *Burgundy Club* Book," *Texas Studies in Literature and Language* 31 (Fall 1989): 426–50.

5. Sandberg, "'Adjustment of Screens,'" 428.

6. In his edition of the *Collected Poems of Herman Melville* (Chicago: Hendricks House, 1947), Howard Vincent argues that "At the Hostelry" and "Naples in the Time of Bomba" were probably written in the late 1850s (483). Aaron Kramer is convinced that Vincent is wrong and that they come later, but he is unspecific. See *Melville's Poetry: Toward the Enlarged Heart* (Rutherford: Fairleigh Dickinson University Press, 1972), 34. In "Melville's Burgundy Club Sketches," Merton M. Sealts Jr. places the time of their composition at some period before 1876 but suggests that Melville continued to work on them later in his life. *Harvard Library Bulletin* 12 (Spring 1958): 253–67. Reprinted in *Pursuing Melville, 1940–1980* (Madison: University of Wisconsin Press, 1982), 78–90. Leon Howard, in *Herman Melville: A Biography* (Berkeley: University of California Press, 1951), writes that "Naples in the Time of Bomba" may have been finished in the late 1880s but perhaps "partially composed many years earlier." He assumes that "At the Hostelry" was composed after "Naples in the Time of Bomba" but completed before it (328, 329). One of the longest and most ambitious treatments of "At the Hostelry" and "Naples in the Time of Bomba," that of William Bysshe Stein in *The Poetry of Melville's Late Years: Time, History, Myth, and Religion* (Albany: State University of New York Press, 1970), is not much concerned with the thorny problem of composition but deals with them as if they were written at about the same time, somewhere in the second half of the 1880s (227–70). In *The Mystery of Iniquity: Melville as Poet, 1857–1891* (Lexington: University Press of Kentucky, 1972), William H. Shurr argues that "Naples in the Time of Bomba" was begun about 1877 and that Melville was "writing the early stages" of "At the Hostelry" in 1878 (209,

221). In his edition, *At the Hostelry and Naples in the Time of Bomba*, Gordon Poole provides an excellent summary of various theories and concludes that with regard to "Naples in the Time of Bomba" especially, "no definite conclusion can be drawn . . . for dating" ([Naples: Istituto Universitario Orientale, 1989], li).

7. Kramer, *Melville's Poetry*, 38.

8. As Robert A. Sandberg points out, Melville composed two prefaces for the unfinished Burgundy Club book, one suggesting that "At the Hostelry" and "Naples in the Time of Bomba" would be accompanied by a number of prose sketches delineating among other things the Marquis de Grandvin and Major Jack Gentian, and the other suggesting that the various sketches would not be included ("'Adjustment of Screens,'" 426).

9. For a concise summary of the history of the term, see Shurr, *Mystery of Iniquity* (208–10), who also presents a detailed synopsis of "At the Hostelry" (210–13).

10. Peter and Linda Murray, *The Penguin Dictionary of Art and Artists*, 5th ed. (Middlesex: Penguin Books, 1983), 314. See also J. R. Watson, *Picturesque Landscape and English Romantic Poetry* (London: Hutchinson, 1970), 1–24.

11. For a different view of the function of the picturesque in the symposium, see Stein, who argues that Melville wanted to vent his "contempt for the cheapening of the traditions of painting by the social and economic pressures of the complacent middle class" and to take jibes "at Christianity and divine providence" (232, 238).

12. See Sidney K. Robinson, *Inquiry into the Picturesque* (Chicago: University of Chicago Press, 1991), for an excellent treatment of these aspects of the picturesque.

13. I am grateful to Stanton Garner for pointing out to me that, in his words, "during the Napoleonic era, the brief republic at Naples was known as the 'Parthenopean Republic.'"

14. *Melville's Reading*, rev. and enlarged ed. (Columbia: University of South Carolina Press, 1988), 134.

15. Preface to *Poems*, vol. 16 of *The Works of Herman Melville*, ed. Raymond W. Weaver (London: Constable, 1924), 352.

16. See Robert A. Sandberg, "'House of the Tragic Poet': Melville's Draft of a Preface to His Unfinished Burgundy Club Book," *Melville Society Extracts*, no. 79 (November 1989): 1, 4–7.

17. *Melville's Reading*, 134.

18. Howard, *Herman Melville*, 329.

19. *Reading Billy Budd* (Evanston: Northwestern University Press, 1990), 30.

20. "Melville's 'Geniality,'" in *Essays in American and English Literature Presented to Bruce Robert McElderry, Jr.*, ed. Max F. Schulz with William D. Templeman and Charles R. Metzger (Athens: Ohio University Press, 1967), 3–26, reprinted in Sealts's *Pursuing Melville*, 155–70.

21. *Pursuing Melville,* 155.

22. *The Clubs of New York* (New York: Hinton, 1873; reprint, New York: Arno Press, 1975), 7 (page citations are to the original edition).

23. Paul Porzelt, *The Metropolitan Club of New York* (New York: Rizzoli, 1982), 2–3.

24. James Grant Wilson, ed. *The Memorial History of the City of New-York* (New York: New-York History Company, 1893), 4:236.

25. *King's Handbook of New York City* (Boston: King, 1893), 68.

26. James Grant Wilson reports that the Loyal Legion Club, for example, had "five meetings annually at Delmonico's" (4:239).

27. *Delmonico's: A Story of Old New York* (New York: Valentine's Manual, 1928), 59.

28. Listed in *The Century: 1847–1946* (New York: Century Association, 1947), 393.

29. Quoted in Leyda, *Melville Log,* 2:787.

30. Quoted in Laura Stedman and George M. Gould, *Life and Letters of Edmund Clarence Stedman* (New York: Moffat, Yard, 1910), 2:460.

31. Ibid., 2:465.

32. If Melville had been willing to join the Authors Club, he possibly would have incurred no membership fees at all. On April 9, 1890, Edmund C. Stedman wrote to Charles Henry Phelps that Melville "ought to be an honorary member. He is a sort of recluse now, but we might perhaps tempt him out." Quoted in Leyda, *Melville Log,* 2:823.

33. Quoted in Leyda, *Melville Log,* 2:781. In a book review for the *New York Times* (December 21, 1921), Brander Matthews recalled that "the shy and elusive Herman Melville" came to a meeting of the newly formed Authors Club: "Apparently he did not greatly care for our society; he did not apply for membership and I believe that he was never with us again. I recall that I heard some one say to me, 'There's Herman Melville!' The name meant little to me then, and I gave him only a casual glance. All that I can now recover is a faded impression of an unobtrusive personality, with a vague air of being somehow out of place in our changing and chattering groups." Quoted in Leyda, *Melville Log,* 2:784.

34. Quoted in Stedman and Gould, *Life and Letters,* 2:455.

35. "Melville's Burgundy Club Sketches," in *Pursuing Melville,* 87.

36. For a more recent example of this argument, see Sandberg, "'The Adjustment of Screens,'" who echoes Sealts: "When considering the character and function of the Marquis de Grandvin, we may usefully bear in mind that he functions primarily as a personification of wine" (433).

37. Shurr comments that the Marquis "is the embodiment of Melville's own need for genial conviviality" (*Mystery of Iniquity,* 208), a position somewhat different from mine.

38. Stein, *Poetry,* 239.

39. Ibid., 247.

40. All page references to the Burgundy Club sketches are to the Constable edition of Melville's works, vol. 13.

41. "Now without doubt this Talismanic Secret has never been found" though people "have time and again pretended to have found it." *Pierre, or The Ambiguities,* ed. Harrison Hayford, Hershel Parker, and G. Thomas Tanselle (Evanston and Chicago: Northwestern University Press and the Newberry Library, 1971), 208.

42. In *Reminiscences of Rufus Choate* (New York: Mason Brothers, 1860), Edward G. Parker comments admiringly that Choate's words in conversation were "rare and high-sounding. . . . He delighted in long words. . . . He did not accord at all in Mr. Webster's veneration for the Saxon element of our language,—the words short, simple and strong. He rather agreed with Thomas de Quincey, that the Latin element of the tongue is needed, to bear in upon the mind an impression of general power" (24).

43. Michael Paul Rogin, *Subversive Genealogy: The Politics and Art of Herman Melville* (New York: Knopf, 1983), 293.

44. Howard, *Herman Melville,* 329.

45. However, he did have, like Jack Gentian, sympathy and tolerance for the South, as Stanton Garner has shown. *The Civil War World of Herman Melville* (Lawrence: University Press of Kansas, 1993).

46. "The Melvilles, the Gansevoorts, and the Cincinnati Badge," Melville Society *Extracts,* no. 70 (September 1987): 1, 4.

47. Sealts compares Major Melvill with Major Gentian in "The Ghost of Major Melvill," *New England Quarterly* 30 (September 1957): 291–306, reprinted in *Pursuing Melville,* 67–77.

48. Stein, *Poetry,* 227.

49. According to Minor Myers Jr., a national drive for more members began in the late 1840s. Officers in the organization "realized that if the society were to recover from the doldrums of the 1830s, more members were needed" (226). They hoped to recruit new members by relaxing the old rules for joining. In 1851, a committee studied the issue and "concluded that inheritance of membership 'by title of primogeniture, is wholly subordinate to the claim of worth and merit on the part of the applicant.'" They not only recommended that the practice of primogeniture be discontinued, but "they also urged admission of descendants of eligible officers who had never joined" (227). By the "Rule of 1954" each state established its own membership requirements. Those of both Massachusetts and New York were liberalized to the extent that Melville, as a descendant of General Gansevoort, would have been eligible to join if such a possibility had occurred to him and if he had been so inclined. In fact, if Major Melvill had wanted to be a member, he probably could have despite the fact that he did not quite serve the required three years in the Continental army. His original assignment was with a local (Massachusetts) artillery unit. Myers re-

ports that exceptions were not uncommon even in accepting original members: "Virginia admitted Col. Theodoric Bland in 1785 even though he had served as a Continental officer less than half a year. Massachusetts took Capt. Samuel Newman, by special vote allowing service in the state artillery to 'supply the place' of the missing year of Continental service" (121–22). Despite such bending of rules for membership, in most states less than half of those who were eligible or who could be made eligible (surely Major Thomas Melvill was of the latter group) chose to join—47 percent in Massachusetts and 48 percent in New York (123). *Liberty without Anarchy: A History of the Society of the Cincinnati* (Charlottesville: University Press of Virginia, 1983).

50. *Reading Billy Budd,* 18.

51. See, for example, William Braswell, who writes that Daniel Orme is Melville's "symbolic self-portrait." *Melville's Religious Thought* (Durham: Duke University Press, 1943), 124.

52. "Melville's Good-Bye: 'Daniel Orme,'" *Studies in American Fiction* 16 (Spring 1988): 5. Reprinted as "The Last Good-Bye: 'Daniel Orme'" in *The Private Melville* (University Park: Pennsylvania State University Press, 1993), 146–58.

53. "Daniel Orme," *Billy Budd and Other Prose Pieces,* vol. 13 of *The Works of Herman Melville* (London: Constable, 1924), 118. Future page references to "Daniel Orme" are to this edition and are given in the text.

54. *White-Jacket,* ed. Harrison Hayford, Hershel Parker, and G. Thomas Tanselle (Evanston and Chicago: Northwestern University Press and the Newberry Library, 1970), 157.

55. *Billy Budd, Sailor,* ed. Harrison Hayford and Merton M. Sealts Jr. (Chicago: University of Chicago Press, 1962), 122.

56. Frank Pisano has shown that the place where Orme chooses to die is old Fort Tompkins on Staten Island. "Melville's 'Great Haven': A Look at Fort Tompkins," *Studies in American Fiction* 17 (Spring 1989): 111–13.

57. Ibid., 113.

Two: Disenchantment

1. *Melville's Reading,* rev. and enlarged ed. (Columbia: University of South Carolina Press, 1988), 120.

2. J. Hampden Dougherty, "Ten Years of Municiple Vigor," *The Memorial History of the City of New-York from Its First Settlement to the Year 1892,* ed. James Grant Wilson (New York: New-York History Co., 1893), 3:406.

3. This brilliant and prolific writer was also the author of a two-volume *Life of Edwin Forrest: The American Tragedian* (1877; reprint, New York: Arno Press, 1977).

4. *The Solitudes of Nature and Man; or, the Loneliness of Human Life* (Boston: Roberts, 1869), 185.

5. Ibid., 187, 199, 200.

6. Ibid., 200.

7. Ibid., 202.

8. Ibid., 194.

9. Ibid., 195.

10. Ibid., 194.

11. Ibid., 196.

12. Ibid., 195.

13. Ibid., 199.

14. Ibid., 194.

15. Humankind has not been changed by the "tender sage," however, according to the character Unger, who remarks that corruption continues as Buddhism has become mostly a ritual.

16. (New York: Hurst, 1879). Entry 15 in Sealts, *Melville's Reading*: "Examined by Ramond Weaver; present location unknown."

17. Quoted in Jay Leyda, *The Melville Log: A Documentary Life of Herman Melville, 1819–1891* (New York: Gordian Press, 1969), 2:784.

18. *Interpreter of Buddhism to the West: Sir Edwin Arnold* (New York: Bookman, 1957), 73.

19. Ibid., 11.

20. Ibid., 73–75.

21. Ibid., 104.

22. *Poetical Works of Edwin Arnold: Containing the Light of Asia, The Indian Song of Songs, Pearls of the Faith* (New York: Alden, 1883), viii.

23. Ibid., v, vi.

24. Ibid., 70, 119.

25. Ibid., 129–30.

26. *Herman Melville: A Biography* (Berkeley: University of California Press, 1951), 316.

27. Edwin Arnold, *Poetical Works*, 164.

28. The volumes of Balzac's works are *Louis Lambert*, trans. Katharine Prescott Wormeley (Boston: Roberts, 1889); *The Magic Skin*, trans. Katharine Prescott Wormeley (Boston: Roberts, 1888); and *Seraphita*, trans. Katharine Prescott Wormeley (Boston: Roberts, 1889).

29. Introduction to *Seraphita*, xlv.

30. "Affinities of Buddhism and Christianity," *North American Review* 136 (May 1883): 477.

31. *Ten Great Religions: An Essay in Comparative Theology* (Boston: Houghton, 1882), 153.

32. Ibid., 153–54.

33. Ibid., 157.

34. Ibid., 160.

35. Ibid., 166.

36. *The Mystery of Iniquity: Melville as Poet, 1857–1891* (Lexington: University Press of Kentucky, 1972), 7.

37. "Buddha and Early Buddhism," *Atlantic Monthly* 48 (December 1881): 840. The degree to which Western interest in Buddhism was rising is suggested by the statement that opens this review: "Within two years, or since the appearance of Mr. Edwin Arnold's Light of Asia, the world of London was amused to learn that an eminent native Hindu Buddhist had come among them to examine the field with a view to making English converts" (840).

38. *Buddhism and Its Christian Critics* (Chicago: Open Court, 1894), 249.

39. F. Max Müller, "Buddhist Charity," *North American Review* 140 (March 1885): 221.

40. This is the reviewer's summation of Lillie's position. "Buddha and Early Buddhism," *Atlantic Monthly*, 840.

41. "Buddha and Early Buddhism," *Nation* 33 (October 27, 1881): 340.

42. See "Review of Seydel's *Die Buddha-Legende und dus Leben nach den Evangelien*," *Nation* 42 (May 27, 1886): 155.

43. Carus, *Buddhism*, 168.

44. "Socrates, Buddha, and Christ," *North American Review* 140 (January 1885): 63–77.

45. Clarke, *Religions*, 163.

46. *North American Review* 113 (October 1871): 429.

47. *Philsosophy of the Buddha* (New York: Putnam's, 1969), 120.

48. Bahm, *Philosophy of the Buddha*, 148.

49. *The Philosophy of Disenchantment* (New York: Brentano's, 1885), 223.

50. Ibid., 219.

51. "Optimism and Pessimism; Or the Problem of Evil," *Contemporary Review* 18 (1871): 67.

52. *Pessimism: A History and a Criticism* (London: Henry S. King, 1877), 2.

53. *Aspects of Pessimism* (Edinburgh: Blackwood, 1894), 250.

54. "Some Aspects of Pessimism," *Atlantic Monthly* 60 (December 1887): 759.

55. Ibid., 758.

56. Saltus, *Philosophy of Disenchantment*, 218.

57. J. H. Whitfield, *Giacomo Leopardi* (Oxford: Basil Blackwell, 1954), 5.

58. Sully, *Pessimism*, 27.

59. See Sealts, *Melville's Reading*, 223, and *Clarel*, ed. Walter E. Bezanson (New York: Hendricks House, 1960), 566.

60. *Essays and Phantasies* (London: Reeves and Turner, 1881), 52.

61. *The World as Will and Idea*, 2nd ed., trans. R. B. Haldane and J. Kemp (London: Truber, 1888), 3:401.

62. Alger, *Solitudes*, 307.

63. Ibid., 363.

64. Introduction to *Seraphita*, xxii.

65. Introduction to *Louis Lambert*, clii.

66. Ibid., cl.

67. See, for example, Richard T. Stavig, "Melville's *Billy Budd*: A New Approach to the Problems of Interpretation" (Ph.D. diss., Princeton University, 1953), 124–29.

68. Letter of December 1, 1884, *Correspondence*, ed. Lynn Horth (Evanston and Chicago: Northwestern University Press and the Newberry Library, 1993), 484. The book of poems was *Vane's Story, Weddah and Om-el-Bonain, and Other Poems* (1881).

69. Letter of January 22, 1885, *Correspondence*, 486.

70. Ibid., 492.

71. Ibid., 492.

72. See letters of April 2, 1886; December 31, 1888; January 12, 1890; and February 25, 1890, *Correspondence*, 497, 514, 522, 526.

73. *Essays and Phantasies*, 188.

74. "Sayings of Sigvat," *Essays and Phantasies*, 214.

75. Stavig observes in passing that "Bumble is surprising similar to Captain Vere!" (138).

76. *Billy Budd, Sailor*, ed. Harrison Hayford and Merton M. Sealts Jr. (Chicago: University of Chicago Press, 1962), 62.

77. Thomson, *Essays and Phantasies*, 113. Like Thomson, Melville uses Guy Fawkes in *Billy Budd* (80) to suggest subversiveness.

78. *Billy Budd*, 63.

79. Ibid., 128.

80. *Essays and Phantasies*, 120.

81. Eleanor Melville Metcalf, *Herman Melville: Cycle and Epicycle* (Cambridge: Harvard University Press, 1953), 284.

82. *Essays and Phantasies*, 218.

83. Ibid., 214–15.

84. Ibid., 216.

85. "Worldly Fortune," *Essays*, trans. T. Bailey Saunders (London: George Allen and Unwin, 1951), 85.

86. Ibid., 85.

87. Ed. Harrison Hayford, Hershel Parker, and G. Thomas Tanselle (Evanston and Chicago: Northwestern University Press and the Newberry Library, 1971), 284.

88. *Essays and Phantasies*, 131–32.

89. Ibid., 136.

90. Ibid., 115.

91. Ibid., 115.

92. Ibid., 214. In "Open Secret Societies," Thomson wrote: "Were I required to draw a practical moral, I should say that all proselytism is useless and absurd. Every human being belongs naturally, organically, unalterably, to a certain species or society; and by no amount of repeating strange formulas,

ejaculations, or syllogisms, can he really apostatise from himself so as to become a genuine member of a society to which these are not strange but natural" (211–12).

93. Ibid., 217–18: "Very well-meaning and stupid people nowo'days are doing their best (a poor little ludicrous best it is) to get us civilised off the face of the earth; they don't see that we need some very tough and rough savagery to keep a firm hold upon it. Nature is savage enough, and is likely to continue so; I don't think that she has made her arrangements specially for our placid and inane comfort, nor do I find that the saints and goody philosophers are her darlings. . . . To think that there are grown men always talking treacle and pap! men who have seen and heard a thunderstorm, and are not ignorant of the existence of shark and crocodile and tiger."

94. Ibid., 206–7, and *Moby-Dick,* ed. Harrison Hayford, Hershel Parker, and G. Thomas Tanselle (Evanston and Chicago: Northwestern University Press and the Newberry Library, 1988), 148.

95. Sealts, *Melville's Reading,* 210 (entry 435a).

96. H. S. Salt, *The Life of James Thomson ("B. V.")* (London: Reeves and Turner, 1889), 288.

97. *Schopenhauer* (New York: Dodge, 1909), 1.

98. Shurr, *Mystery of Iniquity,* 155–57.

99. *World,* 3:339.

100. Ibid., 2:421.

101. Ibid., 2:422.

102. Ibid., 2:422–23.

103. *"There is something so penetrating in the shaft of envy that even men of wisdom and worth find its wound a painful one"* ("Position, or A Man's Place in the Estimation of Others," *Essays,* 83).

104. "Human Nature" is an essay in the section entitled "On Human Nature" of *Essays,* 20–21.

105. "On Human Nature," *Essays,* 22.

106. Ibid.

107. *World,* 1:520.

108. "Our Relation to Ourselves," *Essays,* 23.

109. *Billy Budd,* 74.

110. Chapter 4, "Worldly Fortune," *Counsels and Maxims,* trans. T. Bailey Saunders (London: Sonnenschein, 1890), 121. This is the edition Melville owned.

111. Leyda, *Melville Log,* 2:750.

112. Ibid., 2:791.

113. See Merton M. Sealts Jr., *The Early Lives of Melville* (Madison: University of Wisconsin Press, 1974), 179–85. This account by Melville's granddaughter, Frances Cuthbert Thomas Osborne, was first printed as "Herman Melville through a Child's Eyes," *Bulletin of the New York Public Library* 69 (December 1965): 655–60.

114. Arthur Schopenhauer, *The Wisdom of Life,* 2nd ed., trans. T. Bailey Saunders (London: Sonnenschein, 1891), xxv.

115. Sir John Lubbock, *The Pleasures of Life* (New York: Alden, 1887), 20, 21.

116. Howard, *Herman Melville,* 322.

117. *Essays and Phantasies,* 231.

118. "Personality, or What a Man Is," *Essays,* 38.

119. Ibid.

120. *World,* 3:226.

121. Bryan Magee, *The Philosophy of Schopenhauer* (New York: Oxford University Press, 1983), 318.

122. *Religion: A Dialogue, and Other Essays,* 2nd ed., trans. T. B. Saunders (London: Sonnenschein, 1891), 92. According to Walter Sutton, "The Buddhist idea of the illusory nature of human existence is integral to Melville's final point of view." "Melville and the Great God Budd," *Prairie Schooner* 34 (Summer 1960): 133.

123. Alger, *Solitudes,* 120.

124. *Billy Budd,* 129. Sealts does point out the importance of ambition in Vere's characterization. *Early Lives,* 80.

125. "On Books and Reading," *Religion,* 55.

126. For background on the poem, see Hennig Cohen, ed. *Selected Poems of Herman Melville* (Carbondale: Southern Illinois University Press, 1964), 255.

127. Alger, *Solitudes,* 394.

128. Salt, *Life of Thomson,* 303.

129. Ed. Harrison Hayford, Hershel Parker, and G. Thomas Tanselle (Evanston and Chicago: Northwestern University Press and the Newberry Library, 1970), 279–80.

130. Letter of December 13, 1850, *Correspondence,* 174.

131. *The Endless, Winding Way in Melville: New Charts by Kring and Carey,* ed. Donald Yannella and Hershel Parker (Glassboro: Melville Society, 1981).

132. Leyda, *Melville Log,* 2:731.

133. "Position, or a Man's Place in the Estimation of Others," *Essays,* 62.

134. Ibid., 66.

135. Ibid., 67.

136. Vere addresses the court on how "we officially proceed" (*Billy Budd,* 111).

137. Ibid., 113.

138. "Position," *Essays,* 62–63.

139. *Billy Budd,* 106.

140. "Position," *Essays,* 64.

141. Ibid., 74.

142. Letter of [June 1?] 1851, *Correspondence,* 193.

143. *Early Lives,* 79.

144. "Per Contra," *Essays and Phantasies,* 138–40.

145. *Essays and Phantasies,* 123.

146. Salt, *Life of Thomson,* 69.

147. "Position," *Essays,* 58.

148. Ibid., 53–54.

149. Ibid., 95.

150. Letter of December 20, 1885, *Correspondence,* 492–93.

151. Leyda, *Melville Log,* 2:686.

152. Sealts, *Early Lives,* 81.

153. Quoted in Sealts, *Early Lives,* 24.

154. Leyda, *Melville Log,* 2:823.

155. Quoted in Sealts, *Early Lives,* 99, 100.

156. Quoted in Sealts, *Early Lives,* 121.

157. "Surviving the Gilded Age: Herman Melville in the Customs Service," *Essays in Arts and Sciences* 15 (June 1986): 11.

158. Leyda, *Melville Log,* 2:782. However, Leon Howard warns against taking this passage seriously: "Julian made most of his father's friends almost as 'nervous' as he represented Melville as being" (315).

159. Quoted in Sealts, *Early Lives,* 100.

160. Alger, *Solitudes,* 71.

161. Ibid., 170.

162. "Sayings of Sigvat," *Essays and Phantasies,* 216.

163. *Studies in Pessimism,* 2nd ed., trans. T. Bailey Saunders (London: Sonnenschein, 1891), 28.

164. "Personality, or What a Man Is," in *The Wisdom of Life, Essays,* 28.

165. "Psychological Observations," *Religion,* 90.

166. "The Ages of Life," *Essays,* 102.

167. See "Our Relation to Ourselves," *Essays,* 34. Schopenhauer wrote in a passage that Melville marked: "Ordinary society is very like the kind of music to be obtained from an orchestra composed solely of Russian horns. Each horn has only one note; and the music is produced by each note coming in just at the right moment. In the monotonous sound of a single horn, you have a precise illustration of the effect of most people's minds" (28).

168. "Our Relation to Ourselves," *Essays,* 35.

169. Letter of September 5, 1877, *Correspondence,* 464.

170. *Essays and Phantasies,* 157–58.

171. Ibid., 157.

172. Ibid., 133.

173. "Indolence," *Essays and Phantasies,* 147.

174. "Personality, or What a Man Is," *Essays,* 38.

175. Ibid., 39.

176. See Metcalf, *Herman Melville,* 259.

177. Howard, *Herman Melville,* 318.

178. Shurr, *Mystery of Iniquity,* 155–57.

Three: The Weaver

1. Letter of March 31, 1877, *Correspondence*, ed. Lynn Horth (Evanston and Chicago: Northwestern University Press and the Newberry Library, 1993), 452.

2. William H. Shurr perceptively argues after a study of the changes in the manuscript that "the poem was originally a study of religious devotion" but evolved into "a study of the kind of devotion demanded by art." *The Mystery of Iniquity: Melville as Poet, 1857–1891* (Lexington: University Press of Kentucky, 1972), 245–46.

3. "Melville's Reading of Arnold's Poetry," *PMLA* 69 (June 1954): 365–91.

4. Matthew Arnold, General Introduction to *The English Poets,* ed. Thomas Humphry Ward (New York: Macmillan, 1924), 1:xvii.

5. Ibid.

6. *Arnold and God* (Berkeley: University of California Press, 1983), 266.

7. Matthew Arnold, General Introduction to *English Poets,* 1:xix.

8. Bezanson, "Melville's Reading," 380.

9. "Ionian Form and Esau's Waste: Melville's View of Art in *Clarel,*" *American Literature* 54 (May 1982): 213.

10. Kenneth Allott, ed., *The Poems of Matthew Arnold,* 2nd ed. (London: Longman, 1979), 251.

11. Melville marked with a vertical line and an X the passage containing these words in his copy of Arnold's *Poems* (Boston: Ticknor and Fields, 1856), 25.

12. Ibid.

13. *Mixed Essays, Irish Essays and Others* (New York: Macmillan, 1883), 49.

14. *Billy Budd, Sailor,* ed. Harrison Hayford and Merton M. Sealts Jr. (Chicago: University of Chicago Press, 1962), 125.

15. Bezanson, "Melville's Reading," 370.

16. Fred Eastman, "Matthew Arnold," *Men of Power* (Nashville: Cokesbury, 1958), 104.

17. Matthew Arnold, General Introduction to *English Poets,* 1:xxviii.

18. *Aristotle's Treatise on Rhetoric. . . . Also, the Poetic of Aristotle . . . ,* trans. Theodore Buckley (London: Bell and Daldy, 1872), 424.

19. Ibid.

20. Letter of December 20, 1885, *Correspondence,* 492.

21. Letter of February 23, 1884, to Abraham Lansing. Melville Family Papers. New York Public Library.

22. Commenting on one lecture, John Henry Raleigh states that the "*Daily Princetonian* reported that the lecture was 'a fine specimen of polished English' but said that the speaker was hindered by defects of oratory and that 'the lecture was entirely devoid of any systematic analysis.' In fact, Arnold's oratory moved the students to amusement: 'Prof. E. declares that he can improve Matthew Arnold's delivery one hundred per cent in five lessons. Who

couldn't.'" *Matthew Arnold and American Culture* (Berkeley: University of California Press, 1961), 73.

23. Quoted in Merton M. Sealts Jr., *Melville as Lecturer* (Cambridge: Harvard University Press, 1957), 74.

24. October 31, 1883, p. 5, col. 3.

25. Herbert W. Paul, *Matthew Arnold* (London: Macmillan, 1920), 154.

26. Quoted in Paul, *Matthew Arnold,* 154.

27. 27 (November 1883): 155.

28. Hugo von Hofmannsthal. Quoted in Richard Friedenthal's Postscript to Stefan Zweig, *Balzac,* trans. William and Dorothy Rose (New York: Viking, 1946), 400.

29. *Honoré de Balzac: A Force of Nature* (Chicago: University of Chicago Press, 1932), 82.

30. *Ten Novels and Their Authors* (London: Heinemann, 1954), 101.

31. *Reviews,* vol. 13 of *The First Collected Edition of the Works of Oscar Wilde, 1908–1922,* ed. Robert Ross (London: Dawson's of Pall Mall, 1969), 79.

32. *Honoré de Balzac: A Biography* (London: Athlone, 1957), 183.

33. "Creative Reading: Balzacian Imagination at Work," *Critical Essays on Honoré de Balzac,* ed. Martin Kanes (Boston: G. K. Hall, 1990), 152–53.

34. *The Melville Log: A Documentary Life of Herman Melville, 1819–1891* (New York: Gordian Press, 1969), 2:828.

35. *The Correspondence of Honoré de Balzac; With a Memoir by His Sister, Madame de Surville,* trans. C. Lamb Kenney (London: Bentley, 1878), 1:382.

36. Ibid., 2:113.

37. Ibid., 2:50.

38. Ibid., 1:159.

39. Melville placed brackets around the final two lines of this passage. In his essay "Obermann," Arnold quotes Senancour as stating: "Everything that a mortal heart can contain of life—weariness and yearning, I felt it all. . . . I have made an ominous step toward the age of decline. . . . Happy [is he] . . . whose heart is always young." *The Complete Prose Works of Matthew Arnold,* ed. R. H. Super (Ann Arbor: University of Michigan Press, 1965), 5:302.

40. *Mixed Essays,* 434.

41. "A French Critic on Milton," *Mixed Essays,* 194.

42. *The Yale Manuscript,* ed. S. O. A. Ullmann (Ann Arbor: University of Michigan Press, 1989), 168.

43. Ed. Howard Foster Lowry, Karl Young, and Waldo Hilary Dunn (Oxford: Oxford University Press, 1952), 313.

44. Introduction to *Louis Lambert,* trans. Katharine Prescott Wormeley (Boston: Roberts, 1889), cxxvi.

45. "Rip Van Winkle's Lilac" was left unpublished at Melville's death as part of his collection of verse *Weeds and Wildings.*

46. Leyda, *Melville Log,* 2:806.

47. Melville's possible indebtedness to *Seraphita* in his creation of Billy Budd is discussed in John S. Haydock, "Melville's *Seraphita: Billy Budd, Sailor,*" Melville Society *Extracts,* no. 104 (March 1996): 2–13, which appeared as this book went to press.

48. *Seraphita,* trans. Katharine Prescott Wormeley (Boston: Roberts, 1889), 20.

49. Ibid., 20.

50. Ibid., 21, 29–30.

51. Ibid., 30.

52. Ibid., 81.

53. Ibid., 88.

54. Ibid., 88.

55. Balzac, *Correspondence,* 2:191.

56. Shurr points out that "an earlier version of the title spelled out the name as Coleridge, but the attempt to read the poem as an insight into Coleridge distracts one from the true lines of thought in the poem. The manuscript shows that several other names were considered" (163).

57. See Howard P. Vincent, ed. *Collected Poems of Herman Melville* (Chicago: Hendricks House, 1947), 474, and Hennig Cohen, ed. *Selected Poems of Herman Melville* (Carbondale: Southern Illinois University Press, 1964), 231–32.

58. The compass is perverted because swords captured from the enemy are placed too near to it.

59. *Moby-Dick,* ed. Harrison Hayford, Hershel Parker, and G. Thomas Tanselle (Evanston and Chicago: Northwestern University Press and the Newberry Library, 1988), 307.

60. *Poems of Matthew Arnold,* 535.

61. Quoted in *Poems of Matthew Arnold,* 535.

62. Melville's characterization of Vere, however, is not all negative. In many ways, he is an admirable figure, so much so that some scholars have theorized that this ambiguity derives from the unfinished state of the manuscript at Melville's death, that is, that Melville never decided whether Vere should be presented mainly in a positive or a negative light. Whatever the reality, if Vere's characterization as we have it reflects the negative attributes of James Thomson's Bumble, it may also mirror the positive aspects of Arnold's "Falkland," an essay that Melville read in *Mixed Essays, Irish Essays and Others.* In a passage that Melville marked, Arnold writes that Lucius Cary, Lord Falkland (1610–44) "has for the imagination the indefinable, the irresistible charm of one who is and must be, in spite of the choicest gifts and graces, unfortunate,—of a man in the grasp of fatality" (166). He was "surely and visibly touched by the finger of doom" (167). Slain in battle, the English nobleman did not live to see forty. Arnold points out that Falkland manifested a "passion" both for the military and for "letters" (157). Like Captain Vere, he

was a staunch believer in forms: "Falkland was born a constitutionalist, a hater of all that is violent and arbitrary" (160). One contemporary lauded him for his rational thinking "amidst the excesses" of the time (167). Like Vere, however, he appeared to some as "capricious and unstable" (167). Arnold indicates that the *Spectator* contrasted Falkland unfavorably with Fairfax and others (167–68). Though Arnold praises Lord Falkland for his "lucidity of mind and largeness of temper" (177), he depicts him here and there as much like Melville's Vere, that is, as a tragic figure trying to stay the course "to which 'honesty,' he thought, bound him" but which he did not in his deepest heart approve of (174).

63. "Hebraism and Hellenism," *Culture and Anarachy: An Essay in Political and Social Criticism and Friendship's Garland . . .* (New York, Macmillan, 1883), 122.

64. Park Honan, *Matthew Arnold: A Life* (New York: McGraw-Hill, 1981), 300.

65. *Matthew Arnold* (London: Unwin, 1939), 83.

66. Ibid., 97.

67. In his reading of Arnold, Melville marked numerous references to Senancour.

68. "Obermann," 300.

69. "Amiel," *The Complete Prose Works of Matthew Arnold,* ed. R. H. Super (Ann Arbor: University of Michigan Press, 1977), 11:272, 273.

70. *The Complete Prose Works of Matthew Arnold,* ed. R. H. Super (Ann Arbor: University of Michigan Press, 1968), 6:382.

71. "Amiel," 11:270.

72. Ibid., 11:271.

73. Ibid.

74. Eleanor M. Tilton, "Melville's 'Rammon': A Text and Commentary," *Harvard Library Bulletin* 13 (Winter 1959): 55. "Rammon" was first published in *Collected Poems of Herman Melville,* 411–16.

75. "Rammon," text established by Tilton, "Melville's 'Rammon,'" 56.

76. See Tilton, "Melville's 'Rammon,'" 80, and Shurr, *Mystery of Iniquity,* 143.

77. Shurr, *Mystery of Iniquity,* 144.

78. In describing the Enviable Isles, Melville possibly had in mind Sir Edwin Arnold's "silver islands of a sapphire sea" mentioned in *The Light of Asia* (New York: Alden, 1883), 117.

79. Shurr comments that "the poem is Melvile's version of 'The Lotus-Eaters'" (*Mystery of Iniquity,* 143), but later he seems to argue that the people in the work are dead and in the state of nirvana (145). See his discussion of the Buddha's final trance, 144–45.

80. Vincent states: "Rammon is an important statement, coming late in his life, of Melville's philsophy, especially on the problem of Evil which so con-

cerned him" (*Collected Poems,* 487). Tilton finds Vincent in error and argues that "Rammon" deals "directly with the theme of immortality" ("Melville's 'Rammon,'" 90).

81. "Rammon," 63.

82. Shurr, *Mystery of Iniquity,* 145.

83. See Edward Conze, *Buddhism: Its Essence and Development* (New York: Harper and Row, 1959), 181–82.

84. See chapter 5, "*Omoo:* Trial by Pleasure," in William B. Dillingham, *An Artist in the Rigging: The Early Work of Herman Melville* (Athens: University of Georgia Press, 1972), 79–102.

85. Melville wrote: "But, as to the resolute traveler in Switzerland, the Alps do never in one wide and comprehensive sweep, instantaneously reveal their full awfulness of amplitude . . . so hath heaven wisely ordained, that on first entering into the Switzerland of his soul, man shall not at once perceive its tremendous immensity. . . . Only by judicious degrees . . . does man come at last to gain his Mont Blanc and take an overtopping view of these Alps." *Pierre,* ed. Harrison Hayford, Hershel Parker, and G. Thomas Tanselle (Evanston and Chicago: Northwestern University Press and the Newberry Library, 1971), 284.

86. December 1881, 842.

87. *Moby-Dick,* 374.

88. William Rounseville Alger, *The Solitudes of Nature and Man* (Boston: Roberts, 1869), 194.

89. The vampire siren may be a recurrent figure in Melville's poetry. Though readers have often assumed that the female figure in another poem "Pontoosuc" delivers a message of wholeness and harmony, she may also be a seductive siren. Like the speaker of "Lamia's Song," she espouses integration with nature and with its never-ending restful rhythms, and she gives her message in a similar incantational mode that is seductively hypnotic.

90. Melville doubtlessly knew that Ulysses was not literally the son of Venus, goddess of love and beauty, but referred to him in this way to suggest that the great warrior was intimately familiar with the methods and appeal of Venus.

91. *Matthew Arnold: Prose and Poetry* (New York: Scribner's, 1927), v. "On religious themes," continues Bouton, "Arnold spoke as a layman seeking the vital essence of Christianity, freed from the swaddling bands of miraculous legend and the traditional dogmas of theology" (xxxi).

92. *The English Notebooks,* ed. Randall Stewart (New York: Modern Language Association of America, 1941), 433.

93. *Matthew Arnold* (New York: Eaton & Mains, 1906), 5.

94. Quoted in Paul, *Matthew Arnold,* 130.

95. Paul, *Matthew Arnold,* 133.

96. Ibid., 136.

97. Ibid., 138.

98. Ibid., 144.

99. *Essays and Phantasies* (London: Reeves and Turner, 1881), 137.

100. *The Life of James Thomson ("B. V.")* (London: Reeves and Turner, 1889), 305.

101. T. Bailey Saunders (London: Sonnenschein, 1891), xi.

102. Saunders, *Wisdom*, xi.

103. *The Idea of Tragedy in Ancient and Modern Drama* (Westminster: Constable, 1900), 97.

104. See James Whitlark, "Matthew Arnold and Buddhism," *Arnoldian* 9 (Winter 1981): 5–16.

105. Ed. Van Wyck Brooks (Boston: Houghton, 1933), 353.

106. Trilling, *Matthew Arnold*, 83.

107. Preface to *Last Essays, The Complete Prose Works of Matthew Arnold*, ed. R. H. Super (Ann Arbor: University of Michigan Press, 1972), 8:159–60.

108. Ibid., 8:160.

109. Ibid., 8:162.

110. Melville described a like situation in *Clarel* when he depicted the influence of Derwent's "easy skim" faith on Clarel, who responds more positively to Mortmain's open defiance of God:

Truth bitter: Derwent bred distrust
Heavier than came from Mortmain's thrust
Into the cloud—

(III.xxi.69–71)

111. *The Malady of the Ideal: Obermann, Maurice de Guerin and Amiel* (Philadelphia: University of Pennsylvania Press, 1947), 42–43.

112. Stanton Garner, "Surviving the Gilded Age: Herman Melville in the Customs Service," *Essays in Arts and Sciences* 15 (June 1986): 8. Jay Leyda notes in *The Melville Log* for June 30, 1877: "*After nearly being dismissed from the Customs service, M's working hours are increased*" (2:763). During the summer of 1877, an article appeared in the *New York Daily Tribune* under the heading "Custom-House Pruning: Selecting the Victims." The specter of severance had hovered over Melville for some time. In 1873 John C. Hoadley wrote to an influential acquaintance, George Boutwell, to try to make Melville's employment secure. The letter (*Melville Log*, 2:730–31) offers a rare and invaluable insight into Melville's response to his surroundings in the Customs Service:

There is one person in the employment of the Revenue Service, in whom I take so deep an interest, that I venture a second time to write you about him;—not to solicit promotion, a favor, or indulgence of any sort,—but to ask you, if you can, to do or say anything in the proper quarter to secure him permanently, or at present, the undisturbed enjoyment of his modest, hard-earned salary, as deputy inspector of the Customs in the City of New York—Herman Melville.—Proud, shy, sensitively honorable,—he had much to overcome, and has much to endure; but he strives earnestly to so perform his duties as to make the slightest censure, reprimand, or even reminder,—impossible from any superior—Surrounded by low venality, he puts it all quietly aside,—quietly declining offers of money for special services,—quietly returning money which has been thrust into his pockets behind his back, avoiding offence alike to the corrupting merchants and their clerks and runners, who think that all men can be bought, and to the corrupt swarms who shamelessly seek their price;—quietly, steadfastly doing his duty, and happy in retaining his own self-respect—

By the rules of any conceivable "civil service," he must be secure against removal.—Advancement or promotion he does not seek,—nor would his friends seek it for him.—The pittance he receives ekes out his slender income and that of his wife, (who is a daughter of the late Lemuel Shaw, C.J. of Mass—) and affords him the quiet, simple livelihood he values—The lost of $5000.—by the Boston fire, carrying with it an income of $500.—part of the small property left by her Father, making Mrs. Melville additionally solicitous that Mr. Melville should retain his place—I most earnestly wish that representations might be made in the proper quarter so that in the event of any general change in the Custom House in New York, Mr. Melville might find a sheltering arm thrown over him.—Pardon me: my sincere feeling must be my excuse.

113. Garner, "Surviving," 8.

114. Balzac, *Bureaucracy*, trans. Katharine Prescott Wormeley (Boston: Roberts, 1889), 23.

115. *Seraphita*, 182.

116. Balzac, *Bureaucracy*, 324.

117. Ibid., 38.

118. Parsons, Introduction to *Louis Lambert*, xxiv-xxv.

119. Balzac, *Eugénie Grandet*, trans. Katharine Prescott Wormeley (Boston: Little, Brown, 1906), 129.

120. Quoted in Harry Levin, *Toward Balzac* (Parsippany, N.J.: Dudley Kimball, 1947), 32.

121. Levin, *Toward Balzac*, 32.

122. "Balzac and Reality," *Critical Essays on Honoré de Balzac*, 57.

123. Dargan, *Balzac*, 82.

124. *Literature and Western Man* (New York: Harper, 1960), 169.

125. Balzac, *Correspondence*, 2:132.

126. Ibid., 2:43.

127. Balzac, *Facino Cane*, trans. Katharine Prescott Wormeley (Boston: Little, Brown, 1905), 2.

128. Andre Maurois, *Prometheus: The Life of Balzac*, trans. Norman Denny (New York: Harper & Row, 1965), 548.

129. Balzac, *Correspondence*, 1:368.

130. Ibid., 1:370.

131. Ibid., 1:402.

132. Ibid., 1:414.

133. *Life of Honoré de Balzac* (London: Walter Scott, 1890), 33.

134. Balzac, *Correspondence*, 2:75.

135. Ibid., 2:76.

136. *Balzac's Concept of Genius* (Geneve: Librairie Droz, 1969), 38.

137. Zweig, *Balzac*, 134, 135.

138. Ibid., 139.

139. Ibid., 140. According to George Saintsbury, Balzac's "favorite plan (varied sometimes in detail) was therefore to dine lightly about five or six, then to go to bed and sleep till eleven, twelve, or one, and then to get up, and with the help only of coffee (which he drank very strong and in enormous quantities) to work for indefinite stretches of time into the morning or afternoon of the next day. He speaks of a sixteen hours' day as a not uncommon shift of work, and almost a regular one with him; and on one occasion he avers that in the course of forty-eight hours he took but three of rest, working for twenty-two hours and a half continuously on each side thereof." Introduction to *The Works of Honoré de Balzac* (New York: Harper, n.d.), 1:16.

140. Balzac, *Correspondence*, 2: 117–18.

141. Ibid., 2:214.

142. Ibid., 2:275.

143. Schopenhauer also greatly admired and extolled Scott, calling him "the incomparable Sir Walter Scott." Melville probably would not have known this fact, however, until after he read Scott under the influence of Balzac, for the bulk of his reading of Schopenhauer came a little later.

144. *Works of Honoré de Balzac*, 7:182.

145. Trans. Katharine Prescott Wormeley (Boston: Roberts, 1885), xiv.

146. Balzac, *Correspondence*, 2:77.

147. Ibid.

148. Gansevoort Melville owned an eight-volume set of Scott's *Tales of a Grandfather*, and he once compared the temporary laziness of his brother Herman to that "which so constantly beset one of the most industrious men of the age—Sir Walter Scott" (*Melville Log*, 1:103). Irritated with his English publisher John Murray for requesting proof of his actually having been in the South Seas, Melville wrote in 1848: "Bless my soul, Sir, will you Britons not credit that an American can be a gentleman, & have read the Waverly Novels, tho every digit may have been in the tar-bucket?" (Melville, *Correspondence*, 107).

149. Melville's choice of these particular novels by Scott is interesting in light of the fact that he was writing and rewriting *Billy Budd* at the time he read them. Quentin Durward is, like Billy, a youth (he is about twenty) and is

characterized by striking good looks, openness, and courage. In *Peveril of the Peak*, a Fairfax is mentioned, as is a Vere. The novel is centered on the so-called Popish Plot instigated by the notorious Titus Oates, who appears as a character in the novel. Melville, too, makes reference to this historical episode in *Billy Budd* and to Oates. Both novels by Scott are about young men—boys really—who are strong, handsome, and morally untainted.

150. (New York: John Wurtele Lovell, 1860), 164.

151. "The Greatest Living American Writer," *New York Press*, April 15, 1894.

152. Reprinted in *Critical Essays on W. D. Howells, 1866–1920*, ed. Edwin H. Cady and Norma W. Cady (Boston: G. K. Hall, 1983), 103.

153. Quoted in Van Wyck Brooks, *Howells: His Life and World* (New York: Dutton, 1959), 161.

154. *The Letters of Henry James*, ed. Percy Lubbock (New York: Scribner's, 1920), 1:73.

155. Olov W. Fryckstedt, *In Quest of America: A Study of Howells' Early Development as a Novelist* (Upsala: Boktryckeri, 1958), 216.

156. Kenneth S. Lynn, *William Dean Howells: An American Life* (New York: Harcourt, 1971), 185.

157. *The Immense Complex Drama: The World and Art of the Howells Novel* (Columbus: Ohio State University Press, 1966), 215.

158. Alger, *Solitudes*, 270.

159. Ibid., 268.

Four: Associating with the Rose

1. See Richard Bridgman, "Melville's Roses," *Texas Studies in Literature and Language* 8 (Summer 1966): 235–36.

2. *The Gulistan, or Rose-Garden*, trans. Francis Gladwin (London: Kingsbury, Parbury, and Allen, 1822), x.

3. *The Gulistan*, trans. Edward B. Eastwick (London: Trubner, 1880), 4.

4. *Herman Melville: A Biography* (Berkeley: University of California Press, 1951), 316. Elizabeth Melville's allergy was diagnosed as hay fever, but apparently she continued to refer to her ailment as rose cold. See her reference to it in Jay Leyda, *The Melville Log: A Documentary Life of Herman Melville, 1819–1891* (New York: Gordian Press, 1969), 2:385.

5. *Correspondence*, ed. Lynn Horth (Evanston and Chicago: Northwestern University Press and the Newberry Library, 1993), 280.

6. *A Book About Roses* was first published in 1869. Melville owned the seventh edition (1883).

7. S. Reynolds Hole, *A Book About Roses*, 7th ed. (New York: Gottsberger, 1883), 104. All future page references to Hole are to this edition and are included in the text.

8. Melville marked this passage with a vertical line in the margin.

9. *Moby-Dick,* ed. Harrison Hayford, Hershel Parker, and G. Thomas Tanselle (Evanston and Chicago: Northwestern University Press and the Newberry Library, 1988), 274.

10. Jim McIntyre, *The Story of the Rose* (London: Ward Lock, 1970), 69. An array of interesting interpretations is available on "The New Rosicrucians." Howard states that the poem is simply about the whimsicality and contentment of Melville's old age (317). William H. Shurr, *The Mystery of Iniquity: Melville as Poet, 1857–1891* (Lexington: University Press of Kentucky, 1972), argues— as have other critics—that it is an attack on shallow optimistic thinkers (197). William Bysshe Stein, *The Poetry of Melville's Late Years: Time, History, Myth, and Religion* (Albany: State University of New York Press, 1970), believes the poem to be sexually oriented and "wickedly" anti-Christian (207).

11. See chapter 1 for a discussion of problems in determining the exact date this work was completed.

12. Shurr posits that the speaker is not Melville, who (he argues) took the course represented by the attar (*Mystery of Iniquity,* 201).

13. Stein comments that in these lines Melville is "faintly echoing Coleridge's "Kubla Khan" but that he "has only one purpose in mind—to establish the sexual symbolism of the garden" (*Poetry of Melville's Later Years,* 219). Shurr remarks that in the poem, Melville "is able to . . . parody Coleridge's 'Kubla Khan'" (*Mystery of Iniquity,* 202).

14. Shurr suggests that the line of the poem "I came into my roses late" refers to the circumstances that allowed Melville to retire on December 31, 1885, from his customhouse position and to his ensuing dilemma about what to do with his life now that he had free time (203). Shurr's interpretation differs from my own, however, in its insistence that Melville is not the speaker and that he actually chose the way of the Parsee in the poem.

15. All references to quatrain numbers in the *Rubáiyát* are given in the text and, unless otherwise indicated, are to FitzGerald's third edition, which Melville owned.

16. Dorothee Metlitsky Finkelstein has correctly observed that "the theme of the Rubáiyát is Death. Again and again Melville marked Omar's death images in the poems." *Melville's Orienda* (New Haven: Yale University Press, 1961), 105.

17. The preface to *Polonius* has become the most famous and highly praised section of the book. Edmund Gosse speaks for many when he claims that "the value" of *Polonius* "now rests in its elegant and familiar preface." Introduction to vol. 1, *The Variorum and Definitive Edition of the Poetical and Prose Writings of Edward FitzGerald* (New York: Phaeton Press, 1967), xv. Originally published in 1902.

18. *Polonius: A Collection of Wise Saws and Modern Instances,* vol. 5 of *The Variorum and Definitive Edition of the Poetical and Prose Writings of Edward FitzGerald,* 203.

19. Ibid., 204.

20. Ibid., 204–5.

21. Ibid., 205.

22. Ibid., 206. FitzGerald quotes from *II Henry IV.* 3.2.38–40. Shallow is speaking to Silence and bemoaning the fact that many of his old acquaintances are dead.

23. Ibid., 207.

24. Melville owned three copies of FitzGerald's version of the *Rubáiyát:* the First American Edition from the Third London Edition (Boston: Houghton, Osgood, 1878); Elihu Vedder's *Rubáiyát* with accompanying drawings (Boston: Houghton Mifflin, 1886); and a "semi-manuscript" copy that James Billson sent to Melville. See Entry 393 in Merton M. Sealts Jr., *Melville's Reading,* rev. and enlarged ed. (Columbia: University of South Carolina Press, 1988), 203.

25. *Edward FitzGerald* (Boston: Twayne, 1977), 100. "As for the philosophical content of FitzGerald's *Rubáiyát,*" states Jewett, "the diversity of thought in the Persian original far outstrips that of the English version. . . . The freedom of the *rubai* form allowed Omar to indulge in satire, parody, veiled jokes sometimes taken as serious observations by critics, and in piety as well as skepticism" (100).

26. *Edward FitzGerald* (London: Longmans, Green, 1960), 23.

27. Robert Bernard Martin, *With Friends Possessed: A Life of Edward Fitz-Gerald* (London: Faber and Faber, 1985), 203.

28. *Edward FitzGerald* (New York: Macmillan, 1905), 201. "For disguise it as we will by activities and by pleasures," writes Benson in explaining FitzGerald's position, "we live under a shadow of doom. We may beguile it, we may banish it, but the tolling of the bell that heralds the end beats in our ears. . . . He is wisest who can face the solemn music" (199).

29. Melville cited the source of the quotation as anonymous.

30. Shurr conjectures that the poem may have been written at the time Melville was about to be married or shortly after (*Mystery of Iniquity,* 197). Stein does not speculate on the date of composition but argues that the poem praises sex and condemns Christianity (101–3).

31. Finkelstein believes that Melville's inspiration for the angel with the rose came from FitzGerald's preface to the *Rubáiyát,* "in which one of Omar's disciples describes the poet's death: 'My tomb shall be in a spot where the north wind may scatter roses over it'" (*Melville's Orienda,* 112).

32. Though Shurr does not make the specific connection that I make here between the rose and the creative imagination, he observes that roses "are symbolic of some force able to transform the ordinary realities of life," and he makes the point that the lines quoted here intimate "a sacramental transformation" (*Mystery of Iniquity,* 200).

33. Shurr makes this identification (ibid., 199). In part, 2 Corinthians 6:2 reads: "Now is the accepted time."

34. "Under the Rose," *Billy Budd and Other Prose Pieces,* vol. 13 of *The Works of Herman Melville,* ed. Raymond W. Weaver (London: Constable, 1924), 342. Future page references to "Under the Rose" are to this edition and are given in the text.

35. Finkelstein quotes this quatrain as the likely source for Melville's angel with the wine-jar (*Melville's Orienda,* 112).

36. *Moby-Dick,* 344.

37. "Omar Khayyám, the Astronomer-Poet of Persia," introductory to the *Rubáiyát of Omar Khayyám,* in *The Variorum and Definitive Edition of the Poetical and Prose Writings of Edward FitzGerald* (New York: Phaeton Press, 1967), 2:15.

38. Ibid., 2:18.

39. Ibid., 2:19–20.

40. Ibid., 2:9.

41. Quoted in A. J. Arberry, *The Romance of the Rubáiyát* (London: George Allen & Unwin, 1959), 35.

42. Jane Dillenberger, "Between Faith and Doubt: Subjects for Meditation," *Perceptions and Evocations: The Art of Elihu Vedder* (Washington: Smithsonian Institution Press, 1970), 130.

43. Quoted in Regina Soria, *Elihu Vedder: American Visionary Artist in Rome (1836–1923)* (Rutherford: Fairleigh Dickinson University Press, 1970), 188.

44. Quoted in Soria, *Elihu Vedder,* 188.

45. *Reading Billy Budd* (Evanston: Northwestern University Press, 1990), 25.

46. Quoted in Soria, *Elihu Vedder,* 183.

47. Dillenberger, "Between Faith and Doubt," 130.

48. The one area in which Vedder apparently did not have his way was the method of reproducing his drawings. At first, he wished them engraved, but this proving financially prohibitive to the publisher, he agreed to have them photographed by a new process that closely resembled engraving.

49. Quoted in Soria, *Elihu Vedder,* 183.

50. Dillenberger, "Between Faith and Doubt," 131.

51. See Howard, *Herman Melville,* 336.

52. *Harper's New Monthly Magazine* 59 (September 1879): 495.

53. Ibid.

54. "Vedder's Accompaniment to the Song of Omar Khayyám," *Century Magazine* 29 (November 1884): 4.

55. Coincidentally, Vedder dedicated his edition of the *Rubáiyát* to his wife just as Melville dedicated *Weeds and Wildings* to his Elizabeth, whom he refers to as "Winnifred."

56. Dillenberger, "Between Faith and Doubt," 128.

57. Foreword to *Perceptions and Evocations: The Art of Elihu Vedder,* vii.

58. Howard, *Herman Melville,* 332.

59. David Jaffe, "'Sympathy with the Artist': Elizabeth Melville and Elihu Vedder," Melville Society *Extracts,* no. 81 (May 1990): 10.

60. Pages in Vedder's edition of the *Rubáiyát,* including his section of notes at the end, are not numbered.

61. Quoted in Leyda, *Melville Log,* 2:836. In the medical language of today, according to Dr. Clyde Partin Jr. of the Emory University Clinic, Melville died of congestive heart failure exacerbated by a leaky mitral valve. "Contributory asthenia," Dr. Partin explains, was used by physicians in Melville's day as a general term to denote an overall weakness or debility (letter to author, July 17, 1995).

62. Quoted in Leyda, *Melville Log,* 2:836.

63. Quoted in Leyda, *Melville Log,* 2:837.

64. These three acquaintances were Dr. Titus Munson Coan, Arthur Stedman, and George W. Dillaway. Coan, a physician and minor author, was a persistent admirer of Melville, having first sought him out at Arrowhead. After graduating from the New York College of Physicians and Surgeons, Coan found himself in the same city as Melville, and if he is to be believed, he had some "interesting talks with him" in the 1880s. See Leyda, *Melville Log,* 2:787. Arthur Stedman lived his life in the shadow of his more prominent father, Edmund Clarence Stedman, who had valiantly attempted to draw Melville out during his final years by offering him membership in the Authors Club. Dillaway probably knew Melville only slightly, if at all.

Index

"After the Pleasure Party," 59–60, 93, 130, 173, 174

"Ages of Life, The" (Schopenhauer), 82–83

Alchemy, 151

Alcott, Bronson, 35

Alger, William Rounseville, 32–34, 48–49, 58, 68, 69–70, 81, 139

Allott, Kenneth, 109

All Souls Unitarian Church, 13, 32, 127, 174

"Ambuscade, The," 173, 174

"American Aloe on Exhibition, The," 76–77

Amiel, Henri Frédéric, 112

"Amoroso," 147, 159

Angelico, Fra, 6

apRoberts, Ruth, 92

Aristotle, 95

Arnold, Sir Edwin, 30, 34–37, 38, 124–25, 183 (n. 37)

Arnold, Matthew: as member of Melville's circle, xii, 30; as evangelist for poetry, 92; his linking of poetry and religion, 92; and the creative imagination, 92, 112, 113, 116, 125; his lauding of the ancients, 93–95; his concept of "imaginative reason," 94; his interest in Aristotle, 95; his American tour, 96–98, 124–25; as lecturer, 96–98, 188–89 (n. 22); his distrust of the masses, 97; on

Philistinism, 97; his resentment of aging process, 100–101; his notion of the buried self, 101, 109; youth as concept in, 101–2, 108; importance of self-knowledge to, 108–12, 119, 129; and self-culpability, 110–12; and Buddhism, 112–13, 116, 124–25; his religious views, 122–25, 130; and dogma, 123, 125; and the Pessimists, 124–25; his view of physicians and ministers, 126; as stoic, 127; his belief in best self, 129; his opinion of Lord Falkland, 190–91 (n. 62)

"Art," 8, 90

Aspects of Pessimism (Wenley), 45

"At the Hostelry," 3–9, 10, 12, 17, 21, 30, 177–78 (n. 6)

Authors Club, 14, 15, 79, 179 (n. 32), 200 (n. 64)

"Avatar, The," 70

Bahm, A. J., 42

Balzac (Saltus), 99

Balzac, Honoré de: as member of Melville's circle, xii, 30; his interest in Eastern religions, 37; and Buddhism, 49, 130; imaginative world of, 98–99; death of, 100; his resentment of aging process, 100; his commitment to art, 100, 131–33, 135, 136; his concept of youth, 102,

Hawthorne, Nathaniel, 13, 51, 74, 80, 95–96, 102, 122
"Hawthorne and His Mosses," 95–96
Haydock, John S., 190 (n. 47)
Hayford, Harrison, xii, 54
Hazard of New Fortunes, A (Howells), 138
"Hearth-Roses," 159
Hegesias, 44
Helen of Troy, 151
"Herba Santa," 119–20
Higginson, Thomas Wentworth, 35
Historical, Literary, and Artistical Travels in Italy (Valery), 48
Hoadley, John C., 66, 71–72, 87, 193–94 (n. 112)
Hole, S. Reynolds: as member of Melville's circle, 30, 140; background of, 141; his metaphorical use of the rose, 142; creative urge as subject for, 142–43; his insistence upon devotion, 143–44, 147, 151–52, 153, 154; on the ideal rosarium, 144, 147, 161; as Rosicrucian, 145; his longing for lost Eden, 147–48; as Melville's rose farmer, 149–50; personal characteristics of, 149–50; his treatment of roses as women, 151–52; his similarity to Omar, 152; love as theme in, 153; his fusion of Christianity and New Rosicrucianism, 160
Holmes, Oliver Wendell, 24, 35
Honan, Park, 191 (n. 64)
"Honor," 125–26
Houghton Mifflin Company, 168
"House of the Tragic Poet," 10
Howard, Leon, 1, 11, 18, 37, 65, 85–86, 141, 171, 177 (n. 6), 187 (n. 158), 197 (n. 10)

Howells, William Dean: as member of Melville's circle, 30; as controversial figure, 138; as the American Balzac, 138; and literary realism, 138; recurrent characters in his fiction, 138
Hugo, Victor, 100, 143
Human Comedy (Balzac), 98–99, 131, 134, 138
"Human Nature" (Schopenhauer), 61–62
Hunt, Herbert J., 99

Idylls of the King, The (Tennyson), 35
Imagination, 3, 9, 10, 27, 30, 43, 87–92, 94, 98, 100, 101, 102, 103–6, 107–8, 110–13, 116, 117, 119, 121, 122, 123, 125, 127, 131, 132, 134, 135, 139, 140, 153, 154, 160, 162, 170, 171, 174
Imaginative reason, 94
"Immolated," 69, 72
"In a Bye-Canal," 120–22
"Indolence: A Moral Essay" (Thomson), 84
"Inscription," 85
"In the Garret," 90–91
Ishmael, 164–65
Italy, as metaphor, 7

Jacob (Bible), 90
Jaffe, David, 200 (n. 59)
James, Henry, 25, 138
Jesus, 33, 41, 69–70, 112, 125, 146
Jewett, Iran B. Hassani, 156
"Jimmy Rose," 140
Job (Bible), 89
"John Marr," 80
John Marr and Other Sailors, 35, 47, 68, 71, 72, 106, 113, 114
Johnson, Samuel, 154
"Jolly Corner, The" (James), 25

1, 63–64, 79, 85; retirement, 1,
79–80, 85–86, 95, 197 (n. 14);
impact of old age on, 2–3, 87–88,
90, 92, 98, 100, 101, 102, 104, 105,
117; as conscious artist, 3; his
commitment to art, 3, 4, 7, 8, 27,
30, 55, 87–92, 100, 108, 119, 122,
123, 124, 127, 139, 140, 143–44, 145,
154, 170, 171; his devotion to the
imagination, 3, 4, 9, 10, 27, 30,
87–92, 94, 98, 100, 101, 102, 103–6,
107–8, 110–13, 116, 117, 119, 121, 122,
123, 125, 127, 131, 134, 135, 139, 140,
153, 154, 160, 162, 170, 171, 174; and
artistic experimentation, 4, 10,
30; his bipartite works, 4, 21; and
sociality, 10; his love of privacy,
11; and geniality, 11, 14–15, 15–16,
17, 30, 80; residence of, in New
York, 12; and New York clubs,
13–15, 79; and the Society of the
Cincinnati, 18, 180–81 (n. 49); and
Jack Gentian, 18–19; and Daniel
Orme, 26–30; and Sir Edwin
Arnold, 30; and Buddhism,
30, 32–44, 113–20, 122, 174, 186
(n. 122); and Pessimism, 30, 43;
and Arthur Schopenhauer, 30,
48–49, 58–63, 124, 174; and James
Thomson, 30, 49–58, 95, 123–24,
184–85 (n. 92); and Honoré de
Balzac, 30, 92, 98–100, 103,
127–36, 174; and Matthew Arnold,
30, 92–98, 100–102, 108–13,
122–25, 127, 136, 174; and William
Dean Howells, 30, 136, 138–39,
174; and Sir Walter Scott, 30,
136–37, 174; and S. Reynolds Hole,
30, 140, 141–52, 153–54, 160, 161,
162; and Omar Khayyám, 30, 140,
153–54, 156–59, 160, 161, 162,
163–64, 165, 166, 167, 172, 174; and
Elihu Vedder, 30, 167–74, 198

(n. 24); his interest in
comparative theology, 36; his
knowledge of Leopardi, 43,
48; as "instinctive pessimist," 47;
his rejection of Pessimist label,
50; and optimism, 50, 65, 86;
independence of, 51, 52, 58, 86;
his objections to dogma, 52–53,
123; his view of self-fidelity,
53–54; his opinion of books, 55;
his view of the masses, 55;
position of, on the elusiveness
of truth, 55; his distrust of
journalism, 55–56; his view of
missionaries, 56; his belief in
self-understanding, 59–60, 110,
192 (n. 85); as student of human
nature, 62–63; and the nature
of fate, 63; self-absorption of,
63–68, 87, 154; retention of
powers, 64; his response to
family deaths, 65–66; his
perception of reality, 67–68; his
susceptibility to shame, 68,
70–74; ambition of, 68, 71, 77, 87;
his attitude toward fame, 68,
74–78, 87; his view of his career,
68–78; his sensitivity to criticism,
69–70, 71–72, 81; his marriage, 71,
126; his reclusiveness, 78–83, 87,
179 (n. 32); and personal
relationships, 80, 88–89; his
nervousness, 81; his attitude
toward work, 83–84;
attractiveness of leisure to, 83–85,
87; as stoic, 87, 127; his use of
religious imagery, 88–91; his
concept of youth, 89, 101–5, 108;
his respect for classical literature,
93–95; and Aristotle, 95; as
lecturer, 96, 98; his use of sleep
as metaphor, 105–8, 116, 121, 131;
as insomniac, 107–8, 131; his

Optimists, 65, 86

Organan, The (Aristotle), 95

Original character, 8

Orme, Daniel, 18

Osborne, Frances Thomas, 64

"Palladium" (Matthew Arnold), 108

Papist plot, 196 (n. 149)

"Paracelsus" (Browning), 129

"Paradise of Bachelors and the
    Tartarus of Maids, The," 4, 21

Parerga and Paralipomena
    (Schopenhauer), 58

Parker, Edward G., 180 (n. 42)

Parker, Hershel, 11, 25, 167–68, 186
    (n. 131)

Parsons, George Frederic, 37, 49, 102,
    129

"Parthenope," 9

Partin, Clyde, Jr., 200 (n. 61)

Paul, Herbert W., 123

"Pausilippo (in the Time of
    Bomba)," 6

"Pebbles," 47, 86

Peebles, Mary L., 96

"Per Contra: The Poet, High Art,
    Genius" (Thomson), 55, 84–85,
    123–24

Père Goriot (Balzac), 136, 138

Pessimism: school of and Melville's
    reading, 30; life as illusion in, 43,
    46, 47; basic doctrines of, 43, 46,
    86; its similarity to Buddhism,
    43–44, 67, 123; as distinguished
    from ordinary pessimism, 44;
    popularity of, in America and
    Europe, 44–46; as a movement,
    45, 49–50; in contrast to
    Buddhism, 46; unreality of life
    in, 67–68; its contempt for fame,
    68, 74; its approval of
    reclusiveness, 81–83; its views on
    genius, 82–83; its stance on

leisure, 83, 84; and Christianity,
    123; and the artistic impulse, 124

Pessimism: A History and a Criticism
    (Sully), 45

Peveril of the Peak (Scott), 137, 196
    (n. 149)

Phelps, Charles Henry, 179 (n. 32)

Philosophy of Disenchantment, The
    (Saltus), 43–44, 47

Picturesque, 5, 7–9, 10

Pierre, 16, 55, 88, 139

Pisano, Frank, 181 (n. 56)

Pleasures of Life, The (Lubbock), 65

Plutarch's Lives, 78

Poe, Edgar Allan, 14

Poems (Matthew Arnold), 92, 94

Poems of Edwin Arnold, The, 34

Poetic, The (Aristotle), 95

Poetry of the East, The (Alger), 32

Polonius (FitzGerald), 154, 155, 156,
    197 (n. 17)

"Pontoosuc," 192 (n. 89)

Poole, Gordon, 178 (n.6)

"Poor Man's Pudding and Rich
    Man's Crumbs," 4

"Portrait of a Gentleman, The," 20,
    23

Porzelt, Paul, 179 (n. 23)

Poussin, Gaspar, 7

Price, Uvedale, 7

Priestly, J. B., 130

"Profundity and Levity," 67–68

"Proposals for the Speedy Extinction
    of Evil and Misery" (Thomson),
    48

Protestant work ethic, 83–84

Quentin Durwood (Scott), 137,
    195–96 (n. 149)

Rabourdin, Xavier, 128

Raleigh, John Henry, 188–89
    (n. 22)

Thomson, James (*cont.*)
74–75, 76; on reclusiveness, 82; on
leisure, 84–85; on genius, 84–85;
in indolence, 84–85; and popular
taste, 95; and Balzac, 100; his
rejection of a personal God, 123;
his attutude toward art, 124; on
proselytism, 184–85 (n. 92)
Thoreau, Henry David, 13
Thrale, Hester Lynch, 154
"Thy Aim, Thy Aim?" 77
Tilton, Eleanor, 114
"Timoleon," 77–78
Timoleon, 33, 72, 94, 107, 118, 120, 169,
170, 171
Tintoretto, 13
"To ———," 67
"To Major Jack Gentian, Dean of the
Burgundy Club," 20–21, 22
"To Ned," 42–43
Transubstantiation, 160, 161
Treatise on Rhetoric (Aristotle), 95
Trilling, Lionel, 110, 112, 124
"Two Temples, The," 4

Ulysses, 115, 122, 192 (n. 90)
"Under the Ground," 158–59
"Under the Rose," 162–66
Unger, 182 (n. 15)
Union Club, 13
Urania, 59–60
"Urania" (Matthew Arnold), 93

Valery, Antoine Claude Pasquin, 48
Vampires, 118–19, 120
Vane's Story (Thomson), 184 (n. 68)
Vauquer, Madame, 138
Vedder, Elihu: as a member of
Melville's circle, 30, 140; his
Rubáiyát as unique
accomplishment, 167, 168; his
calligraphy, 168; his arrangement
of quatrains, 168–69; depth and

strangeness of his paintings, 169;
his religious questionings, 169; as
expatriate, 169, 170; his
reputation, 169–70; and
Christianity, 170; and FitzGerald,
170; his similarity to Melville, 170;
his devotion to the imagination
and art, 170, 171, 172; his wife, 170,
199 (n. 55); his use of the rose,
171–72; his treatment of death,
172; his nudes, 172, 173; his dislike
of hypocrisy, 173
Venice, 120
Venus, 122, 151
Vere, Captain, 18, 52–54, 68, 72–74,
110, 190–91 (n. 62)
Verecundia, 72–74
"Vial of Attar, The," 153, 165
Vincent, Howard, 177 (n. 6), 191–92
(n. 80)

Walker, H. H., 99
Walton, Izaak, 153
Watson, J. R., 178 (n. 10)
Watteau, Antoine, 6
Waverly novels (Scott), 195 (n. 148)
Weaver, Raymond, 1, 26
"Weaver, The," 88
*Weddah and Om-el-Bonain, and
Other Poems* (Thomson), 184
(n. 68)
Wedmore, Frederick, 133
Weeds and Wildings, 67, 70, 77, 85,
102, 144, 147, 148, 158, 162, 173
Wenley, R. M., 45
White, Richard Grant, xii
White-Jacket, 28, 70–71
Whitfield, J. H., 183 (n. 57)
Whitlark, James, 193 (n. 104)
Whitman, Walt, 7
Whittaker, Thomas, 58
Whittier, John Greenleaf, 14
Wilde, Oscar, 98–99

Williams, Theodore Chickering, 13, 127, 174–75
Wilson, James Grant, 179 (n. 24)
Wisdom of Life, The (Schopenhauer), 61, 65, 66, 72, 75–76, 85, 124
"Wise Virgins to Madam Mirror, The," 104
"Wish, A" (Matthew Arnold), 126
World as Will and Idea, The (Schopenhauer), 48, 59–60, 62, 63, 67

Wormeley, Katherine Prescott, 100
Wright, Brooks, 35, 36

Yannella, Donald, xii, 186 (n. 131)
Young, Philip, 26, 27
"Youth and Calm" (Matthew Arnold), 108

Zweig, Stefan, 133–34